Missing
Measures

D0141045

Missing Measures

MODERN POETRY AND THE REVOLT AGAINST METER

Timothy Steele

The University of Arkansas Press
Fayetteville · London ·· 1990

Copyright © 1990 by Timothy Steele
All rights reserved
Manufactured in the United States of America
94 93 92 91 90   5 4 3 2 1

DESIGNER: Chiquita Babb
TYPEFACE: Linotron 202 Granjon
TYPESETTER: G & S Typesetters, Inc.
PRINTER: Braun-Brumfield, Inc.
BINDER: Braun-Brumfield, Inc.

The paper used in this publication meets the minimum requirements of the American National Standard for Permanence of Paper for Printed Library
Materials Z39.48-1984. ∞

LIBRARY OF CONGRESS CATALOGING-IN-
PUBLICATION DATA

Steele, Timothy.
    Missing measures : modern poetry and the
revolt against meter / Timothy Steele.
            p.   cm.
    Bibliography: p.
    Includes index.
    ISBN 1-55728-125-4. — ISBN 1-55728-126-2
(pbk.)
    1. Free verse—History and criticism.
    2. Poetry, Modern—History and criticism.
    3. Poetics. I. Title.
PN1059.F7S74   1990
809.1—dc20   89-34918
                                        CIP

for Victoria

CONTENTS

ACKNOWLEDGMENTS

To the John Simon Guggenheim Memorial Foundation, I am indebted for a fellowship for 1984–85, during which time some of this book was written. Thanks are also owed to *The Southwest Review,* in whose pages an early version of the first chapter of the book appeared, and to Wayne State University Press, in whose anthology *Conversant Essays,* edited by James McCorkle, a version of the second chapter was published. I have additionally benefited from the encouragement and learning of many friends, among them R. L. Barth, Edgar Bowers, the late J. V. Cunningham, the late Henri Coulette, Dick Davis, Kenneth Fields, R. S. Gwynn, Jack Hagstrom, X. J. Kennedy, Anthony Olcott, Nancy Huddleston Packer, Margaret Peterson, Terry Santos, Alan Shapiro, Donald E. Stanford, Helen Pinkerton Trimpi, Wesley Trimpi, and Clive Wilmer. Special thanks go to Vikram Seth, whose interest in the project and whose good-natured prodding kept the author going when otherwise he might have dropped by the way. Special thanks go as well to Charles Gullans: throughout the period of this book's writing, he and I have discussed the issues explored in it, and his sympathy and intelligence have been of incalculable help. I feel a similarly great debt to Paul G. Naiditch, who read the manuscript chapter by chapter and who was unfailingly generous with suggestions and constructive criticism. I should also like to express deep gratitude to Joshua Odell for his friendship and for his singularly heartening concern for this project.

Be it noted, finally, that without the support of my wife Victoria, this book would not have been written. Its dedication to her reflects my good fortune in her faith and companionship.

*

I should like to thank these publishers for permission to reprint the following poems:

"The Aim Was Song" from *The Poetry of Robert Frost*, edited by Edward Connery Lathem, copyright 1969. Reprinted with the permission of Henry Holt and Company, Inc.

"For My Contemporaries" from *The Collected Poems and Epigrams of J. V. Cunningham*, Swallow Press, copyright 1971. Reprinted with the permission of The Ohio University Press, Athens, OH.

Ezra Pound's "Coda," from *Personae*, copyright 1926, is reprinted by permission of New Directions Publishing Corporation and Faber & Faber Limited.

The prefatory poem to David Antin's *talking at the boundaries,* copyright 1976, is reprinted by permission of New Directions Publishing Corporation.

"After Haymaking" by Robert Wells from *The Winter's Task,* Carcanet Press, Manchester, England. Reprinted by permission of Carcanet Press.

Missing
Measures

Introduction

In an interview with Jules Huret in March of 1891, Stéphane Mallarmé remarks:

> We are now witnessing a spectacle which is truly extraordinary,
> unique in the history of poetry: every poet is going off by himself
> with his own flute, and playing the songs he pleases. For the first time
> since the beginning of poetry, poets have stopped singing bass. Hith-
> erto, as you know, if they wished to be accompanied, they had to be
> content with the great organ of official meter.[1]

This book endeavors to explain why poets stopped singing
bass. It examines why modern poets, a great many of them at

least, abandoned *mètre officiel* in favor of free verse. It explores ideas and conditions that led to the development of verse without meter—of verse without the regularly measured units of rhythm that had, from pre-Homeric times onward, defined the structures of poetic lines.

To be sure, anticipations of free verse exist prior to the modern period. In our language, the King James Psalms and, to use George Saintsbury's term, the "stave-prose poetry"[2] of James Macpherson's Ossianic epics, William Blake's "Prophetic Books," Martin Farquhar Tupper's *Proverbial Philosophy,* and Walt Whitman's *Leaves of Grass* may be adduced as examples of proto-free verse. Experiments in poetical prose or prose poetry by writers in German and French, from Salomon Gessner to Arthur Rimbaud, could be cited as well. But poets did not consciously write free verse until the mid- to late-1880s. At this time, Gustave Kahn, Jules Laforgue, Édouard Dujardin, Jean Moréas, Francis Vielé-Griffin, and others began to publish *vers libre,* and discussions expounding it and attaching to it that particular phrase, in Parisian journals such as *La Vogue* and *La Revue Indépendante* and in Albert Mockel's Belgian journal, *La Wallonie.* In his *Premiers Poètes du Vers Libre,* Dujardin gives 1886 to 1888 as the period of the seminal publications; and he marks the "definitive establishment of free verse" with the book publication in 1889 of Vielé-Griffin's *Joies* and with its prefatory manifesto beginning, "Le vers est libre." At this point, according to Dujardin, "The battle had been, in effect, won."[3] He adds that during and after 1889 the publications of vers-libristes became too many to number. Mallarmé's comment, in his interview with Huret two years later, that "every poet is going off by himself" indicates how rapidly and widely the medium had been adopted.

Subsequently, favorable and unfavorable analyses of *vers libre* are common. Two important discussions, important because they are conducted by the two leading French poets of the time, date from 1894. The first is Paul Verlaine's poem, *"J'admire l'ambition du Vers Libre,"* which appears in his *Épigrammes* and which is gently skeptical of the new movement. The second and more sympathetic is the "Music and Letters" lecture which Mallarmé delivers at Oxford and Cambridge and in which he announces: "I bring news—and most amazing and unprecedented news. We have been experimenting with verse."[4] And, referring to *vers libre* by name, Mallarmé tells his audiences, maybe the earliest English-speaking ones to hear of the medium, about the innovation.

Details of these developments have been or could be debated. For instance, was Marie Krysinska, as she affirmed in the introduction to her 1890 *Rythmes Pittoresques,* which featured poems that had appeared in magazines during the previous decade, the first vers-libriste to have gotten into print? What role should be assigned to Rimbaud's "Marine" and "Mouvement," two pieces in his *Illuminations,* pieces evidently written in the early 1870s, but not published until 1886? These are sometimes said to be *vers libre*. However, the poet's own view of them is unknown, and when *La Vogue,* under Kahn's editorship, printed the first of the pieces, it was set in the Roman type that the journal customarily used for prose rather than the italic that it used for verse, a fact which suggests that the earliest readers of the work were uncertain of its nature.

Yet this much is clear. It was at this juncture, in the mid- to late-1880s, that poets articulated and started to cultivate a specific mode of versification free of meter. (Shortly, I shall say more about the terms *vers libre* and "free verse.")

To note these circumstances is not to minimize the fact that the revolt against meter had a considerable prehistory. Indeed, this study stresses that if one is to understand the free verse movement, one must examine it in light of ideas about poetry which developed in earlier periods and which in many instances go all the way back to the ancients. Neither would one wish to deny the relevance to the emergence of free verse of forerunning works such as those mentioned a few moments ago. However, these works represented for the most part special or somewhat isolated cases. More to the point, their authors did not call them "free verse."

Though the free verse movement was international and was part of that general revolution in the arts which occurred at the end of the nineteenth and the beginning of the twentieth century, this book directs its attention principally to the leaders of the free verse movement in England and America. Two related considerations have led to this approach. First, the views of the English and American experimentalists illustrate, in fundamental respects, the international movement at large; this fact will be especially evident in the fourth and fifth chapters, which correlate more frequently than is the case in the earlier chapters ideas expressed by English and American poets with ideas voiced by their counterparts in continental Europe. Second, the poetic and critical writings of the English and American experimentalists will be more familiar and more readily available to most of the readers of this book. And I hope that this book will move some of them to reexamine those writings, and the issues they raise, in ways that they perhaps have not done previously.

Because modern poetry's break with meter involves fairly complicated issues in literary history, it may be helpful to summarize them before proceeding, so as to orient the reader and to acquaint him or her with the itinerary that will be followed.

*

The first of the book's five chapters examines the way in which the modern revolution in English and American verse differed from earlier revolutions. Most earlier revolutions involved, as the modern one did in part, a revolt against outmoded poetic diction and subject matter. Such was the case, to cite two instances to which T. S. Eliot refers in discussing his own practices, with the revolutions led by Dryden and Wordsworth. In the modern period, however, the English and American experimentalists identified the florid idiom characteristic of much Victorian verse with meter itself. As a result, they believed that in order to get rid of Victorian style they had also to get rid of meter, which of course had been employed by the Victorians but which was not specifically Victorian, having been used by centuries of earlier poets. When Dryden and Wordsworth objected to overly-poetical mannerisms, they did not include conventional metric among the qualities they wished to remove from verse; they continued to write in the traditional measures of English poetry. In contrast, modern poets, in overthrowing Victorian style, overthrew meter as well.

The first chapter also analyzes the manner in which the modern revolutionaries identified meter not only with Victorian style, but also with a method of reading aloud and scanning English verse that had developed in the nineteenth century. This method of scansion, which became common when English poetry entered school curricula and which was designed to serve as a teaching equivalent to the traditional study of classical prosody, involved speaking lines of verse in a heavily artificial and sing-song way to bring out their metrical identity. For instance, to demonstrate that Keats's famous line in "The Eve of St. Agnes" was an iambic pentameter, one would read it as follows:

The *hare* limp'd *trem*bling *through* the *fro*zen *grass*

And one would render the second line of Shakespeare's sonnet 76 thus:

So *far* from *varia*tion *or* quick *change*

This method of reading and scanning clarifies the metrical norm of conventional lines of verse. It obliterates, however, natural degrees of relative speech stress within lines, and it produced a widespread feeling that conventional verse was necesarily "metronomic" and "rigid." This feeling in turn produced the belief that to introduce rhythmical life into verse, one needed to depart to some degree from metrical norms.

Toward the end of the first chapter, other matters are noted, among them the following one. That the modern revolutionaries did not entirely recognize what they were doing—that they believed they were merely engaging in the kinds of necessary renovations of poetic speech that poets must undertake from time to time to keep poetry vital—is of the utmost significance. This circumstance explains why, in the wake of the triumph of the modern revolution, there ensued not a period of stability and consolidation (which the leaders of the revolution had hoped for and anticipated), but a period of increasing prosodic restlessness and increasing anxiety about the nature and status of poetic structure.

The first chapter, then, establishes two facts: (1) that the modern revolutionaries identified diction with meter and (2) that, having made this identification (and having identified metrical composition with scansion), they deposed meter in the course of deposing Victorian style. By documenting and analyzing this aspect of the modern movement and by contrasting the movement with earlier revolutions—revolutions which criticized dated idiom and subject matter, but which did not call meter into question—the chapter specifies the singularity of the modern attack on meter. As important as this specification is, however, it is only a first step in our study. For the singularity of the attack indicates that there must have been factors that did not exist in earlier periods that did exist in the modern period which helped to give rise to and supported the concept of free verse. The book's next four chapters explain some of these factors.

The second chapter discusses the historical relationship between verse and prose and the influence of the modern novel on modern poetry. Though traditions of prose fiction go back at least as far as Aesop, the fiction of prestige, from the Greeks to the eighteenth century, is mostly in meter. Moreover, serious prose writers, from Gorgias forward, have looked to the older art of poetry for ways of giving prose shape and order. Much of the history of prose style concerns efforts to make prose as memorable and as attractive as verse and to secure for prose a quasi-metrical integrity so that it can achieve an emotional power comparable to that of poetry. "The enthusiastic admirers of Isocrates," Cicero tells us in *Orator* 174, "extol as the greatest of his accomplishments that he was the first to introduce rhythm into prose. For when he observed that people listened to orators with solemn attention, but to poets with pleasure, he is said to have sought for rhythms to use in prose as well, both for their intrinsic charm and in order that monotony might be forestalled by variety."[5] Cicero reminds us here that, historically, prose develops not merely alongside of verse, but in reference to poetic style and metric. Poetry is the primary art, and prose imitates it.

The last two hundred years, however, mark a change. Many of the finest fiction writers of the age compose in prose rather than in meter, and the modern novel acquires a popularity and respectability formerly accorded to epic, verse drama, and lyric. Indeed, by the end of the nineteenth century, the novel is the dominant form of fiction. Modern poets commonly urge that poetry has lost much of its material to prose fiction and that if poetry is to recover that material, it must assimilate characteristics of the novel. Whereas in earlier times prose writers experimented with incorporating verse cadences into prose, poets now begin to experiment with integrating the relative rhythms of prose into verse. Prose becomes, in short, the primary art. In this context, Ford Madox Ford and Ezra Pound's assertion that, as Ford puts it, "verse must be at least as well written as prose if it is to be poetry,"[6] gets transmuted into the notion that verse might profitably be written as the novel is written—without meter.

The second chapter traces the steps of this process. And the chapter concludes with a discussion of the relation of modern theories of free verse to ancient theories of prose, particularly the ancient idea that artistic prose should suggest and, at the same time, avoid metrical pattern. The chapter also makes the point that the modern argument that free verse is more sophisticated than metrical poetry—and thus in a sense supersedes it—is related to the ancient notion, evidently first sounded by Isocrates, that artistic prose is the rightful successor to the more "primitive" form of composition represented by poetry.

The third chapter examines the modern distinction between "verse," meaning metrically competent writing which lacks poetic fire, and "poetry," meaning inspired composition which is independent of conventional rules of versification. Though poetry was always, before the modern period, associated with meter, many critics of different eras have urged that great poetry involves something more than metrical skill. "Imitation," "passion," "concentration": these are just a few of the qualities that poets and their readers have at one time or another felt to be as essential as (or even more essential than) meter to true poetry. Yet an unusual thing happens in the modern period. The commonplace that poetry is something *more* than meter is transformed into the idea that poetry is something *other* than meter. One finds in much modern criticism, especially in that of Eliot, the belief that conventional metrical composition is less admirable than poetry which eschews regular meter in preference for some more "difficult" quality of rhythm.

The third chapter demonstrates that the distinction between verse and poetry originated in the Renaissance, when readers of Aristotle's then recently recovered *Poetics* conflated two of its passages with a passage in Quintilian's *Institutes of Oratory*. In the later Middle Ages, this passage had itself been conflated with Servius's judgment, in *On the Aeneid,* that Lucan's epic about the Roman civil wars is a history, not a poem. In addition, though to a lesser extent, a passage from Plutarch's *Moralia* figures in this matter. Neither Aristotle nor Quintilian (nor Servius nor Plutarch) makes a distinction between verse and poetry. When the ancient authorities are combined, however, the distinction occurs. Having made the distinction, Renaissance readers explore it with reference to the role of imitation in poetry, arguing for and against three related propositions: (1) that imitation is more important to poetry than is verse; (2) that writers like Dante and Fracastoro, who write in meter but do not imitate, are "versifiers" instead of "poets"; and (3) that those who compose prose romances and prose dramas, and who in that process imitate action and life, have a right to the title of "poet," despite the fact that they do not compose in "verse." After the Renaissance, when the controversy over imitation dies down, the verse-poetry distinction is adapted to different and changing contexts. Eventually, it becomes an important tool for advocates of poems, short poems as well as longer narrative and dramatic works, without meter.

The fourth chapter deals with aesthetics and the ways in which it contributes to the rise of nonmetrical poetry. "Aesthetics" is here to be understood in its historical sense, that is, in reference to the theory developed in the eighteenth century that art is concerned with (to use Kant's formulation) "taste" and "judgment" and can be studied and practiced independently of ethical analysis (or "practical reason") and rational understanding (or "pure reason"). Aestheticism facilitates the development of nonmetrical poetry in several ways. For one thing, the aesthetic doctrine that poems are "autonomous" creations results in an emphasis on internal as opposed to external qualities of poetry. Ford, Pound, William Carlos Williams, and Eliot all argue that the free verse movement involves, in Eliot's words, "an insistence upon the inner unity which is unique to every poem, against the outer unity which is typical."[7] If every poem is defined in terms of an independent internal unity, it follows that every poem may or even should create its own prosody.

Aestheticism encourages the development of nonmetrical verse in another respect. In elevating music as the purest of the arts, writers in the aesthetic tradition produce a literary environment in which many poets aspire to musicality. The leaders of the free verse movement almost unanimously explain the medium in terms of music, and they argue that what free verse lacks in metricality it makes up for in musicality. In this regard, Pound's remark that the poet should "compose in the sequence of the musical phrase, not in sequence of a metronome"[8] is doubly significant. In the first place, it indicates the degree to which music has, in Pound's mind, supplanted meter as the measure of verse. In the second place, it suggests the degree to which meter (the root word of "metronome") has come to be viewed as monotonous and inferior.

The aesthetic tradition's concern with organic form also contributes to the development of free verse. For early exponents of organicism—Goethe and Coleridge may serve as examples—organic form and meter are in harmony. This is because nature is regarded as producing attractive products in an orderly fashion. During the nineteenth century, however, interpretations of organic theory alter. Rather than urging that poets should create, as nature does, according to certain regulating principles of development, some observers contend that poets should function, as nature functions, unconsciously. And rather than imitating the comeliness of natural objects, some poets, such as D. H. Lawrence, seek to suggest the internal processes that determine those objects. To the extent that these processes are regarded as being elementally turbulent or chaotic, verse that is intentionally confused comes to be considered truer to nature than is verse of a more orderly kind. To the extent that metrical speech embodies clear structural principles, it is therefore disparaged as not only unnecessary to poetical-natural truth but as inappropriate to it.

Finally, Aestheticism encourages the development of nonmetrical verse because it frees poetry not only from ethical and rational understanding, but from its own history. In stressing the poet's autonomy, Aestheticism has the effect, even when it addresses matters of artistic métier, of depreciating laws of composition external to the poet's individual imagination. Discussing his verse, Williams remarks: "I have never been one to write by rule, even by my own rules. Let's begin with the rule of counted syllables, in which all poems have been written hitherto. That has become tiresome to my ear."[9] So clipped and confident a dismissal of nearly three millennia of conventional craft would not have been possible without a climate of opinion in which each poem and each poet could claim aesthetic autonomy.

The fifth chapter treats the influence of modern science on poetry. As early as the seventeenth century, one encounters the idea that poetry and art are not making the kinds of advances that science is making. This circumstance troubles poets, and one finds a figure like Dryden speculating uneasily that, whereas the ancient world was distinguished by great poetry, the modern world is distinguished by great science. This uneasiness among writers grows over time. By the end of the nineteenth century, it is widely argued that art, in order to insure itself a central position in modern culture, should attempt to achieve the kinds of quantitative progress of which science is capable. Poetry, it is said, should be "experimental" and produce "breakthroughs" and "discoveries."

This concern with "experiment" turns many poets away from the traditional idea that poetry derives its novelty less from its techniques than from its subject matter, the always-changing moral and social conditions of the race and the always-fresh spectacle that those conditions present. Looking to modern science and observing that its achievements often result from inventions or refinements of apparatus, poets seek novelty in the structural elements of their art. Many adopt the view that poetry must, as T. E. Hulme says, "find a new technique each generation. Each age must have its own special form of expression."[10]

The assertion that poetry requires continual technical innovation is frequently accompanied by more specific assertions to the effect that this or that new way of writing reflects the latest developments in science or technology and is thus especially useful or sophisticated. Certain proponents of automatic free verse, for example, urge that their poems embody Freud's theories and illuminate the workings of the unconscious mind. Other poets writing unmeasured verse argue that they are expressing, in a literary sphere, Einstein's relativity theories. With the growth of particle physics, yet other poets contend that they, by breaking up verse forms, are looking to achieve insights and to release energies analogous to those achieved and released by physicists splitting atomic nuclei. Such notions are detrimental to conventional versification because they imply that meter is intellectually backward or instrumentally inferior to newer methods of poetic composition.

Science also influences modern poetry in a related fashion. In most cases, the newer a scientific theory is, the better and more comprehensive it is. The modern movement's leaders transferred to poetry this model of scientific history. This transferral undermined the older view that, in poetic composition, the safest guides are provided by the examples of earlier masterpieces. In addition, the transferral encouraged the notion that the literary past is, like the scientific past, largely irrelevant to present practice. An assumption grew that though a Virgil and a Shakespeare certainly merit great respect, it would be as absurd for a modern poet to write, as they had written, in conventional meter as it would be for a modern scientist to adhere to Ptolemy's concept of planetary motion or Galen's doctrine of the four humors. Imposing the model of scientific progress on poetry was especially crucial to Pound and Eliot, who, even as they wrote poems like the *Cantos* and *The Waste Land,* vigorously and sincerely professed an allegiance to tradition. The model of science persuaded them that in breaking with conventional versification, they were contributing to "progress"—were serving poetry as earlier masters had—and that those who continued to write in meter were, in contrast, contributing to poetic stagnation.

The fifth chapter ends with a discussion of Thomas Mann's *Doctor Faustus,* which provides an acute analysis of the modern attempt to make art "scientific." Mann observes, in his portrait of Adrian Leverkühn, that when modern art has aimed for scientific novelty and for radical refinements of apparatus, it has tended to derail, paradoxically, into magic and barbarism. Mann's theme is relevant to the issue of meter and modern poetry, in that, as much as one sympathizes with the objectives of the modern movement, its results have sometimes proved detrimental in ways that Mann describes. Though the modernists abandoned meter out of a genuine wish to renovate verse and reconnect it to a real world and a real audience, the effect to a great extent has been to deprive poetry of resources that enable it to examine human experience appealingly, distinctively, and meaningfully.

The various issues discussed in this study are related in various ways. One of the study's aims is to clarify the relationships between apparently conflicting impulses of the modern movement. Superficially, modern poetry presents a fragmented and tangled spectacle: poets and poetry appear to be flying off in all directions at once. While acknowledging this multiplicity, the remarks that follow will endeavor to reveal deeper qualities that comprehensively characterize the modern revolution in verse.

It probably should also be said that this study does not deal much with three issues often considered highly pertinent to the modern revolution in verse. I refer to the First World War, to the American rejection of what Emerson called "the courtly muses of Europe,"[11] and to the suspected influence of moveable type and printing on poetic composition. These issues do not receive detailed attention here for two reasons. First, the issues have hitherto been frequently discussed, whereas the matters examined in these pages have not. Second, it is possible that undue weight has been laid on these issues. It is legitimate to argue that the free verse movement might not have triumphed had it not been for the First World War and for the distrust of authority that the war occasioned. Yet the free verse movement began well before the war. What is more, to urge that the trauma of World War I accounts for free verse begs the question of why earlier poets (e.g., Sophocles and Andrew Marvell) who lived through similar social upheaval and violence nevertheless kept writing in meter.

Related statements may be made about the ascription of free verse to American literary nationalism. Americans played a key role in establishing free verse as the dominant means of poetic expression in our time. The international success of *The Waste Land* was particularly important in raising free verse to a position of virtual orthodoxy. It is useful to explore these facts. And, to return to a point touched upon earlier, I would not devote as much attention as I do to Pound, Eliot, and Williams did I not believe that their views are centrally illustrative of tendencies in modern verse in general.

But the free verse movement was transatlantic, and some of the earliest developments in or anticipations of the movement are European. Two English examples that may be usefully cited here are Macpherson's Ossianic poems and Tupper's now largely forgotten but once (in the mid-nineteenth century) enormously popular *Proverbial Philosophy*. Macpherson's work stimulated early experiments with prose-poetry; and, without downplaying Whitman's originality, we may observe, as Whitman's contemporaries often did, that his long loose line owes a debt not only to the King James Bible, but also to Tupper's "Rhythmics."[12]

Moreover, the very term "free verse" derives from the French *vers libre*. Indeed, English and American poets were generally slow to naturalize the term into their own language. The French term predominated for some time. For instance, Eliot, in his 1917 essay, "Reflections on *Vers Libre*," employs solely the French term. In contrast, by the time of his 1942 "The Music of Poetry" essay, which also discusses the revolution in modern versification,

Eliot speaks of "free verse." An early important document in English to discuss free verse in just those words is the unsigned preface (1915) to the first of the three anthologies of Imagist poetry arranged by Amy Lowell; and it is significant that when the term is introduced in the preface, the principal author of which was evidently Richard Aldington, it appears between quotation marks and in hyphenated form. "We do not insist upon 'free-verse' as the only method of writing poetry," the preface states. "We fight for it as for a principle of liberty."[13] The phrase, that is, is translated, but the quotation marks and hyphen would seem to indicate its still foreign character.

Delays in adopting the Anglicized term may partly be explained by the fact that "free verse" sounds, as Eliot and Williams noted, self-contradictory. This difficulty seems to have been less felt in France, perhaps because *vers libre* derived from and was homophonic with *vers libres,* a type of classical French poetry exemplified by La Fontaine's *Fables* and Molière's *Amphitryon,* which was perfectly metrical. *Vers libres,* that is, are not "free verses" in the twentieth-century sense; they merely feature a mixture of different but conventional meters and a mixture of different sorts of rhymes—*plates* (couplet), *croisées* (crossed), *embrassées* (enveloped), and so forth. For a comparable kind of versification in English poetry of the same period, we might think of Abraham Cowley's Pindaric odes. To the extent that *vers libres* used its changes in meters and its varying arrangements of rhymes for purposes of emphasis, and for highlighting changes in mood and meaning, we might also think of later poems such as Matthew Arnold's "Dover Beach," Coventry Patmore's "Departure," and Robert Frost's "After Apple-Picking."

When the French experimentalists dropped the "s" from *vers libres,* they did so to advocate a new kind of poetry, a poetry which, in Dujardin's words, "pushing liberation to its extreme limit, admits an indeterminate number of syllables, . . . allows assonance in the place of rhyme and even the absence of all appearance of rhyme."[14] Yet because of its resemblance to and aural identity with the traditional term, the French *vers libre* did not jar the ear and mind in the way that the English term did.

As an aside, one might note that shortly before the advent of *vers libre,* the Symbolists had used an additional phrase, *vers libérés,* to indicate verses that—though "liberated" from certain classical conventions of French poetry, especially the proscription against lines of longer than Alexandrine length—were still rhymed and syllabically correspondent. Acceptance of the term *vers libre* may have been facilitated by the currency of this additional phrase and by the fact that the poetry it described exhibited, as *vers libres* did, traditional features of verse.

Furthermore, much free verse practice, American and otherwise, reflects ideas about poetry and art traceable back not only to European Aestheticism but to late-ancient Neoplatonism and to the Neoplatonic belief, memorably elaborated by Plotinus in his *Enneads,* that the indeterminate is mystically liberating, while the determinate is materially confining. Then, too, it must be said that poets like Horace followed metrical conventions of previous periods and even other countries while insisting as forcefully as Williams that writers should deal with native subjects and not rely on materials from foreign models. To urge that free verse resulted from American literary nationalism leaves unexplained, that is, the fact that literary nationalists of former ages did not abandon meter.

As for modern printing, it obviously has affected our ways of looking at and, in some cases, of composing verse. Eliot, to cite a well-known instance, composed poems at the typewriter; to appreciate his work, one must recognize that some of it is written almost as much for the eye as for the ear. Metrical verse can appeal to the eye, but its fundamental appeal is to audial perception. "Now is the winter of our discontent" and "The Hiker's Companion to California" both occupy thirty-five spaces of type. One is a conventional iambic pentameter; the other is not. A poet accustomed to measure lines in a visual manner may lose sight of this distinction more quickly than one who retains an ear for the measure.

Nevertheless, one should be cautious of overestimating the effects of type and typography on the development of free verse. The visual appearance of the poem on the page has long been appreciated. Shaped or pattern poetry, for example, goes back to the Alexandrian period, and shaped poems were popular in the Renaissance. Yet in neither case did the interest in the visual effects of shaped verses undermine metric. For example, the shaped verse of a poem such as George Herbert's "Easter Wings" has regular linear pattern and stanzaic structure as well as a specific visual aspect. And with regard to moveable type itself, one might observe that it existed for over four centuries before free verse came into being. Free verse is more likely to flourish in an age of printing than in an age in which literary culture is more closely connected to speech and oral traditions. Yet to praise or to blame Gutenberg for free verse is probably to exaggerate the influence of printing.

Having explained why I do not discuss certain issues sometimes considered highly pertinent to the modern revolution in verse, I should explain why I do devote a good deal of attention to classical texts rarely associated with the subject. Literary issues are not like scientific ones. They can never be solved once and for all. A chemist may determine definitively the properties of a mineral. A poet or critic, however, cannot achieve similar exactitude in determining what constitutes a fine poem or by what means it may be produced. Proximate solutions are the best that writers can hope for. Moreover, literary issues, like moral, political, religious, and legal ones, must be continually reexamined; in addressing them, we must attend both to our unique and living moment and to the guidance of earlier wisdom and precedent. New answers are always needed; old ones are always relevant. What previous writers have said about their art is illuminating since their remarks indicate the ways in which they sought to resolve matters that writers of every age must address; we can learn from their successes and disappointments.

No less important is the fact that the very terms with which modern debates about poetry have been pursued are terms that were first hammered out and given significance by Greek and Latin authors. To the extent that we understand the original meanings of these terms and understand the ways in which they have altered and have been adapted to changing circumstances over time, our understanding of our situation will be richer.

An additional observation about the word "poetry" is in order. We live with the legacy of the ancient Greek view of the art. This view was dual. On the one hand, poetry was *metron,* metrical composition. On the other hand, poetry was *mimēsis,* imitation— or, we might say, "fiction." A particular writer, such as Plato or Isocrates, might stress the metrical element; another writer, such as Aristotle or Plutarch, might stress the mimetic element. Yet there was no conflict in the duality. Not only was most fiction in ancient Greece written in verse, but medical, ethical, philosophical, political, and cosmological works were commonly written in verse as well. One reason that Plato was so concerned about the moral and social effects of poetry was that poetry was in his time regarded as a medium for the communication of knowledge in general. One reason Aristotle argued that poetry could be more usefully regarded as fictional composition than as metrical composition was that fiction was, in his day, a much more specifying characteristic than meter was.

Today the situation is reversed. Non-literary subjects are rarely treated in meter. Narrative and dramatic works are usually in prose. To the extent that it is possible to apply the older terms for short poems to what is currently published, we may say that even lyrics, satires, epigrams, elegies, and the like are mostly written without meter. Whereas for the Greeks, metrical composition was the broad base of the literary pyramid, meter in our era is more like its narrowing tip. Whereas ancient writers sometimes complained that verse is all-too-widely practiced, modern writers may ask, in the words of the title of Edmund Wilson's essay, "Is Verse a Dying Technique?"

As will become evident in this study, certain confusions in modern discussions of verse have resulted from the fact that the legacy of the Greeks has not been adequately recognized and that the difference between their situation and ours has not been sufficiently appreciated. We cannot ask of others or ourselves absolute precision when we speak of "poetry," and we should not damn such terminological imprecisions as must inevitably attend any general discussion of the art. Yet we should be aware of something of the history of the word and should bear this history in mind when we use the word.

Though the term "meter" presents fewer problems than "poetry," it may bear comment as well. The first of the *OED*'s definitions of the word reads, "Any specific form of poetic rhythm, its kind being determined by the character and number of the feet or groups of syllables of which it consists."[15] Meter involves more than merely a vague property of rhythm. As the definition indicates, the rhythm has specific form. It repeats. Its patterns can be discerned and anticipated. Its principles are recognizable. It is true that, for a time in the Middle Ages, *metra* applied to Latin verse in then-declining quantitative meters, as opposed to *rithmici versus,* Latin verse in the rhymed and accentual measures that had started to develop in late antiquity. Yet when, in the later Middle Ages, the quantitative measures further declined—and when, moreover, poetry written in the vernaculars was gradually eclipsing verse in Latin—"meter," in the original sense of "poetic measure," was coined afresh by the modern languages.

To the extent that vernacular poets in the later Middle Ages came to adopt the principle of regulating the number of syllables in their lines, a principle central to ancient versification as well, the re-minted term may have seemed especially appropriate, even though in vernacular verse it was dynamic stress instead of duration that provided a defining element for the individual syllables in the line. The re-minting proved additionally appropriate to the degree that modern meters such as iambic pentameter are, as Aristotle says of the ancient *metra,* "sections of rhythms" (*Poetics* 1448b21).[16] Just as, for example, the ancient dactylic hexameter was a line with a certain kind of rhythm (dactylic) cut into sections of a certain length (six feet), so the modern iambic pentameter is a line with a certain kind of rhythm (iambic) measured into segments of a certain length (five feet). In any case, "meter" has continued to carry the meaning of "poetic measure" down to the present day.

A key difference between ancient versification and modern English versification might be mentioned here. This difference involves rhyme. Generally speaking, ancient Greek and Latin poets employ rhyme only occasionally and ornamentally. Following practices developed in late antiquity and the Latin Middle Ages, poets in the modern languages often employ rhyme to mark line-endings. Regular use of "end rhyme" appears in verse in the Romance languages earlier than it does in verse in English. Indeed, end rhyme does not become prominent in English verse until after the Norman conquest and after the gradual transformation of the English language and its literature by Romanic influences.

In one sense, end rhyme has allowed poets in English a certain latitude in metrical practice. Admittedly, for the most part, end rhyme has simply supplemented the traditional procedure of regulating the number of syllables per line. When, for instance, Anne Bradstreet uses end rhyme in "Verses upon the Burning of our House" or Christina Rossetti uses it in "A Pause for Thought," the device reinforces and emphasizes the structure of the lines by making them agree with each other in their terminal syllables. Yet on occasion, end rhyme has served as a kind of alternative to the strict regulation of syllabic equivalences from line to line or from stanza to stanza. Especially in poems in short lines or in simple stanzaic forms, where the structural units are compact and readily apprehensible to the ear, rhyme may provide a definition such that the observance of syllabic equivalences may be relaxed somewhat.

Consider, for example, one of Thomas Hardy's early poems, "Neutral Tones." The poem consists of four quatrains with an *abba* rhyme scheme; the first three lines of each quatrain are tetrameters, while the fourth and final line is a trimeter. Yet it is difficult to fix a definite term to the rhythm of the lines. If we scan them, we will find that Hardy mixes iambs and anapests almost equally, as in the poem's third stanza:

> The smile on your mouth was the deadest thing
>
> Alive enough to have strength to die;
>
> And a grin of bitterness swept thereby
>
> Like an ominous bird a-wing . . .[17]

However, the variations in rhythm and syllable count do not disrupt the poem's structural integrity. Only one of the poem's lines, the fourteenth, is enjambed. Otherwise, the linear units correspond throughout to syntactical units, and the reader pauses at the ends of the lines and hears clearly the four-four-four-three pattern of stresses. (This is true even in the first stanza, where the fourth line is noticeably longer than the corresponding lines in the other stanzas; however, there are still three stresses in the line, and it is clear which of the syllables are stressed.) More important, the end rhymes knit the lines together securely. A metrician might say that the rhythm of the poem is "iambic-anapestic"; or since the iambs outnumber the anapests by a slight margin, he or she might call the rhythm "iambic with frequent anapestic substitutions." But such terms do not entirely suit a poem like Hardy's, which approaches the condition of a sort of rhymed accentual verse.

Such a technique may reflect the influence of the accentual procedure of the old Germanic tradition, though in that tradition it was customarily internal alliteration rather than end rhyme that clarified the structure of the line. Yet the point to be made here is merely that end rhyme has sometimes served in English verse to clarify the structures of comparatively loose lines. Though examples of this technique may be found in all periods from the later Middle Ages forward, it is practiced with particular frequency in the nineteenth century. It is possible that in this area the example of nineteenth century poets encouraged experiments in free verse. (The special case of Gerard Manley Hopkins will be discussed in chapter two.) It should be noted, however, that the freedoms involved in work such as Hardy's are considerably less than those involved in the practice of a Pound or Williams. Hardy retains a recognizable measure, even if it is not strictly isosyllabic. For that matter, isosyllabic measures themselves have always permitted certain variations. Ancient poets, for instance, were at points allowed to resolve a long syllable into two shorts or to contract two shorts into a long; English poets have always been allowed occasional substitutions of variant feet for the dominant foot in the line. Moreover, the free-versers were for the most part opposed not only to conventional meter, but also to end rhyme.

To avoid any appearance of authorial presumption, I should add that I am keenly aware of the complexities of the questions this book examines and of the fact that there is no absolutely right or wrong way of resolving them. I entertain no hard and fast definition of poetry itself, nor do I think that such definitions contribute to the health of the art. At the same time, I believe that our ability to organize thought and speech into measure is one of the most precious endowments of the human race. To throw away this endowment would be a tragedy. It is unfortunate that in recent years, many proponents of free verse, who have long since overwhelmingly outnumbered the defenders of meter, have adopted the view that meter is entirely obsolete and that anyone who questions this view should be squelched at all costs. Such individuals have imposed, or have attempted to impose, an ortho-doxy as rigid and as intolerant as any that the modernists encoun-tered when they undertook to reform poetry.

I should like to make some further observations concerning the modernists. If in writing this book I have found myself obliged at points to make judgments critical of them, I think they would want the evidence and arguments to be given a fair hear-ing. In suggesting that the modernists may have been misguided in some respects, I do so simply in hopes that the suggestion will help to bring about a clearer understanding of the revolution they led and a richer consideration of issues that current poetic practice and theory might address. I admire the modernists' devotion to poetry and their achievements. But for several generations we have been living with a phenomenon which I have elsewhere called recycled novelty. In ever-narrower ways, the procedures and ideas of the modern movement have been appropriated and deployed as if they were still brand-new and untried. Unless we gain a more informed awareness of the modern movement and of its liabilities as well as its admirable vitalities, we will continue to repeat its shortcomings without capturing its virtues.

Another point regarding the modernists should be mentioned. Some of their programs were to an extent promulgated to shock the middle-brow. And certain readers may feel that it is therefore naive to take their statements and ideas too much at face value. Though a healthy caution to the literalist, this view is in other senses unsound. To begin with, it is unjust to the modernists themselves, who were more than mere controversialists. In addi-tion, some statements and ideas that may have been advanced in the heat of polemical engagement or daredevil iconoclasm have been adopted in a much more solemn fashion by later commen-tators. Perhaps it is wise to consider the possibility that, for in-stance, Pound was not entirely serious when he urged that con-ventional iambic verse was "metronomic." (Since he returns to this concept on several occasions at different times in his career, one suspects that he was dead serious.) Yet whatever the case may be, the concept has been tremendously influential. For fifty years now, textbooks of one kind or another have, sometimes citing Pound directly, informed readers that regular meter and individual rhythm are mutually exclusive. There is thus good reason to examine the concept and Pound's exposition of it as clearly as possible.

On a different and more simply descriptive note, I should also say that this study is not centrally concerned with analyzing different species of free verse and with speculating about the ways in which these do or do not work. This is not to disparage the fruits that analyses of this type might yield. Yet T. V. F. Brogan's bibliography, *English Versification, 1570–1980,* has fifteen pages of entries for such analyses, some of them highly insightful, and similar analyses have continued to appear more or less regularly since Brogan's work was published.[18] There are, I realize, many varieties of free verse, from the long scriptural lines of Whitman to the short and frequently enjambed lines of Williams, from the suavely cadenced free verse of Stevens' "Snow Man" and some of Pound's *Cantos* to the scattery, all-over-the-page compositions of E. E. Cummings; in the cases of Ford and Eliot, we sometimes see, in a single poem, passages in free verse alternating with passages in regular meter or in lines that hover around a metrical norm without committing themselves to it. Such differences are worth noting. Yet, as was indicated at the outset, my object here is to explain why many modern poets, around and shortly after the turn of the century, abandoned the practice of writing metrically, a practice which had informed poetic composition for nearly three millennia. I do not aim to provide a taxonomic examination of the multiplicity of heterogeneous modes that arose during the modern movement or that have ramified in subsequent poetic practice. Such an examination would require an additional and entirely different book.

It would also require an additional and entirely different book to examine all the connections between free verse in modern poetry and comparable phenomena in other modern arts. This is not to dispute the fact that many of the ideas that supported the rise of free verse encouraged the rise of, for example, abstractionism in painting and atonality in music. The emphasis in modern aesthetics on the value of the indeterminate influences the visual and musical arts no less than it influences poetry. The same may be said of the interest in novelties of method suggestive of scientific progress. And I discuss, especially in the fifth chapter of this study, these ideas in relation to music and painting as well as verse. However, to draw at every possible point analogies between developments in modern poetry and developments in other arts would detract from this study's efforts to explain as specifically and clearly as possible why many modern poets were moved to break with the compositional conventions of their own art and to abandon meter in favor of free verse.

Finally, it may be helpful to remember, in the course of this study, an obvious but easily forgotten point. Meters themselves are abstractions from or selections of certain patterns of speech in a language. Ancient and modern writers alike testify that metrical systems establish themselves gradually by trial and error. Writers do not sit down and invent them. They are invented, so to speak, by the languages they serve. This is true, for instance, even of Latin metric and its appropriations from Greek. Ennius's great achievement was not that he arbitrarily willed the hexameter onto the Latin tongue; rather, he demonstrated how the line could be suited to Roman speech and to a language richer in long syllables and more accentual than Greek. Negative demonstration of this point is supplied in our language by the unsuccessful experiments with classical measures by Sidney, Dyer, Drant, Spenser, and their "Areopagus" circle. Stress plays too large and quantity too small a role in English: the attempted adaptation, in this case, would not work.[19]

One of the hopes of the modern movement's leaders was that if they overthrew the traditional system of English metric, a new system would generate itself out of the ruins. It may be observed, by way of concluding this introduction, that the history of postmodern poetry is to a great extent the history of the consequences of this hope.

CHAPTER I

Poetry and Precedent:
The Modern Movement
and Free Verse

The revolt against meter is perhaps the most striking feature of the modern revolution in poetry, and free verse is probably the most significant legacy of that revolution. As was noted in the introduction, one can cite from earlier periods a number of works—among them the King James Psalms, Blake's "Prophetic Books," Tupper's *Proverbial Philosophy,* and Whitman's *Leaves of Grass*—which prefigure free verse and which have sometimes had that term retrospectively applied to them. But it was the theory and practice of modern authors, such as T. E. Hulme, Ford Madox Ford, Ezra Pound, T. S. Eliot, and William Carlos

Williams, that made free verse a dominant medium for poetic composition in our literature. In an interview in *Antaeus* in 1978, Stanley Kunitz remarks, "Non-metrical verse has swept the field, so that there is no longer any real adversary from the metricians."[1] Though Kunitz may be overstating the case, and though circumstances may even now be altering again to allow the metricians a voice in contemporary poetry, Kunitz's assessment of prevailing practice is accurate: most verse published today is not metrical. And this situation reflects, among other things, the success of the modernists' revolt against meter.

To understand how free verse developed and why so many modern poets adopted it, one must first examine what the modern movement's leaders believed their revolution represented. The most crucial point in this regard is that the modern revolutionaries believed that their movement was essentially like earlier literary revolutions. The modern movement's leaders commonly argue that theirs is a rebellion against an antiquated diction and subject matter, and is, as such, precisely the rebellion that "modernists" of all ages have had to undertake to keep poetry vitally engaged with the speech and life of its time. Free verse, according to this argument, does not signify a rejection of traditional poetic discipline, but is rather an innovation of the kind which normally accompanies changes in style and taste.

In one respect, this argument is valid. Poetic conventions evolve and flourish; if, having become established, they are used too widely and perfunctorily, they may weaken and fail. When poetry suffers a period of decline, it is only right that poets should try to revive it. This is what good poets have always done; this is what the modernists were doing when they urged that the styles of Victorian verse had grown slack and feeble and needed to be replaced by an idiom better equipped to treat modern life.

In another respect, however, the argument is not sound. In its advocacy of free verse, the modern revolution differed from earlier revolutions. It differed from the revolution Euripides led against Aeschylean style and the revolution Horace led against the literary conservatism of his day; and it differed from—to refer to Eliot's favorite examples—the revolution which Dryden led against Cleveland and the metaphysicals and the revolution which Wordsworth led against the Augustans. To be sure, earlier revolutions frequently entailed the elevation of certain verse forms at the expense of once-prominent ones. Wordsworth and the Romantics, for instance, cultivated sonnets, ballad stanzas, and blank verse—forms relatively neglected by the previous age—and generally shunned the balanced couplet, in which so much of the poetry of the previous age had been composed. Yet Wordsworth did not argue, as the modernists of this century did, that abandoning meter was a suitable means of reforming the faults of predecessors. Indeed, historically speaking, free verse is nothing if not singular. Until this century, virtually all Western poetry is informed by the distinction, perhaps most memorably enunciated by Aristotle (*Rhetoric,* 3.8.2–3),[2] that prose is organized in the general patterns and periods of rhythm (*rhythmos*) and poetry in the specifically and regularly ordered rhythmical units of meter (*metron*).

The modern movement's leaders did not entirely comprehend or admit the singularity of free verse. One reason they did not is that they identified the Victorian diction against which they were rebelling (and the subject matter associated with the diction) with metrical composition *per se*. Having made this identification, they felt that to dispose of objectionable Victorian idiom, they had to dispose of meter. This feeling in turn led the modernists to regard free verse more as an element of reformed speech than as a prosodic matter. They thus overlooked or minimized, especially in the earlier stages of their revolution, the prosodic oddity of free verse. This chapter will explore the modernists' identification of idiom and meter and will clarify the singularity of free verse as an antidote to dated diction and matter.

1. The Identification of Meter with
Dated Diction and Subject Matter

We may begin with Eliot. Though anticipated or influenced by Ford, Hulme, and Pound, Eliot became the most popular and prestigious figure of the modern movement. Much sought-after as a public spokesman for the movement, he consequently had the opportunity and encouragement to explain it in a more systematic fashion than his co-revolutionaries. Eliot's views of the modern revolution and of free verse appear most tellingly in two lectures delivered in the forties, "The Music of Verse," and the second of his Milton papers. In these lectures, Eliot surveys the modern movement retrospectively, taking for granted its triumph and describing what the movement meant to one who participated in it.

Eliot insists in these lectures that the modern revolution had three basic and related objectives: (1) the reformation of an idiom which was obsolete and unrelated to common speech, (2) the reorientation of poetry's subjects and imagery toward contemporary life, and (3) the incorporation into poetic diction of "modern" words and phrases, words and phrases which had not been previously used in poetry but which had the capacity to relate poetic speech to modern life in ways that earlier forms of diction could not. Eliot also states that in having these objectives and in pursuing them, the modern revolution was no different from the revolutions led by Dryden and Wordsworth.

In his Milton lecture, Eliot discusses the modern movement in broad terms, sounding the theme that it was like earlier revolutions in that it involved an effort to empty poetry of hot air and to connect poetry to contemporary speech:

> I have on several occasions suggested, that the important changes in the idiom of English verse which are represented by the names of Dryden and Wordsworth, may be characterized as successful at-

tempts to escape from a poetic idiom which had ceased to have a relation to contemporary speech. This is the sense of Wordsworth's Prefaces. By the beginning of the present century another revolution in idiom—and such revolutions bring with them an alteration of metric, a new appeal to the ear—was due.

(OPP, 159)

It is important to note that Eliot links "idiom" with "metric." He frequently makes this connection, as, for instance, when he discusses his feeling that *Murder in the Cathedral* was too ceremonial to suggest a basis for a truly modern verse drama. "Here, then," he remarks, "were two problems left unsolved: that of the idiom and that of the metric (it is really one and the same problem)" *(OPP,* 80). It is equally important to note that Eliot asserts that in literary revolutions, an alteration of idiom entails an alteration of metric.

Eliot's association of idiom and metric is questionable. Though what a poet says is related to the way in which he says it, idiom and metric are different. Idiom is immediate and fluid; it tends to change from generation to generation. Differences of idiom may appear among different groups of contemporaries speaking the same language. It may be helpful, in this regard, to think of the word in the original Greek sense of *idiōma,* "peculiarity" or "distinctive property." Even a poetic idiom highly informed by standards of verbal propriety remains a part of language and will vary and evolve as language does.[3]

Metric is more stable and less local. It is an abstraction; it comprises a measure or measures by means of which speech can be organized into particular rhythmical patterns. Poets far apart in time can use the same meter. Shakespeare and Wordsworth, though of different eras and outlooks and idioms, both employ iambic pentameter. Indeed, different languages can share the same meters. Greek and Latin share the dactylic hexameter, and Russian, German, and English share the iambic tetrameter. (Variations from language to language in phonological and other matters will naturally lead to differences in compositional practice: for example, Roman hexameter poets generally avoid the feminine third-foot caesura often employed by Homer and Hesiod; Russian tetrameters tend to feature fewer actual speech stresses—tend to be, as Vladimir Nabokov puts it, "scudded" more frequently—than English tetrameters.[4]) Furthermore, poets who are contemporaries or near-contemporaries can use the same metrical form to entirely different effects. The heroic couplet, for instance, appears to fine advantage in Robert Frost's haunting "Once by the Pacific," as well as in some of J. V. Cunningham's satirical epigrams.

As for Eliot's assertion that alterations of idiom inevitably bring alterations of metric, the assertion is not borne out by the testimony of literary history, certainly not by the testimony Eliot himself cites. As we shall see, Wordsworth, throughout the revolution he led, defended conventional meter as earnestly as he decried the vices of "POETIC DICTION."[5] Whereas Wordsworth tried to reform poetry by bringing to traditional metrical composition a more vigorous language and a more genuine subject matter than were in fashion at the time, Eliot endeavored to reform poetry, at least in part, by abandoning conventional meter.

To put the matter more comprehensively, we may say this of the leaders of the modern revolution. With the best of motives and intentions, they objected to the diction and attendant subject matter of Victorian verse. Yet they identified Victorian poetry with the metrical system which the Victorians used but which was not in itself Victorian, having been used for centuries by a variety of poets working in a variety of styles. Hence, the modernists' attack on Victorian idiom led to an attack on meter and to the suggestion that metrical composition was outmoded in the same manner that Victorian style was outmoded.

In view of the vague and overly decorative lyricality of much Victorian verse, the identification of diction with metric is understandable up to a point. Furthermore, though metrical composition does not necessarily cause inflated rhetoric, it accommodates it more readily than prose. An insipid poet may be encouraged to indulge in exaggerations of style as a result of the special character of metrical structure; and a more serious poet, observing this practice, may consequently identify rhetoric with meter. At the same time, one should note that such an identification confuses properties which have been recognized as distinguishable for most of literary history.

To return to Eliot: discussing the objectives he and early associates entertained, he goes on to say, in his Milton lecture, that they wanted to create a poetry which spoke unaffectedly and which took its subjects and vocabulary not from dated canons of taste, but straight from modern life, regardless of its evidently "non-poetic" qualities. Eliot more specifically observes that this process of poetic modernization was to include the incorporation into verse of elements of speech which had not been employed by earlier poets:

> [I]t was one of our tenets that verse should have the virtues of prose, that diction should become assimilated to cultivated contemporary speech, before aspiring to the elevation of poetry. Another tenet was that the subject-matter and the imagery of poetry should be extended to topics and objects related to the life of a modern man or woman; that we were to seek the non-poetic, to seek even material refractory to transmutation into poetry, and words and phrases which had not been used in poetry before.
>
> (OPP, 160)

In "The Music of Poetry," Eliot advances arguments much like those he advances in his Milton paper. Here, too, Eliot urges that the modern movement represents, as he puts it in the last paragraph of the essay, "a period of search for a proper modern colloquial idiom" (OPP, 38). He contends, as he does in the Milton paper, that the modern revolution is identical to the revolutions led by Dryden and Wordsworth:

> Every revolution in poetry is apt to be, and sometimes to announce itself to be a return to common speech. That is the revolution which

Wordsworth announced in his prefaces, and he was right: but the same revolution had been carried out a century before by Oldham, Waller, Denham and Dryden; and the same revolution was due again something over a century later.

(*OPP,* 31)

In addition to speaking to the modern movement in general, Eliot speaks in this essay of free verse in particular. And, with regard to the latter, he suggests that those who question the legitimacy of free verse are misguided, because they fail to see that the distinction between metrical and non-metrical verse is basically trivial compared to the more profound distinction between good writing and bad:

> As for "free verse", I expressed my view twenty-five years ago by saying that no verse is free for the man who wants to do a good job. No one has better cause to know than I, that a great deal of bad prose has been written under the name of free verse; though whether its authors wrote bad prose or bad verse, or bad verse in one style or in another, seems to me a matter of indifference.
>
> (*OPP,* 37)

Similar arguments appear, it is interesting to note, in two of Eliot's earlier essays, "Reflections on *Vers Libre*" and "Ezra Pound: His Metric and Poetry," both of which were originally published in 1917 and both of which are collected in *To Criticize the Critic.*[6] In his essay on Pound, Eliot comments on the great proliferation of free verse that was then occurring, and he says: "Who is responsible for the bad free verse is a question of no importance, inasmuch as its authors would have written bad verse in any form." Later he adds, "There are not, as a matter of fact, two kinds of verse, the strict and the free; there is only a mastery which comes of being so well trained that form is an instinct and can be adapted to the particular purpose in hand." And he concludes his "Reflections" by asserting that "the division between Conservative Verse and *vers libre* does not exist, for there is only good verse, bad verse, and chaos" (*TCC,* 167, 172, 189).

36

We will return to Eliot's view of free verse toward the end of this chapter. For the moment, it is enough to observe that Eliot embodies attitudes also held by other leaders of the modern movement. These attitudes are especially evident in the literary criticism of Ford Madox Ford. Though mainly remembered today for his novels, Ford began writing *vers libre* in the nineties, and he could rightly characterize himself, in his 1921 memoir *Thus to Revisit,* as "the doyen of living writers of *Vers Libre* in English" (*TTR*, p. 198). In the present study, I will refer to Ford frequently, not only because his views are representative, but also because his influence on the development of modern poetry is not sufficiently recognized, despite the fact that Pound repeatedly stressed the importance of Ford's contributions.[7]

Ford's views about the modern movement and free verse appear most clearly in his preface to his 1911 *Collected Poems,*[8] in a long essay entitled "The Battle of the Poets" in *Thus to Revisit,* and in some notes for a lecture on *vers libre* which he delivered in the twenties in New York City and which Frank MacShane has preserved in his *Critical Writings of Ford Madox Ford.*[9] Ford emphasizes, as Eliot does, that the modern revolution in verse principally represented a protest against an idiom which had no relationship to living language, a desire to connect poetry with modern life, and a desire to incorporate in poetry the diction of contemporary colloquial speech. Ford, like Eliot, urges that the modern revolution, in possessing these aims, was just like earlier literary revolutions; and Ford argues, too, that free verse should be regarded simply as an instrument for reforming poetic speech and as a medium which allows a greater genuineness of diction than that allowed by meter.

Ford's family was related by marriage to the Rossettis, and as a child Ford was compelled to attend private readings by poets including Browning, Tennyson, and the Rossettis themselves. In his lecture on *vers libre,* Ford describes these readings, and his account offers good insight into the reasons for Ford's subsequent literary rebellion. When the poets started to recite, Ford tells us, the most horrible changes came over these normally nice people. They had, all, always, on these occasions the aspects and voices, not only to awful High Priests before Drawing Room altars—but they held their heads at unnatural angles and appeared to be suffering the tortures of agonising souls. It was their voices that did that. They were doing what Tennyson calls, with admiration: "Mouthing out their hollow O's and A's."

And it went on and on—and on! A long, rolling stream, of words no-one would ever use, to endless monotonous, polysyllabic, unchanging rhythms, in which rhymes went unmeaningly by like the telegraph posts, every fifty yards, of a railway journey.

(CW, 157)

Such experiences soured Ford not only on Victorian verse, but on traditional poetry in general. He came to feel, as others in the modern movement did, that metrical composition was inevitably fustian. He asked himself, "Is there something about the mere framing of verse, the mere sound of it in the ear, that it must at once throw its practitioner or its devotee into an artificial frame of mind? . . . [M]ust it necessarily quicken them to the perception only of the sentimental, the false, the hackneyed aspects of life?" The answer was clearly, Yes, which led Ford to the conclusion "that all poets must of necessity write affectedly, at great length, with many superfluous words—that poetry, of necessity, was something boring and pretentious" (*CP,* 333, 336).

For Ford, the affected diction of the Victorians was accompanied by a related literary malady. The Victorians failed, in Ford's view, to bring an original spirit to the material they treated: "What worried and exasperated us in the poems of the late Lord Tennyson, the late Lewis Morris, the late William Morris, the late—well, whom you like—is not their choice of subject, it is their imitative handling of matter, of words, it is their derivative attitude" (*CP,* 340). Ford argues, too, that his own experiments in verse are a reaction against such derivative writing and that they attempt to address the contemporary world as opposed to the mythologial and medieval worlds so frequently addressed by the Victorians. He speaks of having "one unflinching aim—to register my own times in terms of my own time" (*CP*, 327), insisting, as Eliot does, on the importance of a specifically modern diction which can render modern subjects. Discussing his development as a poet, he tells us that by 1898 he had worked out a "formula" for writing poems, and some of the features of his formula are similar to the "tenets" Eliot mentions in his Milton essay. The individual articles of the formula, Ford writes, were:

> that a poem must be compounded of observation of the everyday life that surrounded us; that it must be written in exactly the same vocabulary as that which one used for one's prose; that, if it were to be in verse, it must attack some subject that needed a slightly more marmoreal treatment than is expedient for the paragraph of a novel; that, if it were to be rhymed, the rhyme must never lead to the introduction of unnecessary thought; and, lastly, that no exigency of metre must interfere with the personal cadence of the writer's mind or the pressure of the recorded emotion.
>
> (*TTR*, 206–07)

As does Eliot, Ford suggests that free verse is a logical response to a dissatisfaction with "dead form" and is a natural expression of the desire for a more contemporary and colloquial poetic speech. Speaking of imagism (of which he was one of the eleven charter members included in Pound's *Des Imagistes* anthology of 1914), Ford contends that imagistic *vers libre* is not a rebellion against poetic rigor, but against the rhetorical vices of the previous age. "The work is free," Ford comments of the Imagists' poems, "of the polysyllabic, honey-dripping and derivative adjectives that, distinguishing the works of most of their contemporaries, makes nineteenth-century poetry as a whole seem greasy and 'close,' like the air of a room" (*TTR*, 157). Ford argues that his modernism and free verse embody the same goals and aspirations that good poets have always had: "I would rather read a picture in verse of the emotions and environment of a Goodge Street anarchist than recapture what songs the sirens sang. That after all was what Francois Villon was doing for the life of his day" (*CP,* 333).

In his *vers libre* lecture, Ford describes free verse more generally in terms of the modern need for a reform of poetic diction. Perhaps recalling Wordsworth's definition of a poet as "a man speaking to men," Ford asserts, "I said then—and I say now—if a man cannot talk like an educated gentleman about things that matter in direct and simple English let him hold his tongue." And it is apparent here, as it is in his preface, that Ford believes that the poet, in order to speak unaffectedly, must shed conventional verse as well as Victorian style. Oddly, Ford cites as a credo for *vers libre* Wordsworth's pentameter, "Shine, Poet! in thy place, and be content," about which he comments: "That is really what vers libre is. It is an attempt to let personalities express themselves more genuinely than they have lately done." With respect to the poetic status of free verse, Ford simply asserts at the end of his lecture that it is a perfectly legitimate "form": "Objections to vers libre. . . . None. More forms in the world the better" (*CW,* 157, 161, 162).

Many of the ideas one finds in Eliot and Ford are to be found as well in Pound. For Pound, too, the modern revolution represents a repudiation of Victorian style and an attempt to re-direct poetry toward modern speech and life. In "A Retrospect," Pound looks back on the beginnings of imagism and suggests that imagistic free verse was a salutary protest against the poetry of the nineteenth century, a period he describes as being "a rather blurry, messy sort of a period, a rather sentimentalistic, mannerish sort of a period." Regarding the modern movement, Pound says that it aims at replacing the obsolete bric-a-brac of Victorian style with a truer and sharper-sighted verse. "As to Twentieth century poetry, and the poetry which I expect to see written during the next decade or so, it will, I think, move against poppy-cock, it will be harder and saner. . . . At least for myself, I want it so, austere, direct, free from emotional slither" (*LE,* 11, 12).

Pound also suggests, in his "Retrospect," that the modern revolution bears a healthy resemblance to previous revolutions. He tells us that when he and H. D. and Richard Aldington decided in 1912 to form a group dedicated to revitalizing poetry, they adopted as their first principle, "Direct treatment of the 'thing' whether subjective or objective." And evidently this, in Pound's mind, is exactly the principle earlier poets have embraced when they forged new styles. "In the art of Daniel and Cavalcanti," Pound comments, "I have seen that precision which I miss in the Victorians, that explicit rendering, be it of external nature, or of emotion. Their testimony is of the eyewitness, their symptoms are first hand." Much the same theme informs Pound's 1913 essay, "The Serious Artist," in which he argues that the "new sort of poetic art" he is advocating "is not a new sort but an old sort . . . a poetry that can be carried as a communication between intelligent men" (*LE*, 3, 11, 55).

No less emphatic on this subject is Pound's 1914 article for *Poetry* on Ford's verse. Pound praises Ford for trying to bring the language of verse up-to-date, and Pound argues that if modern poets wish to refresh their art, they would do well to follow Ford's attempt to integrate real speech and real life into poetry. Pound hails Ford's "On Heaven" as "the best poem yet written in the 'twentieth-century fashion'" and concludes his consideration of Ford by saying: "I find him significant and revolutionary because of his insistence upon clarity and precision, upon the prose tradition; in brief, upon efficient writing—even in verse" (*LE*, 373, 377).

With respect to free verse, Pound presents ideas similar to those presented by Eliot and Ford. In his "Retrospect," Pound stresses the virtues of "technique," though he does so in a vague manner, and he seems to feel that conventional technique may be jettisoned if it does not suit the poet's purposes: "I believe in technique as the test of a man's sincerity; in law when it is ascertainable; in the trampling down of every convention that impedes or obscures the determination of the law, or the precise rendering of the impulse." The clearest portion of the "Re Vers Libre" section of Pound's "Retrospect" is a one-sentence paragraph which runs: "Eliot has said the thing very well when he said, 'No *vers* is *libre* for the man who wants to do a good job.'" Pound also cites Eliot's dictum in his review of *Prufrock and Other Observations* for *Poetry* in 1917, and here Pound suggests, as does Eliot himself, that distinctions between formal and free verse are not significant when compared to distinctions between good and bad writing. "A conviction as to the rightness or wrongness of *vers libre*," says Pound at the start of that section of his review devoted to Eliot's versification, "is no guarantee of a poet" (*LE*, 9, 12, 421).

Reading critical statements of others in the modern movement, one hears the themes that Eliot, Ford, and Pound develop. This is especially true of T. E. Hulme and William Carlos Williams. Both identify antiquated diction with meter in the same manner as Eliot, Ford, and Pound do, and both contend that to reform idiom it is necessary to reject traditional versification. One sees this identification and contention in Hulme's "Lecture on Modern Poetry," which appears to have been first delivered in 1908 or 1909 (the exact date is not clear; the lecture was revised and redelivered in 1914). Hulme argues that meter is suitable only to epic subjects and not suitable to the modern poetic spirit, which is intimate, introspective, and impressionistic:

> [W]hat is this new spirit, which finds itself unable to express itself in the old metre? Are the things that a poet wishes to say now in any way different to the things that former poets say? I believe that they are. The old poetry dealt essentially with big things, the expression of epic subjects leads naturally to the anatomical matter and regular verse. Action can best be expressed in regular verse. . . . But the modern is the exact opposite of this, it no longer deals with heroic action, it has become definitely and finally introspective. . . . Regular metre to this impressionist poetry is cramping, jangling, meaningless, and out of place. Into the delicate pattern of images and colour it introduces the heavy, crude pattern of rhetorical verse.
>
> (*FS*, 72–3, 74)

42

This argument implies that metrical composition inevitably entails stylistic exaggeration. It implies that meter and rhetoric are virtually identical. And a little later Hulme explicitly conflates the two in a single phrase, when he speaks of the "metre of rhetoric" (*FS,* 75).

Williams offers a similar argument in a 1932 letter to Kay Boyle. Analyzing the modern movement, Williams remarks, "A minimum of present new knowledge seems to be this: there can no longer be serious work in poetry written in 'poetic' diction. It is a contortion of speech to conform to a rigidity of line" (*SL,* 134). For Williams, fatuous or awkward diction results not so much from misuses of speech as from a property—rigidity—that he attributes to the conventional verse line itself. In 1946, Williams again appears to equate meter with stale speech when he hails the poems of Byron Vazakas' *Transfigured Night* as having "completely done away with the poetic line as we know it," and when he says of Vazakas: "He has been led, more by irritation, I think, than by anything else, to an investigation of the poetic line, to attack the problem of measure, of which the conventional line is such a very bad approximation,—the line in which the worst clichés of the art of poetry lie anchored."[10] The conventional line, in Williams' view, has no independence but is inextricably connected with hackneyed expression. The conventional line is not seen in its traditional sense as a pattern of potentials which may be variously realized in speech. Instead, it is, in Williams' arrestingly mixed metaphor, a harbor filled with clichés.

Like others in the modern movement, Hulme and Williams affirm that abandoning traditional metric is an expression of principles which, though opposed to those of nineteenth-century verse, are deeply traditional. This idea is evident in Hulme's "Romanticism and Classicism," written in 1913–14. In this essay, Hulme objects to the "sloppiness" of Romantic verse, and, in terms resembling those used by Pound, he predicts of the modern movement, "I prophesy that a period of dry, hard, classical verse is coming."[11] Williams, too, construes his attack on traditional meter as an affirmation of time-honored values. In his "Poem as a Field of Action" essay, Williams, having proposed "sweeping changes from top to bottom of the poetic structure," adds: "It may be said that I wish to destroy the past. It is precisely a service to tradition, honoring it and serving it that is envisioned and intended by my attack, and not disfigurement—confirming and *enlarging* its application."[12]

In concluding this section of this chapter, one might make a further observation. At times the belief that an overthrow of conventional metric is needed to produce a new idiom is accompanied by the supposition that the new idiom will in turn create a new metric. For instance, in the last paragraph of his "Music of Poetry," Eliot hopefully envisions an end to the chaotic versification that had become the order of the day: "[W]hen we reach a point at which the poetic idiom can be stabilized, then a period of musical elaboration can follow" (*OPP,* 38). Because Eliot refers to "musical elaboration" rather than "metrical elaboration," one cannot say with certainty that he is urging that stable idiom is a determinant or a precondition of metrical order. But, as will become evident in later chapters, Eliot sometimes uses "music" as an alternative for "meter." And it would seem that he thinks that the establishment of the new idiom will clarify the measures in which the poems in that idiom are to be written.

Yet it is unlikely that a mere change of poetic idiom will alter the basic character of a language or establish grounds for a new metrical system. With regard to the English language specifically, one might note that simply to write in a new idiom does not mean that the iambic pattern will suddenly cease to provide a clearer and more flexible model for speech than other possible patterns. In addition, since idiom is by its nature more or less fluid, it can never be entirely "stabilized." Nor would one wish it to be. If it were, it would petrify—and it was just this tendency towards petrification that the modernists complained of in Victorian verse.

2. Earlier Reformations of
Poetic Diction and Subject Matter

Most literary revolutions are led, as the modern one was, by poets who feel that poetry has grown pompous and must be refashioned so that it can speak directly and truly of life. Yet in abandoning meter to achieve reformation, the modern movement is unique. In order to establish both the way the modern revolution resembled earlier revolutions and the way it differed from them in its identification of outmoded idiom with meter and in its advocacy of a poetry free of conventional versification, we should now turn to the two ancient literary innovators mentioned above, Euripides and Horace, and to the two English ones to whom Eliot appeals, Dryden and Wordsworth.

Though Euripides (as far as we know) did not formally engage in literary criticism, the fact that he consciously revolutionized tragedy in the second half of the fifth century B.C. is borne out by subsequent ancient writers. It is equally apparent that the two traits which most marked his innovations are traits we associate with the modernists of our time. First, Euripides objected to the heroic mode of previous tragedy and insisted on presenting his characters and their world in a "realistic" manner, however much such a presentation involved what traditionalists considered to be qualities inappropriate to tragic drama. Second, he rejected the elevated rhetoric that had characterized tragic style since Aeschylus' time and wrote in a style incorporating the ordinary speech of his day.

The first of these traits is noted by, among others, Dio Chrysostom (*Oration*, 52)[13] and Diogenes Laertius (*Lives*, 4.5.6 [Crantor]).[14] It is noted as well by Aristotle (*Poetics*, 1460b33–34), who records that "Sophocles said that he portrayed people as they ought to be and Euripides portrayed them as they are."[15] The second of these traits—the adept and colloquial novelty of Euripides' diction—receives comment from "Longinus" (*On the Sublime,* 40.2)[16] and from Aristotle (*Rhetoric,* 3.2.5) in his discussion of art-which-hides-art: "Art is cleverly concealed when the speaker chooses his words from ordinary language (*eiōthyias dialektou*) and puts them together like Euripides, who was the first to show the way."

Even if one lacked the evidence of such commentators, one would have ample testimony about Euripides' innovations and about the controversy they excited. This additional testimony is supplied by Aristophanes' *The Frogs,*[17] which provides perhaps the earliest extended examination of a literary revolution and several lines of which, it is interesting to note, Ford uses as an epigraph to "The Battle of the Poets" essay in *Thus to Revisit.* The second half of *The Frogs* consists of a formal debate between Aeschylus and Euripides with Dionysus serving as judge. Aeschylus is cast in the role of the somewhat stodgy defender of older conventions, and Euripides is cast in the role of the wily and newfangled parvenu. The debate takes place in Pluto's palace in the Underworld, where Aeschylus, who has long occupied the honorary Chair of Tragedy, finds his position challenged by the arrival of the recently deceased Euripides. (Aristophanes' play was first staged in 405 B.C., the year after Euripides' death.) The charges which Euripides levels at the older Aeschylus and the terms with which Euripides justifies his own innovations resemble strikingly statements made by the modernists of our time.

For example, Euripides claims that Aeschylus is bombastic (*kompophakelorrēmona,* "boast-bundle-phrased") (839) and argues (907 ff.) that Aeschylus' tragedies are the works of an overly poetical impostor (*alazōn*). So wildly inflated is Aeschylus' style, Euripides says (926), that it is at times downright unintelligible (*agnōta*); and, with a colorful metaphor, he alleges (937–44) that, under Aeschylus' influence, tragedy itself grew into a state of sickly bloating (*oidousan*), which, however, has since been happily alleviated by strong doses of modernity. "When I took over Trag-

edy from you," Euripides says to Aeschylus, "the poor creature
was in a dreadful state. Fatty degeneration of the Art. All swollen
up with high-falutin' diction. I soon got her weight down,
though: put her on a diet of particles, with a little finely chopped
logic (taken peripatetically), and a special decoction of dialectic,
cooked up from books and strained to facilitate digestion."

As for his own "new" style, Euripides boasts (959) that he did
not rely on the grandiose and fabulous. Instead, "I wrote about
familiar things (*oikeia pragmat' eisagōn*), things the audience knew
about." Nor did he, he adds (1058), bludgeon the audience with
big words or befuddle them with resonant obscurities; no, he
spoke in "human terms" (*phrazein anthrōpeiōs*, "language man to
man"). Euripides further states (1178) that he avoided inane ornament or "padding" (*stoibēn*) and that his writing was "clear"
(*saphēs*) and "acute" (*leptos*). Indeed, when Euripides speaks (941)
of the way he "reduced" tragedy, the term he employs, *ischnana,*
indicates not only "spare," but suggests the *ischnos charaktēr* of
the classical plain style itself, which Euripides helped to found.
That Euripides ultimately loses the debate—Dionysus favoring
Aeschylus because he is a sounder ethical guide than his more
stylistically sophisticated rival—does not concern us here. What
is important is simply the similarity between Euripides' ideas and
innovations and those of the leaders of the modern movement in
our century.

Issues like those raised by Euripides' work appear in Horace's
literary epistles. It would be wrong to call Horace a Euripidean
figure, for Horace repeatedly urges that poetry should feature
both moral concern and technical finesse, and he seeks to heal the
kinds of breaches between ethics and aesthetics depicted in *The
Frogs.* Horace is nevertheless staunchly opposed to the literary
conservatism of his day. He particularly objects to critical tastes
which encouraged archaizing tendencies and which favored older
Roman poetry at the expense of contemporary verse. In his Epistle
to Augustus (2.1),[18] he protests (18–49) against the sort of critic

who approves only of the old and says (76–77, 90–91): "I am impatient that any work is censured, not because it is thought to be coarse or inelegant in style, but because it is modern (*nuper*). . . . [I]f novelty (*novitas*) had been as offensive to the Greeks as it is to us, what in these days would be ancient?"

Horace insists furthermore that poetry ought to assimilate contemporary usage and ought to aim at a plausible treatment of life. Poetic diction is not, he urges, a static and time-hallowed dialect; it must change as language itself changes and must stay related to living speech. In the second of his Epistles to Julius Florus (2.2), for instance, Horace contends (115–119) that the poet is at liberty to renew and alter the language of verse when the need arises: "Terms long lost in darkness the good poet will unearth for the people's use and bring into the light. . . . New ones he will adopt which Use has fathered and brought forth (*quae genitor produxerit usus*)." And Horace expatiates on this point in Epistle 2.3, the *Art of Poetry.* "[A]ll mortal things shall perish," he says (68–72), "much less shall the glory and glamour of speech endure and live. Many terms that have fallen out of use shall be born again, and those shall fall that are now in repute, if Usage so will it (*si volet usus*), in whose hands lies the judgment, the right and the rule of speech."

In the *Art of Poetry,* Horace also makes the point, as Eliot does in his Milton lecture, that periodic renovations of poetic diction, far from harming verse, are necessary and healthy. Moreover, just as Eliot observes that he and his fellow modernists wanted to employ "words and phrases which had not been used in poetry before," so Horace affirms (48–53) that the poet may update and transform idiom as his subject matter requires: "If haply one must betoken abstruse things by novel terms, you will have a chance to fashion words never heard of by the kilted Cethegi [ancient Romans], and licence will be granted, if used with modesty; while words, though new and of recent make, will win acceptance, if they spring from a Greek fount and are drawn therefrom but

48

sparingly." In a more personal tone, Horace continues this argument (55–59) by defending his own modernity of speech: "[W]hy should I be grudged the right of adding, if I can, my little fund, when the tongue of Cato and of Ennius has enriched our mother-speech and brought to light new terms (*nova nomina*) for things? It has ever been, and ever will be, permitted to issue words stamped with the mint-mark of the day."

These sentiments are in turn related to Horace's belief that the poet must not simply follow literary conventions, but must directly address life. Horace always stresses the value of literary training. Yet through training alone the poet will achieve little. As Horace in the *Art of Poetry* says (318–23) in his discussion of drama, once the poet has mastered the tools of his trade, he should then "look to life and manners for a model, and draw from thence living words." Significantly, when Horace surveys Roman drama, he expresses the opinion (285–88) that Latin writers have most excelled when they have tackled native subjects instead of rehearsing the standard ones of Greek literature: "Our own poets have left no style untried, nor has least honour been earned when they have dared to leave the footsteps of the Greeks and sing of deeds at home, whether they have put native tragedies or native comedies on the stage." Though the comparison may seem far-fetched, in this respect Horace resembles modern literary nationalists like Williams, who wish to see poets address subjects of their own environment and not rely on plots and subjects imported from other eras and other countries.

There is a related point. Though formidably well-read, Horace is as impatient as Ford is with what Ford calls "imitative handling of matter, of words" and "derivative attitude." In the earlier of his two Epistles to Julius Florus (1.3), Horace inquires after the young poet Celsus Albinovanus and says (14–20) he hopes that Albinovanus is composing poems which reflect his experience and not just his perusals of the works of others in the library in the temple of Apollo on the Palatine: "What, pray, is

Celsus doing? He was warned, and must often be warned to search for home treasures, and to shrink from touching the writings which Apollo on the Palatine has admitted: lest, if some day perchance the flock of birds come to reclaim their plumage, the poor crow, stripped of his stolen colours, awake laughter."[19] In these remarks, Horace is not disparaging a knowledge of tradition. He is, however, insisting that a poet must not be over-bookish and over-literary, but must produce work which is distinctly his.

Horace also resembles the modernists of our time in this respect. As well as objecting to dead diction and convention, he argues that prosaic speech can be serviceably deployed in verse. He says in one of his early *Satires* (1.4) that his diction is "akin to prose" (*sermoni propriora*) and that if his satires were deprived of their "regular beat and rhythm" (*tempora certa modosque*), they would scarcely retain any poetic features whatever. Horace never suggests that this conversational manner represents the only or even the best style. Of his *Satires* themselves, he goes so far as to say (1.4.38–44, 63–65) that in writing them he does not view himself as a poet and raises the question of whether satire can strictly be deemed poetry, so humble is the speech in which it is written.

At the same time, Horace emphasizes in the *Art of Poetry* that plain diction, adroitly managed, is preferable to a continually elevated style. If simple speech is characterized by *iunctura* (a skillful weaving together of words), *calliditas* (an artful dexterity of arrangement), and *urbanitas* (an engaging refinement), it can achieve effects unattainable by a grander manner. Discussing specifically the quality of *iunctura,* Horace speaks (240–43) of his own objectives: "My aim shall be a poetry, so moulded from the familiar that anybody may hope for the same success, may sweat much and yet toil in vain when attempting the same: such is the power of order and connexion, such the beauty that may crown the commonplace." Horace appreciates the middle and high styles, skillfully used; for that matter, he uses them himself in the *Odes*. Yet, regarding style, he appears to share Eliot's view that "diction should become assimilated to cultivated contemporary speech, before aspiring to the elevation of poetry." Until, that is, one can cleverly and effectively manage plain diction, one will not succeed in more rarefied or heroic composition. Horace thus makes the point with respect to poetry that Cicero, in *Orator* 98–99, had earlier made with respect to oratory: competency in plain diction is valuable not only in itself; it is as well the necessary foundation for the speaker who wishes to ascend to the high manner.

Like Aristophanes' Euripides and like Horace, Dryden stresses the value of an unaffected and contemporary poetic idiom. Indeed, this aspect of Dryden's thought provides the governing theme of the three BBC lectures on Dryden which Eliot delivered in 1931: "What Dryden did, in fact, was to reform the language, and devise a natural, conversational style of speech in verse in place of an artificial and decadent one. . . . [H]e restored English verse to the condition of speech."[20] Dryden's emphasis on naturalness is evident in much of his writing, nowhere more so than in two of his earliest and best-known critical pieces, his 1664 dedication of *The Rival Ladies* to the Earl of Orrery and his *Of Dramatic Poesy: An Essay*, which was composed in 1665–66 and published in 1668.[21]

The dedication to *The Rival Ladies* is particularly relevant because in it Dryden explicitly advocates a poetry which has the character of "ordinary speaking" and which possesses "the negligence of prose" (*ODP*, 1:7). Dryden uses the word "negligence," we should note, not in the sense of "carelessness," but in the sense in which Cicero uses the word (*neglegentia*) in his definition of the plain style—in the sense of uncosmetically attractive (*Orator*, 78). Because *The Rival Ladies* is not only in meter, but in rhyme, and because some critics of Dryden's day were arguing that rhyme in dramatic verse produced an inevitably stilted quality, Dryden is specially interested in making the point that rhyme can be harmonized with colloquial expression. Infelicites may occur, Dryden concedes, when a poet uses rhyme ineptly; by the same token, however, when rhyme is expertly employed "the first word in the verse seems to beget the second, and that the next, till that becomes the last word in the line which, in the negligence of prose, would be so; it must then be granted, rhyme has all the advantages of prose besides its own" (*ODP*, 1:7).

The virtues of fluent and flexible style are discussed at greater length in *Of Dramatic Poesy: An Essay*. Among the many topics the four disputants in the dialogue examine are the condition of English verse in the immediately preceding age and the direction in which contemporary verse might profitably move. Eugenius, one of the two characters who express, it is widely felt, Dryden's own views, makes a number of statements resembling those made by Eliot, Ford, and Pound. For example, Eugenius argues that the metaphysical poetry so popular with the previous generation is hopelessly stiff and false. Speaking of John Cleveland's work, Eugenius suggests that using words in an odd or distorted manner may be permissible on occasion, but

> to do this always, and never be able to write a line without it, though it may be admired by some few pedants, will not pass upon those who know that wit is best conveyed to us in the most easy language; and is most to be admired when a great thought comes dressed in words so commonly received that it is understood by the meanest apprehensions, as the best meat is the most easily digested: but we cannot read a verse of Cleveland's without making a face at it, as if every word were a pill to swallow: he gives us many times a hard nut to break our teeth, without a kernel for our pains.
>
> (*ODP*, 1:40)

In another section of the dialogue, Eugenius takes a position which is not unlike that which Pound takes in his "Retrospect" essay. This position involves the argument that the innovations of

newer writers like Waller and Denham are in no way seditious
assaults on the art of poetry, but are instead a healthy reaction
against the vices of a worn-out mode; it is noteworthy that at this
juncture, no one else in the dialogue, not even Crites, who is
generally skeptical of the achievements of modern writers, op-
poses Eugenius. On the contrary, Dryden reports, "every one was
willing to acknowledge how much our poesy is improved by the
happiness of some writers yet living, who first taught us to mould
our thoughts into easy and significant words, to retrench the
superfluities of expression, and to make our rhyme so properly a
part of the verse that it should never mislead the sense, but itself
be led and governed by it" (*ODP,* 1:24–25).

One should also observe that, as well as recommending naturalness of style and (to use Pound's phrase) "efficient writing" in
verse, Dryden is a champion of the literature of his nation and his
time. *Of Dramatic Poesy* reflects issues debated during the Quarrel
of the Ancients and Moderns, which had its origins in the Italian
Renaissance and which continued in England and France down
to the eighteenth century.[22] The Quarrel entailed a comparison of
the achievements of the ancients and moderns in various fields,
including poetry. As we will see in the fifth chapter of this study,
Dryden was uneasily aware of one of the principal points that
emerged during the Quarrel, namely, that the modern sciences
were capable of a cumulative progress unavailable to the modern
arts. At the same time, Dryden stoutly defends the claims of the
modern poets against the claims of the ancients. Modern English
dramatists especially, Dryden feels, deserve credit for the originality of their plots and lively characterizations. Eugenius and his
ally Neander, commonly thought to be the character who most
nearly reflects Dryden himself, argue that the ancients recycled in
their plays the same stories again and again and did not present
the entertaining and realistic varieties of mood found in modern
dramas. If it would be an exaggeration to portray Dryden's views
in terms of the Poundian program of "Make It New," it is never-

theless the case that Dryden is interested in, and values, the contemporary in many of the ways that Pound, Eliot, Ford, Hulme, and Williams do.

Before moving to the final section of this chapter, we may briefly consider Wordsworth, in whom we find many of the ideas we have discovered in the other poets we have examined. In the preface to the second edition of *Lyrical Ballads,* Wordsworth announces that his work is a reaction against "the gaudiness and inane phraseology of many modern writers" and against "arbitrary and capricious habits of expression." Such habits, he suggests, are connected with another literary vice: the turning aside from genuine experience in order "to trick out or to elevate nature" (*SPP,* 446, 447, 454).

Of his own poetry, Wordsworth avows that his object in writing it was "to choose incidents and situations from common life, and to relate or describe them, throughout, as far as was possible in a selection of language really used by men." Wordsworth further stresses that the poet should not dwell in a private lexicon, among a circumscribed set of "poetical" subjects. Rather, the poet's work should partake of a general sympathy, and the poet must remember that "Poets do not write for Poets alone, but for men" (*SPP,* 446, 457).

Like earlier and later poetic innovators, Wordsworth contends that the language of poetry should have what Eliot calls "the virtues of prose." In fact, in his preface, Wordsworth argues "that not only the language of a large portion of every good poem, even of the most elevated character, must necessarily, except with reference to the metre, in no respect differ from that of good prose, but likewise that some of the most interesting parts of the best poems will be found to be strictly the language of prose when prose is well written." And subsequently, he remarks: "We will go further. It may be safely affirmed, that there neither is, nor can be, any *essential* difference between the language of prose and metrical composition" (*SPP,* 450, 451).

Like other innovators, Wordsworth wants to free poetry from stale idiom and wants to write directly and freshly. Of his verse in general, he says: "I have at all times endeavoured to look steadily at my subject; consequently, there is I hope in these Poems little falsehood of description, and my ideas are expressed in language fitted to their respective importance" (*SPP,* 450). The aim is true speech, a poetry that communicates with clarity and energy to readers, a poetry not dependent on antiquated diction and mannerism.

3. *Revolution with a Difference: The Abandonment of Meter*

If a reader of Roman poetry had fallen asleep in 45 B.C. and had awakened twenty-five years later to find at his bedside Horace's *Epodes* and the first three books of *Odes,* he might well have been astonished on unrolling the scrolls. The poet's material and presentation of it would have seemed most unusual. Yet the reader, at least the educated one, would have recognized the verse forms. If he had wished, he could have traced in his mind their continuity all the way back to the misty beginnings of Greek iambic and melic poetry. Similarly, if an English reader had fallen asleep in 1775 and had awakened a quarter of a century later to find the *Lyrical Ballads,* he might well have been startled by the subject and manner of "Tintern Abbey" or "Her Eyes Are Wild." He would, however, have had no difficulty determining that the first was in conventional blank verse and the second mainly in rhymed iambic tetrameters. If a reader had fallen asleep in 1900 and had awakened in 1925 to find Ford's *On Heaven,* Eliot's *The Waste Land,* and Pound's *Draft of XVI Cantos,* it is likely he would have been very confused by the versification in the books.

This is the singularity of the modern movement. It broke with traditional versification. Like earlier revolutionaries, those of this century urged that poetry should free itself of stilted idiom. Like earlier revolutionaries, they wanted a poetry which incorporated colloquial immediacy and genuine feeling. But earlier revolutionaries did not argue, to cite Ford once more, "that no exigency of metre must interfere with the personal cadence of the writer's mind or the pressure of the recorded emotion" (*TTR*, 206–07). Euripides' metrical virtuosity is legendary. Even in the astrophic monodies of the late plays (parodied by Aristophanes in *Frogs* 1331 ff.), one can follow, line by line, what Euripides is doing metrically. The accusations of licentiousness directed against these solo arias seem to have concerned their music and choreography (and their sometimes outlandish emotionalism) as much as their rhythmical character.[23] Horace, however innovative in his treatment of subject matter and in his adaptions of earlier forms, is a master of traditional craft. In fact, in *Epistle* 1.19, he insists that maintaining conventional versification in no way diminishes a poet's claim to originality. "And lest you should crown me with a scantier wreath," he remarks (26–29), discussing his achievements in the *Epodes* and *Odes*, "because I feared to change the measures and form of verse, see how manlike Sappho moulds her Muse by the rhythm of Archilochus; how Alcaeus moulds his, though in his themes and arrangement he differs." As Horace says in *Satire* 2.1.28, "My own delight is to shut up words in feet (*me pedibus delectat claudere verba*)." He is an innovative poet. His experiments, however, are carried out in the context of metrical tradition. To speak a moment of Villon, whom Ford and Pound refer to as a model, he is shockingly original; yet he writes in strict metrical forms, *ballades* and *rondeaux,* which had been bequeathed to him by earlier poets like Deschamps and Machaut.

The same circumstance applies to Dryden. Though a defender of modern practices, Dryden throughout his criticism emphasizes the value of metrical composition. Indeed, one of the common themes of his essays, dedications, and prefaces is that those who have difficulty writing naturally in verse should blame themselves and not their medium. In his dedication to *The Rival Ladies,* Dryden admits that rhyme can result in awkwardness but adds that it does so only "when the poet either makes a vicious choice of words, or places them, for rhyme sake, so unnaturally as no man would in ordinary speaking." This argument appears as well in *Of Dramatic Poesy,* in which Neander comments that "the necessity of a rhyme never forces any but bad or lazy writers to say what they would not otherwise." The fact that Dryden himself, later in his career, abandoned the use of rhyme in his dramatic works is not of consequence in the present context, for he makes much the same arguments about unrhymed metrical composition that he makes about rhymed metrical composition. For instance, in the section of the *Essay* in which Neander discusses rhyme, he also cites a line of blank verse containing two clumsy inversions, "I heaven invoke, and strong resistance make," and remarks: "[Y]ou would think me very ridiculous if I should accuse the stubbornness of blank verse for this, and not rather the stiffness of the poet" (*ODP,* 1:7, 81, 82).

Nor does Dryden see any contradiction between seeking a prose-like directness of speech and writing in conventional measure. This indeed is a point that he makes in the concluding section of the *Religio Laici,* where he ascribes the simplicity of the poem's heroic couplets to his didactic objectives:

> Thus have I made my own opinions clear;
> Yet neither praise expect, nor censure fear:
> And this unpolish'd, rugged verse, I chose,
> As fittest for discourse, and nearest prose.
>
> (451–54)[24]

As Dryden's lines imply, style is not meter. It is as possible to write metrically in the plain style as it is to write in the middle and high styles. Dryden's attitude about meter is summarized in a statement he makes in the last paragraph of a *Defense* which he wrote for his *Of Dramatic Poesy* in the wake of Robert Howard's attack on it. "I have observed," says Dryden, "that none have been

57

violent against verse, but such only as have not attempted it, or have succeeded ill in their attempt" (*ODP*, 1 : 129–30).

Wordsworth, too, is a strong defender of meter, and his preface to *Lyrical Ballads* has an eloquent explanation of its values. Wordsworth carefully distinguishes the conventions of meter from the conventions of "POETIC DICTION"—arguing that the latter create a harmful barrier between reader and poet, but that the former establish a salutary bond between the two:

> [T]he distinction of metre is regular and uniform, and not, like that which is produced by what is usually called POETIC DICTION, arbitrary, and subject to infinite caprices upon which no calculation whatever can be made. In the one case, the Reader is utterly at the mercy of the Poet, respecting what imagery or diction he may choose to connect with the passion; whereas, in the other, the metre obeys certain laws, to which the Poet and Reader both willingly submit because they are certain, and because no interference is made by them with the passion, but such as the concurring testimony of ages has shown to heighten and improve the pleasure which co-exists with it.
>
> (*SPP*, 457–58)

Wordsworth also discusses the nature of meter itself and "the charm which, by the consent of all nations, is acknowledged to exist in metrical language." He speaks of the happy effect of meter for the reader—of the "small, but continual and regular impulses of pleasurable surprise from the metrical arrangement" and of "the pleasure which the mind derives from the perception of similitude in dissimilitude" (*SPP*, 458, 459, 460). And Wordsworth speaks as well of the fundamental and wonderful paradox of successful metrical composition: it is speech which is natural and, at the same time, is ordered within and played off against the norm of a fixed line:

> Now the music of harmonious metrical language, the sense of difficulty overcome, and the blind association of pleasure which has been previously received from works of rhyme or metre of the same or similar construction, an indistinct perception perpetually renewed of

language closely resembling that of real life, and yet, in the circumstance of metre, differing from it so widely—all these imperceptibly make up a complex feeling of delight.

(*SPP*, 460–61)

In view of Dryden's and Wordworth's statements, one may find it hard to comprehend how Eliot could repeatedly justify *vers libre* by appealing to their authority. In a broader sense, one may find it hard to comprehend how the modernists of our time could argue so forcefully that their revolution, which developed and expressed itself—practically speaking—through free verse, was like earlier literary revolutions. Admittedly, the modernists' enterprise was, at least in its initial stages, polemical. They wanted first and foremost their views heard and their poems published and read. Like many polemicists, they may have availed themselves of evidence which supported their cause and suppressed evidence which did not. Yet this is neither a complete nor a fair explanation of their use of the past and their sincere desire to reform poetry. There were factors in the cultural life of their times—factors which did not in earlier periods exist or exert a determining power—that helped give rise to free verse.

Some of these factors are explored in later chapters. Before concluding this chapter, we will look at a single topic related to these matters. The topic involves a certain demonstrable misunderstanding of English versification that seems to have prevailed among the modern revolutionaries, especially the critically energetic and influential Pound. The misunderstanding concerns a confusion of scansion with actual metrical practice. In an interview in a recent issue of *The Iowa Review,* J. V. Cunningham suggests that the misunderstanding occurred in part on account of that method of reading and scanning that developed in the schools in the nineteenth century, when English poetry entered academic curricula and there arose a need for a teaching equivalent to the traditional study of classical prosody. This method of reading and scanning entails speaking lines of verse in a pronounced and sing-song way to bring out their metrical identity:

> And *Melancholy mark'd* him *for* her *own*
> It *is* the *first* mild *day* of *March*
> *This* is the *for*est prime*val*, the *mur*muring *pines* and the
>   *hem*locks

Such reading clarifies the metrical norm of lines, but it obliterates natural degrees of relative speech stress within lines. It also distorts the nature of the English language, for English does not consist of inherently unaccented and accented syllables. It consists of syllables of different degrees and forms of accent, and these are determined by syntactic context as well as by the phonetic and phonemic character of the syllables themselves. Emphatic reading and scanning, whatever its pedagogic virtues, thus produces highly artificial effects. As Cunningham says, "If you tried to talk that way in any other situation, you would be thought to be posturing."[25] Thus, the procedure can easily lead to the impression that meter is stiff and wooden.

Pound seems to have been led to this impression. His remark, "[C]ompose in the sequence of the musical phrase, not in sequence of a metronome" and his related imperative, "Don't chop your stuff into separate *iambs*" (*LE*, 3, 6) are valuable in that they remind the poet that it is incumbent upon him to give his verse rhythmical life. At the same time, the remark misconstrues traditional metrical practice, as does his characterization, in "Treatise on Metre" in the *ABC of Reading,* of the iambic pentameter as "ti tum ti tum ti tum ti tum ti tum . . . from which every departure is treated as an exception."[26] Good poets do not write in a foot by foot or metronomic manner. They compose in phrases and sentences which fit or can be adjusted to fit a meter or a portion of it. When, for example, Shakespeare wrote,

> His life was gentle, and the elements
> So mix'd in him that Nature might stand up
> And say to all the world, "This was a man!"
>
> (Julius Caesar, 5.5.73–75)

it is unlikely that he did so in a "His life . . . was gen . . . tle and . . . the el . . . e ments" fashion. At points a poet may analyze the particular feet of a particular passage with a view to modulating or perfecting a cadence, but this is quite a different thing from counting, syllable by syllable, through a poem.[27]

Furthermore, given the fact that any complete articulation in English has one and only one primarily stressed syllable and a number of syllables receiving varying degrees of secondary stress, it would be rather difficult to write a "metronomic" line, a line, that is, of light and heavy syllables of perfectly equivalent alternating weight. Pound's ti-tumming accounts for the metrical norm of the pentameter line and for the way a student might scan or read the line to bring out its metrical identity. But the ti-tumming does not account for the necessary and happily infinite varieties of rhythmical contour (and they are not "exceptions") that can exist within the norm of the conventional pentameter. Here, for example, is one pentameter line each from poems of Ben Jonson, Rochester, Jane Austen, E. A. Robinson, Robert Frost, and Thom Gunn, pentameters which are metrically the same, but which nevertheless embody different individual rhythms:

> Farewell, thou child of my right hand, and joy
> French truth, Dutch prowess, British policy
> The day commemorative of my birth
> If ever I am old, and all alone
> Snow falling and night falling fast, oh, fast
> Resisting, by embracing, nothingness[28]

In his *Poetics,* Julius Caesar Scaliger observes that meter and rhythm are concurrent, not antithetical, phenomena: "The measure of the verse is invariable, its rhythm variable. . . . It will be therefore the Measure that determines its extent. Rhythm on the other hand determines its temperament" (*mensura versus non mutata, Rhythmus mutabitur. . . . Erit igitur Mensura praescriptio tractus. Rhythmus autem praescriptionis temperamentum*).[29] In ancient Greek one of the meanings of *rhythmos* is "disposition" or "temperament." Jonson, Rochester, Austen, Robinson, Frost, and Gunn all demonstrate in particular English practice what seems to hold true in different ways for different metrical systems in the Indo-European languages: conventional versification accommodates personally distinctive rhythm within the norm of measure.

The method of reading and scanning to which Cunningham refers, however, obscures this quality in English meter, and Cunningham is no doubt correct in observing that the understandable hostility to the method came to be directed at meter itself. Ultimately that hostility led to the idea that the only way a poet can give rhythmical distinction to his verse is to violate meter. It led to the idea, which will be examined in the next chapter, that skillful versification involves departure from a norm rather than variation within it. (This is not to suggest that one cannot draw discriminations between a very "free" free verse, such as one finds in much of the *Cantos,* and some sort of more restricted procedure, of which Eliot's "Gerontion" may serve as an example. "Gerontion" hovers loosely but frequently around iambic pentameter. Yet the freer and more restricted procedures are related, and both undermine the norm itself in the same manner if not to the same degree.)

It might also be observed that the ti-tumming method of reading continues to inform attitudes towards metrical composition. At times, readers who recognize that a poem is metrical will, in reading it silently or aloud, impose the light-heavy, light-heavy pattern across the lines, even when their syntax and rhythm vary considerably from the pattern. For such readers, the alertly fluid verses of, for example, Philip Sidney's "With how sad steps," will sound as crudely mechanical as the most thumping specimens of George Gascoigne's work.

The popularity of musical scanning in the final two decades of the nineteenth century may also have affected the modernists' views of meter. Pound's belief that conventional verse is metronomic recalls Sidney Lanier's argument, in his *Science of English*

Verse of 1880, that pentameters are written in 3/8 time—metri-cally unaccented syllables having the time value of eighth notes, metrically accented syllables having the time value of quarter notes. According to this theory, when the ear hears pentameter it hears tick-*tack,* tick-*tack,* tick-*tack,* tick-*tack,* tick-*tack.*[30]

There is another matter related to scansion that affected the development of free verse. This concerns the exhaustive analyses, undertaken in the late nineteenth and early twentieth century by scholars like Jakob Schipper and Saintsbury, of feet and meters possible in English verse. These analyses appear to have led some poets to regard scansion as generative rather than descriptive. That is, some of the modernists were led into the misapprehen-sion that any piece of writing which can be broken down into feet of one kind or another, and that can be marked out in long and short or accented and unaccented syllables, can claim traditional poetic legitimacy. This is a misapprehension because anything can be scanned. One can break a grocery list, a newspaper column, or a television script into iambs, trochees, anapests, and other feet. This does not make the list or column or script metrical, for metrical composition entails the use of feet in repeated and recog-nizable linear or strophic units.

It is on the mistaken belief that scanning something makes it metrical that Eliot bases many of his "Reflections on *Vers Libre.*" Discussing *vers libre* and contending that no verse is really free, he says:

> If *vers libre* is a genuine verse-form it will have a positive definition. And I can define it only in negatives: (1) absence of pattern, (2) absence of rhyme, (3) absence of metre.
>
> The third of these quantities is easily disposed of. What sort of a line that would be which would not scan at all I cannot say. Even in the popular American magazines, whose verse columns are now largely given over to *vers libre,* the lines are usually explicable in terms of prosody. Any line can be divided into feet and accents.
>
> (*TCC,* 184–85)

63

Near the end of the essay Eliot says of *vers libre* "that it is not defined by non-existence of metre, since even the *worst* verse can be scanned" (*TCC,* 189).

Eliot has equated meter with scansion. According to his analysis, any utterance is metrical. Pound, in his review of *Prufrock and Other Observations,* offers by implication the same equation of meter with scansion and the same all-encompassing definition of metricality. After quoting Eliot's remark, "No *vers* is *libre* for the man who wants to do a good job," Pound suggests that it is virtually impossible for a poet to compose non-metrically:

> Alexandrine and other grammarians have made cubby-holes for various groupings of syllables; they have put names upon them, and have given various labels to 'metres' consisting of combinations of these different groups. Thus it would be hard to escape contact with some group or other; only an encyclopedist could ever be half sure he had done so. The known categories would allow a fair liberty to the most conscientious traditionalist. The most fanatical vers-librist will escape them with difficulty.
>
> (*LE,* 421)

One sympathizes with Pound's impatience with prosodic pedantry. His remarks, however, are misguided. He might just as well say that even the most fanatical stream-of-consciousness prose writer or the most incoherent street-corner orator could not be sure that he was not composing metrically.

Pound and Eliot's appeal to scansion to justify experiments with free verse may seem to contradict their hostility to the ti-tumming exercises of reading and scanning. To be sure, there is a contradiction. The ti-tumming theory holds that metrical composition is inevitably rigid, while the unavoidable-feet theory holds that anything in syllables is metrical. Yet these two theories co-exist in Pound and Eliot (and much subsequent prosodic discussion) because together they constitute a highly efficacious defense of experimental poetry: while the ti-tumming theory discredits conventional meter, the unavoidable-feet theory legitimizes free verse as being metrical.

This legitimization of free verse was important for the modernists. Many poets writing free verse had misgivings about the medium. Any indication that they were following traditional prosody (even as they were at the same time breaking with it) was welcome. It helped to give them the hope that, lurking in their experiments, were forms capable of being developed and passed on to later writers, forms that would become clearer and clearer as the experiments continued and that would eventually constitute as organized and explicable a prosodic system as the traditional accentual-syllabic system of English prosody.

That the leaders of the modern revolution so misunderstood meter is troubling. At the same time, one must remember the world in which the modernists grew up. It was a world in which Swinburne was the chief poet and in which Swinburneanism was the mode most obviously available to the young poet. Swinburne was a dead end. And why was he, and Victorian verse in general, a dead end? It was because of the numbingly emphatic quality of the verse. It was because the metrical effects of the verse, even when they were striking and admirable (as they often were in Swinburne), insisted on themselves as metrical effects in the absence of serious and vital subject matter. It was because the verse almost seemed to preclude mature and flexible expression. Metrical speech, as was noted earlier, by nature produces degrees of emphasis. Moreover, as has already been observed, meter can support elevated diction more readily than prose can, and it may thus encourage the unwary or unskillful writer to employ falsely or indiscriminately elevated diction. It may have been only natural for Ford, Eliot, and Pound, living at the particular historical moment they did, to consider removing meter from poetry in hopes of removing from it everything which seemed overwrought and dull.

One should also note that the modern revolutionaries were

uneasy about their attack on meter and that this uneasiness increased after the triumph of the revolution. The modern movement's leaders were, as the years passed, concerned that their revolution was not followed by a period of consolidation, but by increasingly casual and incoherent experiments with poetic form. As early as his 1918 "Retrospect," Pound cautions his followers, "*[V]ers libre* has become as prolix and as verbose as any of the flaccid varieties that preceded it. . . . I do not think one can use to any advantage rhythms much more tenuous and imperceptible than some I have used" (*LE*, 3, 12–13).

The sentiment expressed by Pound is expressed repeatedly by Eliot and William Carlos Williams in their later criticism and letters. In his 1942 "Music of Poetry" essay, Eliot surveys the contemporary scene and writes that "the craving for continual novelty of diction and metric is as unwholesome as an obstinate adherence to the idiom of our grandfathers." In 1944, in his lecture on Dr. Johnson, he speaks of the "riot of individual styles" in modern poetry and adds that "originality, when it becomes the only, or the most prized virtue of poetry, may cease to be a virtue at all; and when several poets, and their respective groups of admirers, cease to have in common any standards of versification, any identity of taste or of tenets of belief, criticism may decline to an advertisement of preference." In 1947, Eliot remarks in his Milton lecture: "We cannot, in literature, any more than in the rest of life, live in perpetual state of revolution," and he warns his audience of the danger of "a progressive deterioration, and that is our danger today" (*OPP*, 35, 182, 160). It is interesting to note that Eliot lived to see a world in which creative writing and creative free versing became a common feature of academic life, and his response to this world was evidently one of dismay. In 1950, he says in a letter to Janet Adam Smith: "I was shocked when my grand-niece presented me with some verses that she had written as school exercises to find that little girls in an American school were *encouraged* to write in vers libre."[31]

One finds similar statements in the essays and letters that Williams wrote from the early thirties on. In 1932, he characterizes "the present moment" as "a formless interim" and somewhat uneasily observes, "There is no workable poetic form extant among us today." In 1935, he writes to the editor Ronald Lane Latimer, asking him to try to discover an alternate metric in his (Williams') own work, a discovery which Williams himself feels incapable of making: "All right, what then do I want you to do? I want you to DISCOVER not necessarily in my verse, but mine may do, what the new measures are to be." In 1942, corresponding with his son Bill, he gloomily says of his own poems: "I have wanted to link myself up with a traditional art, to feel that I was developing individually it might be, but along with that, developing still in the true evolving tradition of the art. I wonder how much I have succeeded there. I haven't been recognized and I doubt that my technical influence is good or even adequate." In 1948, in his "Poem as a Field of Action" essay, he complains of dull experimentality in contemporary writing, "[T]he tiresome repetition of this 'new,' now twenty years old, disfigures every journal." And in 1953, he writes in his "On Measure—Statement for Cid Corman": "There is nothing interesting in the construction of our poems, nothing that can jog the ear out of its boredom." Of this situation, he sadly and honestly remarks: "I among the rest have much to answer for"; and he continues, "Without measure we are lost. But we have lost even the ability to count. . . . There are a few exceptions but there is no one among us who is consciously aware of what he is doing" (*SL,* 129, 152, 202; *SE,* 280, 338, 339, 340).

These considerations should probably make one skeptical of Eliot's contention that metrical considerations are negligible when compared with the broader question of good writing and bad. As true as it is that meter alone will never produce a fine poem, even a poor poet who writes in meter keeps alive the traditions of versification. When good and bad writers alike devote themselves to free verse, it is possible that all sense of poetic form—and of the memorability and delight its symmetries and surprises can give to readers—will be lost.

Writing of his coming of age in the early years of the twentieth century, Wallace Stevens in his "Noble Rider and the Sound of Words" says that there was a sense "that the Victorians had left nothing behind."[32] Conventional poetry, it was widely believed, was exhausted. Yet the Victorian era had left behind something, something even the leaders of the modern movement admired and wished to emulate. This was prose fiction. And the next chapter will examine how modern prose fiction affected the development of free verse.

CHAPTER 2

"The Superior Art":
Verse and Prose
and Modern Poetry

In the last and longest section of his *Orator,* Cicero takes up the subject of prose rhythm. While speaking of the earliest writers to attempt rhythmical arrangement in prose, he makes the following remarks about Isocrates, remarks which I cited in the introduction to this study but which bear repeating here:

> The enthusiastic admirers of Isocrates extol as the greatest of his accomplishments that he was the first to introduce rhythm into prose. For when he observed that people listened to orators with solemn attention, but to poets with pleasure, he is said to have sought for rhythms to use in prose as well, both for their intrinsic charm and in order that monotony might be forestalled by variety.
>
> (*Orator,* 174)

These observations remind us that ancient prose writers, in developing their art, emulated the older art of poetry. From the fifth century B.C. on, orators and rhetoricians were centrally concerned with establishing quasi-metrical procedures for prose that would give it a structural integrity and attractiveness comparable to that of verse. Gorgias, who is reputed to have been Isocrates' teacher, is generally considered to be the figure who initiated the development of rhythmical prose; Cicero himself, shortly after making the comments cited above, argues that both Gorgias and Thrasymachus preceded Isocrates in the innovations with which the younger man was sometimes credited. Diodorus Siculus makes clear (12.53.2–5)[1] that when Gorgias made his famous embassy and public address to the Athenians in 427 B.C., he had already developed a prose style that incorporated devices suggestive of poetry. "[B]y the novelty of his speech," Diodorus tells us, "he filled the Athenians, who are by nature clever and fond of dialectic, with wonder. For he was the first to use the rather unusual and carefully devised structures of speech, such as antithesis, sentences with equal members [*isocōlon*] or balanced clauses [*parison*] or similar endings [*homoioteleuton*], and the like, all of which at that time was enthusiastically received because the device was exotic." In a similar vein, Demetrius observes (*On Style,* 12–15)[2] that before Gorgias, prose writers employed a loose, disjointed style (*lexis eiromemē*), whereas Gorgias and his followers fashioned a more tightly organized, periodic style (*lexis periodos*) in which, Demetrius says, "the periods succeed one another with no less regularity than the hexameters in the poetry of Homer."

To be sure, ancient writers never insisted that prose actually be composed in meter, that is, in the regularly measured rhythmical units of verse. Yet all major writers on oratory and rhetoric treat prose rhythm as a principal aspect of their subject. And, as Cicero's observations indicate, it was agreed that rhythmical arrangement was a chief means by which poets enchanted their

70

listeners and that something of the same kind of organization would similarly benefit prose writers.

Quite a different phenomenon characterizes recent literary history. Rather than prose emulating the metrical order of poetry, poetry emulates the rhythmical freedom of prose. Whereas in earlier periods prose writers experimented with cadential patterns and other elements associated with verse, many modern poets forgo conventional metric in favor of free verse and replace meter with looser rhythms traditionally associated with prose.

One reason for this development concerns the modern novel of manners. Prior to the nineteenth century, most imaginative literature of prestige is metrical. Its authors are writers of verse, such as Homer, Sappho, Sophocles, Virgil, Horace, Dante, Petrarch, Ariosto, Shakespeare, Jonson, Racine, Pope. But in the late eighteenth and nineteenth century, prose fiction challenges and, to a great extent, triumphs over fiction in verse. In consequence, the modern reformers of poetry pursue their reforms with reference not only to the deficiencies of Victorian verse, but also to the successes of the period's novels. When Ford and Pound urge that, as Ford says, "verse must be at least as well written as prose if it is to be poetry" (*TTR,* 201), their assertion entails more than a frustration with lax poetic style. They are arguing as well that verse must be as engaging as good prose fiction, if it is to hold a central place in modern literature. Given the novel's ascendency in the Victorian period, and given the inflated diction and limited subject matter of much Victorian verse, this aim is perfectly reasonable. Furthermore, as was noted in the last chapter, the aim resembles objectives that earlier poets pursued when they set out to reform a poetic idiom that had lost touch with living speech. In the modern movement, however, prosaic qualities become desiderata not only for poetic diction, but for poetic structure itself. And the idea that verse should be as well written as prose is converted into the very different idea that poetry might be written as the novel is written: without meter.

This chapter will address three related topics: first, the ways in which, in antiquity, prose writers sought to model prose on the structural order of poetry; second, the response of poets, in the modern period, to the novel's success and to their realization that poetry had lost its traditional position as the primary vehicle for fiction; third, the ways in which modern poets, developing a "free" verse designed to compete with prose fiction, employed concepts which ancient writers had employed in developing an artistic prose designed to compete with poetry.

1. *Prose Seeking Order*
on the Model of Poetry

Ancient prose rhythm has been studied extensively.[3] It would be superfluous and impractical to attempt a survey of the matter here. It will be sufficient to consider those issues concerning ancient prose rhythm that indicate the manner and degree to which ancient prose writers looked to poetry for structural order. These issues involve the amount and nature of rhythm believed appropriate to prose, the units of rhythm that were felt suitable to prose and the way these were used by prose writers, and the difficulty that ancient critics sometimes had in maintaining working distinctions between verse and prose.

Regarding the amount of rhythm appropriate to prose, ancient critics affirm that prose should possess perceptible rhythmical structure, but should not embrace the norm of a metrical line. In the third book of the *Rhetoric*, Aristotle addresses this issue in his seminal discussion of prose rhythm:

> The form of diction (*skēma tēs lexeōs*) should be neither metrical (*emmetron*) nor without rhythm (*arrhythmon*). . . . If it is without rhythm, it is unlimited, whereas it ought to be limited (but not by metre); for that which is unlimited is unpleasant and unknowable. Now all things are limited by number (*arithmō),* and the number

belonging to the form of diction is rhythm (*rhythmos*), of which the metres (*metra*) are divisions. Wherefore prose (*logon*) must be rhythmical, but not metrical [i.e., in a specific metre such as trimeter or hexameter], otherwise it will be a poem (*poiēma*). Nor must this rhythm be rigorously carried out, but only up to a certain point.

(3.8.1–3)

Writing on stylistic elegance, Demetrius makes a similar observation, remarking (183) of Plato's prose: "Plato in many passages owes his elegance directly to the rhythm (*rhythmō*). . . . His members (*cōla*) seem to glide along and to be neither altogether metrical (*emmetrois*) nor unmetrical (*ametrois*)." So, too, Cicero says (*Orator,* 187), "It is clear, then, that prose should be bound or restricted by rhythm (*numeris*), but that it should not contain actual verses (*versibus*)." In short, prose should hint at metricality without being in meter.

A corollary of this idea is that prose calls for qualities of movement which, though suggesting the order of metrical composition, are more variable or diffuse than the specific units of verse. Contrasting the comparative freedom of prose with the restrictions of verse, Dionysius of Helicarnassus says (*On Literary Composition,* 19): "[E]pic writers cannot vary their metre, for all the lines must necessarily be hexameters; nor yet the rhythm, for they must use those feet that begin with a long syllable, and not all even of these. The writers of lyric verse cannot vary the melodies of strophe and antistrophe, but whether they adopt enharmonic melodies, or chromatic, or diatonic, in all the strophes and antistrophes the same sequences must be observed. . . . Prosewriting, [however,] has full liberty and permission to diversify composition by whatever changes it pleases."[4]

Similarly, in his dialogue, *De Oratore,* Cicero has Crassus remark (3.184) that, though the prose writer must attend to rhythmical effects, he is not so confined in this respect as the poet:

These points however do not call for such close attention and care as is practiced by the poets; for them it is a requirement of actual

73

necessity and of the metrical forms themselves that the words shall be so framed in the line that there may not be less or more by even a single breath than the length required. Prose is less fettered (*Liberior est oratio*), and its designation as 'free style' (*soluta*) is quite a correct one, only this does not mean that it is free to go loose or to roam about, but that it is not in chains and supplies its own control.[5]

Quintilian sums up the difference between the rhythm of prose and the meter of poetry when he remarks (9.4.50) "that rhythm has unlimited space over which it may range, whereas the spaces of metre are confined" (*quod rhythmis libera spatia, metris finita sunt*). For this reason, Quintilian observes elsewhere (9.4.115–16) that the prose writer is concerned with "the general rhythmical effect of the period" rather than with the specific unit of a verse line. And Quintilian concludes: "Therefore rhythmical structure will hold the same place in prose that is held by versification in poetry" (*Ergo quem in poemate locum habet versificatio, eum in oratione compositio*).

There is a practical reason behind the ancients' belief that prose should suggest metricality without being in meter. A prose writer or orator desires to appeal movingly and memorably to his audience. Rhythmical arrangement enables him to do this. But he also does not want his art to be too obvious. If his rhythms are too readily recognizable and predictable, his audience may consider his composition excessively contrived. Conspicuous refinements of style could prove especially deleterious in forensic oratory, where they might well indicate an absence of conviction on the part of the pleader.

Speaking of this matter, Aristotle remarks (*Rhetoric,* 3.8.1) of prose, "If it is metrical, it lacks persuasiveness, for it appears artificial, and at the same time it distracts the hearer's attention, since it sets him on the watch for the recurrence of such and such a cadence." Quintilian likewise contends that, though the prose writer should attend to rhythmical arrangement, he must avoid too regular a rhythm:

For we shall really be indulging in a species of versification (*versificandi genus*) if we seek to lay down one law for all varieties of speech: further, to do so would lay us open to the charge of the most obvious affectation. . . . [T]he sweeter the rhythm, the sooner the orator who is detected in a studied adherence to its employment, will cease to carry conviction or to stir the passions and emotions. The judge will refuse to believe him or to allow him to excite his compassion or his anger, if he thinks that he has leisure for this species of refinement. It will therefore be desirable from time to time that in certain passages the rhythm should be deliberately dissolved.

(9.4.143–44)

To speak briefly of issues we will be examining in the third section of this chapter, the ancient notion of prose approximating but not being meter is much like modern notions of free verse, especially those advocated by Eliot. Furthermore, ancient discussions of the dangers of seeming overly artificial in prose have their counterparts in the modern period. In the modern period, however, the dangers are discussed with reference not to the prose writer but to the poet, who is often counseled to avoid meter in order to avoid appearing artificial.

Ancient prose also looks to poetry by applying metrical terminology to prose composition. Ancient critics analyze prose rhythm with reference to metrical feet and to their arrangement in clauses and periods. Regarding the metrical feet believed to be most suitable for prose, some ancient critics urge that the *paeon* (most commonly in the form of the so-called First Paeon, $-\smile\smile\smile$, or its inversion, $\smile\smile\smile-$) is especially fitting. Evidently first consciously employed in prose by Thrasymachus, the paeon was favored because it was not notably employed in any of the poetic *metra*, though the paeon, particularly as a resolved form of the cretic ($-\smile-$), was used in lyric verse. This quality's importance is related to the issue mentioned a moment ago: though it was felt that an absence of rhythm would offend the ear of the reader or listener, it was also felt that prose verging too closely on standard metrical lines would sound stilted. A prose writer or orator whose rhythms were largely constructed out of dactyls and spondees, for instance, would run the risk of sounding hexametric, since those feet are especially associated with the hexameter; by the same token, runs of trochees and iambs might suggest the tetrameter and trimeter respectively. The paeon, however, did not have such close associations with the common meters. Aristotle, who spells the word, in contrast with later custom, with an alpha instead of an omega as the fourth letter, puts the matter this way (*Rhetoric,* 3.8.5): "[T]he paean should be retained [for prose], because it is the only one of the rhythms mentioned which is not adapted to a metrical system, so that it is most likely to be undetected."

There are two points to make here. First, though some ancient writers believed that paeons were signally suited to prose, other writers felt that, because all sorts of feet occur naturally in speech, it is misleading to suggest that only certain of them are adaptable to prose. Cicero respectfully discusses (*Orator,* 192–96) Aristotle's endorsement of the paeon but adds nevertheless: "My own feeling, however, is that all kinds of feet are mingled and jumbled together in prose. . . . Prose, then, as I have said before, should be tempered by an admixture of rhythm; it should not be loose, nor wholly rhythmical (*nec dissoluta nec tota numerosa*); the paean [Cicero's follows Aristotle's spelling] is to be the principal measure, because that is the opinion of our greatest authority [Aristotle], but we should combine this with the other rhythms which he disregards." Quintilian is even more skeptical of the notion that the paeon or any other foot can claim overriding efficacy for prose, remarking (9.4.87–91) that he is "surprised that scholars of the highest learning should have held the view that some feet should be specially selected and others condemned for the purposes of prose, as if there were any foot which must not inevitably be found in prose." Quintilian goes on to observe that however dogmatically critics assert that some feet do not belong in oratory, "for all they say, these feet will force themselves upon them against their will. . . . Feet therefore should be mixed, while care must be taken that the majority are of a pleasing character, and that the inferior feet are lost in the surrounding crowd of their superior kindred."

A second point to note with regard to the paeon is that even critics who favored it never suggested that paeonic rhythm should be employed with absolute regularity. To do so would be to violate the nature of prose and to convert prose into a species of metrical composition. Rather, critics like Aristotle (*Rhetoric,* 3.8.6–8) and Demetrius (38–41) urge that it will be enough for the writer simply to use paeonic rhythm at certain key points. In particular, it seems to have been thought that an author might merely begin clauses and periods with a First Paeon and conclude with an inverted or Fourth Paeon, without worrying too much about what happens in the middle sections—the theory being that opening clauses or periods with a long syllable would give them impetus at the outset and that ending them with a long syllable would provide them with a felicitous sense of closure.

This procedure is illustrated by Demetrius in his discussion of the paeon. He cites (39) the observation with which Thucydides starts his account of the plague and argues that the impressive and quiet firmness of the observation results from Thucydides' beginning with a First Paeon and ending with its inverted version:

$$— \cup \cup \; \cup \qquad \qquad \cup\cup —$$

ērxato de to kakon ex Aithiopias.

    (Now it was from Aethiopia that the malady originally came.)

There is an additional point to make with respect to paeonic rhythm. One need not, Demetrius continues, employ exactly the formula just given to achieve a forcefulness comparable to that of Thucydides' statement about the plague's origin. Indeed, if one always employed this construction, one's audience would probably become distracted by the recurrence of the pattern, and the construction would conduce less to impressiveness than to an appearance of affectation. It may therefore be advisable, Demetrius observes, simply to modulate the beginnings and con-

clusions—and, if one wishes, the interiors—of clauses in a
paeonic manner without really resorting to paeons. This latter
technique is well exemplified, to Demetrius' mind, by a clause
Theophrastus once cited for its stylistic elevation:

$$- \quad - \quad \cup\cup\ \cup\ \ -\cup\cup\ -\omega\ \cup\cup\cup\ -\ \ -$$
tōn men peri ta mēdenos axia philosophountōn.
  (Those who philosophize in matters that are worth nought.)

The rhythm of this clause is not strictly paeonic. It is not strictly
anything. Nevertheless, the clause is initiated and terminated
with long syllables, and in two places within the line three short
syllables either precede or follow a long syllable.

The paeon was not the only rhythmical unit which drew special attention from ancient prose writers. Greek and Latin orators
developed additional rhythmical units to highlight the endings
of clauses or periods. These cadential units, called *clausulae,*
consisted of different combinations of feet. For instance, three
clausulae favored by Latin writers were the cretic spondee
($-\cup--\breve{}$), the double cretic ($-\cup--\cup\breve{}$), and the cretic dichoree
($-\cup--\cup-\cup$). In Cicero's *De Oratore,* Crassus discusses (3.173)
clausulae, characterizing them as "pauses (*clausulae*) dictated by
the need to draw breath rather than by complete exhaustion, and
marked not by scribes' punctuation but by the pattern of words
and content."[6]

Concerning the use of *clausulae,* Crassus sounds a theme that
one encounters in discussions of other elements of prose rhythm.
Clausulae should be employed, he says, regularly enough to secure
rhythmical order for speech, but not so regularly as to suggest
verse:

> The key point here is that if the sequence of words causes the
> appearance of verse in prose, there is something wrong: yet at the
> same time we want the sequence of words to end rhythmically, just as
> a verse does, tidily and completely. There is no one thing, out of so
> many, that more clearly marks off the orator from the man who is
> ignorant and unskilled in speaking than that the untutored pour out

all they can shapelessly, letting breath, not technique, dictate the pauses in what they say: while the orator so binds his thought in words that he imposes on it a rhythm at once disciplined and free. Having bound it with balance and rhythm, he relaxes and frees it by changes of order, ensuring that the words are neither subjected like verse to some particular rule nor so free as to wander at large.

(3.175–76)

To the modern student, writing prose with so conscious an eye on rhythmical arrangement may seem peculiar, and he may ask to what extent ancient writers put the ideas we have been examining into practice. The answer is, fairly extensively. The practice of prose rhythm was, in its particulars, never uniform. There was, however, an almost universal agreement about its importance. What is more, the available evidence (e.g., Aristotle, *Rhetoric,* 3.8.1; Dionysius, *On Literary Composition,* 11; Cicero, *De Oratore,* 3.195–96) indicates that even uneducated audiences could appreciate skillful rhythm in an oration and could, by the same token, be irritated and put off by inept rhythm.[7]

Other indications of the degree to which ancient prose emulates the metrical order of poetry are exercises in comparative metrical analysis, such as one finds in the eighteenth chapter of Dionysius' *On Literary Composition.* In endeavoring to demonstrate successful and unsuccessful management of rhythm and meter, Dionysius juxtaposes a passage from the *Iliad* with a passage from Hegesias' *History of Alexander.* The passages deal with similar episodes. In the passage from the *Iliad,* Homer narrates how Achilles, having killed Hector, ties the body to a chariot and drags it before the walls of Troy. In the passage from the *History,* Hegesias tells how Alexander, having been betrayed by a false offer of peace from Batis, has Batis tied to a chariot and hauled at high speed over rough ground so that he is virtually flayed alive. Both episodes are horrifying. It requires great tact, Dionysius notes, to communicate such material in a way that does not sicken but moves the heart. Homer, Dionysius urges, has this tact. His narration of Achilles' shameful treatment of Hector's corpse is affecting, and this quality derives, Dionysius contends, largely from Homer's straightforward language and the unaffected skill with which he manages the hexameter. Hegesias' passage, in contrast, is merely stomach-turning. According to Dionysius, the grotesquerie of Hegesias' account results precisely from his mismanagement of rhythm and from the preciosity in his choice and disposition of feet.

To modern readers raised on New Critical analysis, Dionysius' comparison will seem in many ways familiar. But the comparison will seem striking in one respect: Dionysius is comparing the metrical qualities not of two poems, but of a poem and prose work. So closely does ancient prose look to poetry for structural order—so directly does it seek the kinds of rhythmical effects associated with poetry—that Dionysius can apply the same techniques of prosodic analysis to each art.

Because ancient prose tried to govern itself, as poetry was governed, on some sort of rhythmical basis, and because prose looked to metrics for structural order, it was at times difficult to maintain distinctions between the two arts. This difficulty is evident in the labored efforts Cicero devotes in the *Orator* to distinguishing rhythms of prose from those of verse. The difficulty is also reflected by Quintilian, who expresses (9.4.53) exasperation at having "come across tiresome grammarians who attempted to force prose into definite meters (*varias mensuras*), as though it were a species of lyric poetry (*lyricorum carmina*)." Quintilian is himself at pains to draw boundaries between prose rhythm and poetic versification, and he makes interesting remarks in reference to Cicero's exertions on the same subject:

> Cicero, indeed, frequently asserts that the whole art of prose-structure consists in rhythm and is consequently censured by some critics on the ground that he would fetter our style by the laws of rhythm. . . . Among others they attack Cicero's statement that the *thunderbolts of Demosthenes would not have such force but for the rhythm with which they are whirled and sped upon their way.* If by *rhythmis contorta* he really means what his critics assert, I do not agree

with him. For rhythms have, as I have said, no fixed limit or variety of structure, but run on with the same rise and fall till they reach their end. . . . For my own part, to avoid incurring the calumny, from which even Cicero was not free, I ask my reader, whenever I speak of the rhythm of artistic structure (as I have done on every occasion), to understand that I refer to the rhythm of oratory, not of verse.

(9.4.53–57)

How verse and prose differ has always been a vexed question; Quintilian is dealing with a perennial problem. It is important to note, however, that if Quintilian is distressed that some critics confuse prose and verse, he believes that the art whose identity is thereby threatened is prose. He is not afraid that verse is being treated as if it were a species of prose, but that prose is being treated as if it were a species of verse.

As we will see later in this chapter, this situation is exactly reversed in the modern period. Prose is not drawn towards metric and verse; verse is drawn away from metric and toward prose. Distinguishing between prose and verse remains as perplexing an issue as ever; it is, however, not prose but verse whose nature is unclear and whose independence from its sister art is precarious. Whereas in antiquity writers expressed concern about the tendency of prose to abandon rhythm in its general sense for the particular structure of meter, our time has witnessed the tendency of verse to abandon meter in favor of a more general and vaguer quality of rhythm. Indeed, it is scarcely an exaggeration to say that the prosodic history of modern verse consists of the displacement of *metron* by *rhythmos*.

2. *The Shift from Fiction in Meter to Fiction in Prose*

Cultivation of prose rhythm persists into and through the Middle Ages.[8] In Latin, partly because of the influence of speech qualities of the developing European vernaculars, the classical quantatitive rhythms are gradually overlaid by accentual ones. (Much the same phenomenon characterizes Greek; from the first century A.D. onward, Greek quantitative metric weakens, eventually to be supplanted by versification based on accent.) This development, however, does not signal the end of earlier practices, but rather their adaptation to new linguistic environments. For instance, the ancient *clausulae* are transformed by degrees in Latin prose into the medieval schemes of *cursus*. In other words, as writers neglect or lose sensitivity to the durational values of syllables in Latin, and as Latin itself assumes an accentual character, the quantitative *clausulae* are transferred into an accentual context. To take as examples the three *clausulae* cited earlier, the cretic spondee becomes the *planus* ($-\cup-\underset{\prime}{-}\underset{\smile}{}$), the double cretic becomes the *tardus* ($-\cup-\underset{\prime}{-}\cup\underset{\smile}{}$), the cretic dichoree becomes the *velox* ($-\cup--\cup\underset{\prime}{-}\cup$).

The continued proximity of prose to poetic practice can be seen in the various meanings that attach themselves to *prosa,* which is a medieval contraction for *prorsus oratio* (straightforward speech) and from which we derive our word "prose." During the Middle Ages, *prosa* indicates that kind of carefully composed non-poetic discourse indicated in classical Latin by *numerosa oratio* or *compositio oratio* (rhythmical and/or artistic speech). *Prosa* has, in this sense, definite stylistic ornament and often has construable rhythm. Furthermore, *prosa* is employed in the earlier Middle Ages to describe a poem written in Latin according to accentual measure as opposed to classical quantitative measure. *Prosa* signifies as well the couplet compositions written as texts for the musical sequences of the medieval church. Though these were initially written solely with reference to the musical texts, subsequently *prosae* were produced in conformity with scansion and structural rhyme.

Other evidence of the proximity of medieval prose to poetry includes the medieval interest in *prosimetra*, compositions in which verse is interspersed with prose. This form precedes the Middle Ages. It appears to have originated with Menippus (fl. 3rd c. B.C.), whose now-lost satires were imitated in Varro's *Saturae Menippeae,* of which only fragments are extant. The *Apocolocyntosis* traditionally attributed to Seneca and the surviving section of Petronius' *Satyricon* may also be cited as examples of the form. It was in the Middle Ages, however, that the *prosimetrum* was especially favored, thanks partly to the influence of Martianus Capella's *Marriage of Mercury and Philology* (early 5th c.) and Boethius' *Consolation of Philosophy* (524); both *prosimetra* achieved considerable popularity and became stardard school texts. Another indication of the proximity of prose to verse in the Middle Ages is the frequency with which writers engage in the exercise of paraphrase, of turning prose works into verse and verse works into prose. Yet another sign of the closeness of prose and verse is the fact that as the use of structural rhyme increases in medieval poetry, it increases in medieval prose as well. In fact, in the later Middle Ages, rhymed prose (*mixtum sive compositum*)—prose in which the ends of adjacent or near-adjacent cola are rhymed—is recognized as a distinct stylistic category.[9]

Lastly, it is significant that Dante's *On Vernacular Eloquence,* which is both a summary of much medieval poetics and the first substantial work on literature in modern languages, treats poetry as the primary art and prose as the secondary art. In the first paragraph of Book II, Dante says:

> [W]e declare in the first place that the illustrious Italian vernacular is equally fit for use in prose (*prosaice*) and in verse (*metrice*). But because prose writers rather get this language from poets, and because poetry seems to remain a pattern to prose writers, and not the converse, which things appear to confer a certain supremacy, let us first disentangle this language as to its use in meter (*metricum*).[10]

Because the Middle Ages maintained a tradition in which prose looked to verse for structural order (or continued to share with verse a concern with rhythmical arrangement), one cannot point to any movement in medieval prose analogous to that represented by Gorgias in antiquity. Medieval writers had no need to relate prose to verse. Such a relationship already existed, and Latin itself, in which the relationship had been so long and so firmly established, remained the language of educated Europe. With the Renaissance, however, one again sees prose writers soliciting from verse the means for organizing, clarifying, and elevating prose. This development is reflected in the Ciceronian movement, which arose from a belief that medieval Latinists had barbarized the language. The Ciceronian movement aimed at producing a modern Latin based on ancient rhetorical theory in general and on the model of Cicero in particular. What is more significant, the development is reflected in the various attempts to provide the evolving vernaculars with a sophistication equivalent to that of literary Latin.

In English the attempt to appropriate resources of poetry for prose is most clearly exhibited in John Lyly's *Euphues* and Euphuism. Characteristic of Lyly's book and of Euphuistic style is the following soliloquy, which Euphues delivers when he, having stolen Lucilla from his friend Philautus, has in turn been cast aside by her in favor of Curio:

> O the counterfaite loue of women. Oh inconstant sex. I haue lost *Philautus,* I haue lost *Lucilla,* I haue lost that which I shall hardlye finde againe, a faythfull friende. A foolishe *Euphues,* why diddest thou leaue *Athens* the nourse of wisdome, to inhabite *Naples* the nourisher of wantonesse? Had it not bene better for thee to haue eaten salt with the Philosophers of *Greece,* then sugar with the courtiers of *Italy?* But behold the course of youth which always inclyneth to pleasure, I forsooke mine olde companions to search for new friends, I reiected the graue and fatherly consayle of *Eubulus,* to follow the braine-sicke humor of mine owne will. I addicted my selfe wholy to the seruice of women to spende my lyfe in the lappes of Ladyes, my lands in the maintenance of brauerie, my witte in the vanities of idle Sonnets.[11]

Here we have repetition ("O the counterfaite . . . Oh inconstant"), antithesis ("the nourse of wisdome . . . the nourisher of wantonesse"), rhetorical questions ("Why diddest thou . . . Had it not bene better"), parallelism ("I forsooke . . . I reiected . . . I addicted"), alliteration ("lyfe . . . lappes . . . Ladyes . . . lands"). We even have a classical tricolon crescendo ("I haue lost . . . a faythfull friend"), a succession of three grammatically related clauses in which the final clause is the longest and envelops and encompasses the first two. Lastly, after having gone on for several more sentences like those cited above, the passage closes with Euphues resolving, in a decasyllabic couplet, to forswear Neapolitan decadence: "I will to *Athens* ther to tosse my bookes, no more in *Naples* to lyue with faire lookes."

In trying to give qualities of verse to prose, Lyly may be said to be resuming a tradition that goes back to Gorgias. Yet in the artistic prose of the Renaissance, there is a concern that is not in ancient prose, and this concern is of great importance to recent literary history. Authors like Lyly are not merely attempting to make prose poetic. They are also trying, in an unprecedented way, to compose prose fiction possessing the dignity of verse fiction.

At this juncture, it must be recalled again that in antiquity most fiction of prestige is in meter. This is not to slight ancient prose fiction like that of Achilles Tatius or Heliodorus. Not until the Renaissance, however, does there arise a wide interest in prose as a medium for serious imaginative literature. There are several reasons for this new interest. One involves vernacular drama and the question of whether prose might not be the proper vehicle for modern plays; this topic will be examined in the next chapter. Another is the development of the romance, of which *Euphues* is a notable example and which, though it had ancient antecedents, was viewed by some Renaissance writers as their age's most significant contribution to fiction. The romance was frequently written in and associated with prose. Dante's line (*Purgatorio,* 26.118), "Verses of love and prose romances" (*Versi d'amore e prose di romanzi*)[12] is an early reflection of this association. It should perhaps be added that Dante associated (*On Vernacular Eloquence,* i.x) romance not simply with prose in general but with the French vernacular in particular. Hence Renaissance defenders of contemporary fiction were, to a certain extent, compelled to defend the use of prose in fiction.

Changing attitudes towards prose are anticipated by Boccaccio's introduction to *The Decameron*'s Fourth Day, during which Boccaccio discusses his work. At first he modestly characterizes it as "these little stories of mine, which bear no title and which I have written, not only in the Florentine vernacular and in prose (*non solamente in fiorentin volgare e in prosa*), but in the most homely and unassuming style it is possible to imagine." He shifts his ground, however, when he remarks that well-meaning friends have told him that, rather than scribbling mere prose tales to amuse women, he should devote himself to the higher pursuits of verse, which can claim the genuine sponsorship of the Muses. Though acknowledging that such advice may be sound, Boccaccio slyly suggests that he may not be as far removed from the Muses of poetry as those who counsel him think. The Muses are divine women, and it may be that writing poetry for them and writing prose for human women are in fact closely related enterprises. Indeed, "it is possible that they [the Muses] have been looking over my shoulder several times in the writing of these tales, however unassuming they may be, perhaps because they acknowledge and respect the affinity between the ladies and themselves. And so, in composing these stories, I am not straying as far from Mount Parnassus or from the Muses as many people might be led to believe."[13]

It is, in any case, against a background of changing attitudes towards prose fiction that Philip Sidney writes in his *Apologie for Poetrie:*

> [T]he greatest part of Poets have apparelled their poeticall inventions in that numbrous kinde of writing which is called verse: indeed but apparelled, verse being but an ornament and no cause to Poetry . . . I

speak to shew, that it is not riming and versing that maketh a Poet, no more then a long gowne maketh an Advocate; who though he pleaded in armor should be an Advocate and no Souldier. But it is that fayning notable images of vertues, vices, or what els, with that delightfull teaching, which must be the right describing note to know a Poet by.[14]

Sidney expresses here a concern with writing respectable fiction in prose. Furthermore, in his romance, the *Arcadia*—especially in the unfinished second version—Sidney attempts in his own way what Lyly attempts in *Euphues.* Sidney aims to produce a prose "poem," a prose narrative "fayning notable images of vertues, vices, or what els, with that delightfull teaching." (The verse interludes, though interesting in terms of the history of English metric, represent a small part of the work itself.) Sidney's intentions are disclosed not only by his elaborate style, but also by his formal arrangement of the work, which is determined by the five-act structure for poetic drama that Horace had recommended and which reveals Sidney's wish for the *Arcadia* to be treated with the same sort of seriousness accorded metrical fiction.

Though tastes in prose style change, arguments like Sidney's on behalf of prose fiction persist into the eighteenth century. Of these later arguments, one of the most interesting is Henry Fielding's preface to *Joseph Andrews,* in which Fielding defends the use of prose for "Epic Comedy":

[A]s this Poetry [Epic] may be Tragic or Comic, I will not scruple to say that it may be likewise either in Verse or Prose; for tho' it wants one particular, which the Critic enumerates in the constituent Parts of an Epic Poem, namely Metre; yet, when any kind of Writing contains all its other Parts, such as Fable, Action, Characters, Sentiments, and Diction, and is deficient in Metre only; it seems, I think, reasonable to refer it to the Epic; at least, as no Critic hath thought proper to range it under any other Head, nor to assign it a particular Name to itself.[15]

Today we call the kind of work that Fielding discusses, and that is prefigured by *Euphues* and the *Arcadia,* a novel. Its emergence affects poetry profoundly. An increasingly distinctive and popular form of non-metrical fiction, the novel of manners—an extended narrative that treats the familial, social, political, sexual, and psychological relations of people in modern society—gradually absorbs much of the material and audience formerly devoted to poetry.

It must be stressed that at just the time the novel was coming into maturity, poetry was relinquishing territories it had long occupied. The Romantic movement, though encouraging poets to explore new areas of experience, also encouraged a spontaneous lyricism that proved detrimental to the long poem. Evidence of this may be seen in the unfinished extended works that are produced in the Romantic period, works like *The Recluse, Christabel,* and *Don Juan.* These efforts appear to have been propelled forward in brief bursts of intensity without the supports of the pedestrian but perhaps necessary virtues of perspicuously arranged exposition. Indeed, in the Romantic and Victorian period, the short poem becomes the fundamental poetic form. On occasion it is even urged that long poems are but amalgamations of shorter works, as in Poe's remark, "What we term a long poem is, in fact, merely a succession of brief ones—that is to say, of brief poetical effects."[16] While in earlier periods, narrative and dramatic modes are often considered the most important ones and often attract the best efforts of the best poets, in the Romantic period and the nineteenth century, the long poem, though often attempted, has comparatively little vitality.[17]

It is possible that if a Milton had been living at that hour, circumstances might have taken a different turn. It is also possible, however, that he might have written a monumental novel in the manner of Hugo or Tolstoi rather than a long work in meter. Prevailing ideas about poetry ill sustained the long poem. The fourth chapter of this study will examine these ideas, which derive from German Aesthetic Idealism and from aspects of Neo-platonic thought. It is enough here to note that the ideas tended to narrow poetry to suggestive lyricality. As a result, there was a literary vacuum, which the novel eventually and successfully filled.

The shift of importance from poetry to the novel—from metrical fiction to prose fiction—is cogently summarized by Pound in his "How to Read" essay:

> I mean to say that from the beginning of literature up to A.D. 1750 poetry was the superior art, and was so considered to be, and if we read books written before that date we find the number of interesting books in verse at least equal to the number of prose books still readable; and the poetry contains the quintessence. . . . But, as I have said, the *'fioritura* business' [the florid embroidery of style] set in. And one morning Monsieur Stendhal, not thinking of Homer, or Villon, or Catullus, but having a very keen sense of actuality, noticed that 'poetry,' *la poésie,* as the term was then understood, the stuff written by his French contemporaries, or sonorously rolled at him from the French stage, was a damn nuisance. And he remarked that poetry, with its bagwigs and its bobwigs, its padded calves and its periwigs, its 'fustian à la Louis XIV', was greatly inferior to prose for conveying a clear idea of the diverse states of our consciousness ('les mouvements du coeur').
>
> And at that moment the serious art of writing 'went over to prose' . . .
>
> (*LE,* 31)

In the second half of the nineteenth century, poets developed two responses to the triumph of the novel. The first of these was to pursue a path, already given preliminary exploration by certain of the Romantics, into pure poetry, into a poetic art that accepts and even glories in its progressive attenuation and that turns inward on its own medium for its resources and subjects. Swinburne is the most notable English representative of this response. The second response involved an effort to recover materials increasingly claimed by prose fiction, and this response is best exemplified by Browning, much of whose work aims at accommodating the narrative qualities and tones of the novel. For instance, Browning's most famous long poem, *The Ring and the Book* of 1868–69, attempts to do in pentameters what Wilkie Collins had been doing for a decade in his popular mystery stories. The plot of Browning's poem deals with a famous crime and unfolds, in the manner of Collins, by having interested parties deliver in succession their different and conflicting views of the case. Similarly, many of Browning's other poems are character studies or little novels in meter.

Browning's admirers recognized the unusual enterprise in which he was engaged. This recognition appears in Oscar Wilde's dialogue, "The Critic as Artist," which was published in 1890, the year after Browning's death, and in which one of the characters observes:

> Yes, Browning was great. And as what will he be remembered? As a poet? Ah, not as a poet! He will be remembered as a writer of fiction. . . . The only man who can touch the hem of his garment is George Meredith. Meredith is a prose Browning, and so is Browning.[18]

Though this compliment is, to be sure, cleverly backhanded, it is sincere: in the context of the Victorian era, it indicates Browning's freedom from the sterilities of much of the poetry of the time.

The same view of Browning appears in the criticism of Ford, who favorably contrasts Browning's prosaic qualities with the insipid idiom of most Victorian poets. In *Thus to Revisit,* Ford excepts Christina Rossetti and Browning from his otherwise sweeping censure of Victorian verse, saying: "Christina Rossetti was an infinitely great master of words, but the emotions her work always gave me were those of reading prose—and so it was with Browning." In addition, Ford remarks that Browning and Hardy, by rejecting Victorian diction, were precursors of the

Imagists: "In the matter of language at least, first Browning and then Mr. Hardy, showed the way for the Imagiste group—Browning dragging in any old word from an immense, and Mr. Hardy doing the same thing from a rather limited, vocabulary" (*TTR*, 131, 153).

Among poets who begin to publish in the first two decades of this century, there is an acute awareness of the alternatives represented by Swinburne and Browning, and a sense that it is necessary to choose between them. This situation is particularly observable in the young Pound, who is attracted to the mellifluous suavities of Swinburne and at the same time wants to bring qualities of modern prose fiction into poetry. On the one hand, much of Pound's early work is frankly Swinburnean—full of inversions, archaisms, and thee-ings and thou-ings. On the other hand, a smaller number of poems aim at a colloquial idiom and, in matter and treatment, follow the example of Browning. This stylistic schizophrenia mirrors Pound's attitudes towards the two poets: Swinburne is, for Pound, the figure who rescued English verse from a decline which began at the time of the Puritan revolt, and Browning is, in Pound's eyes, the author of the best single collection of Victorian verse, *Men and Women,* and the creator of the highly suggestive *Sordello.* Though neither writer is completely satisfactory—Browning for all his talent smacks of hucksterish vulgarity and Swinburne for all his melodic dexterity lacks direct engagement with the world—the two combined represent, Pound implies, the "whole or perfect poet" (*LE,* 293).

Early in his career, Pound's divided allegiance is weighted in the direction of Swinburne. The weight shifts, however, in the direction of Browning as time passes. The change is disclosed in *Personae,* the 1926 edition of Pound's shorter work, a collection from which the author suppresses many of his youthful Swinburnean pieces while retaining the material more in Browning's style.[19] The change is also disclosed in the initial version of his first *Canto,* which appeared in *Poetry* in 1917. In this version, Pound opens by addressing Browning and by candidly indicating that he plans to forgo aesthetic purity in favor of the "rag-bag" (later he calls it "hodge-podge") approach to composition exhibited in *Sordello:*

> Hang it all, there can be but one *Sordello!*
> But say I want to, say I take your whole bag of tricks,
> Let in your quirks and tweeks, and say the thing's an art-form,
> Your *Sordello,* and that the modern world
> Needs such a rag-bag to stuff all its thought in;
> Say that I dump my catch, shiny and silvery
> As fresh sardines flapping and slipping on the marginal
>   cobbles?
> (I stand before the booth, the speech; but the truth
> Is inside this discourse—this booth is full of the marrow of
>   wisdom.)
> Give up th' intaglio method. [20]

It is clear from the *Canto,* and from the *Hugh Selwyn Mauberley* sequence of 1920, that Pound regrets giving up "th' intaglio method." Nevertheless, he feels he must follow the course marked out by Browning or yield the field of literature to prose writers. As he says further on in the *Canto,* in lines which resume the theme of the beginning, "[S]hall I do your trick, the showman's booth, Bob Browning, / . . . (Or sulk and leave the word to novelists?)." [21]

In Eliot, too, one sees an early interest in Swinburnean style and an ultimate rejection of it for attitudes associated with prose fiction. Especially revealing in this regard is Eliot's 1920 essay on Swinburne, in which Eliot sympathetically analyzes Swinburne's gifts, but concludes the analysis with the judgment that Swinburne's airily "uprooted" style simply will not do for the modern poet. Eliot goes, however, a step further than Pound does in his *Canto.* For Eliot suggests, as a stylistic alternative to Swinburne, not a poet whose works, like Browning's, resemble prose fiction, but two writers who are in fact novelists:

Only a man of genius could dwell so exclusively and consistently among words as Swinburne. His language is not, like the language of bad poetry, dead. It is very much alive, with this singular life of its own. But the language which is more important to us is that which is struggling to digest and express new objects, new groups of objects, new feelings, new aspects, as, for instance, the prose of Mr. James Joyce or the earlier Conrad.[22]

One sees here in Eliot that which one sees also in Pound's *Mauberley:* the criticism of a deficient poetic style, the escape from which is represented by the style of a novelist or novelists. Of Mauberley, Pound says, "His true Penelope was Flaubert."[23] In the passage just cited, Eliot's Penelopes are Joyce and Conrad. And much the same situation, it may be added, applies to Ford. The three writers whom he consistently recommends as models, to poets and prose writers alike, are Henry James, W. H. Hudson, and Conrad.

This belief in the efficacy of the prosaic and the novelistic is also evident, for example, when Pound, in his essay "The Serious Artist," quotes Stendhal's statement that the novel "is concerned with giving a clear and precise idea of the movements of the spirit" and then says that "if we can have a poetry that comes as close as prose, *pour donner une idée claire et précise,* let us have it. . . . And if we cannot attain to such a poetry, noi altri poeti, for God's sake let us shut up" (*LE,* 54, 55). Ford adopts a similar viewpoint when he argues that the decline of poetry in the Victorian period was due almost entirely to the fact that poets did not adequately appreciate or attempt to master procedures and qualities of sound prose composition: "[T]he reason for the intolerably dull effect produced by nearly all modern and semi-modern verse is simply that the poet as a rule considers himself too important a person to descend to the technique of the creative prose writer." And Ford goes on to say that, if poets are to restore their art, they will have to bring to it some of the attitudes and techniques of the novelist: "[I]f you arrogate to yourself the title of poet and claim that, let us say, a poet is to a story-teller as is a barrister to an

93

attorney—the member of a more technically learned profession—you ought to have at least the skill of the lower members of
the lower branch" (*TTR,* 153–54).

So, too, with Eliot. Cautioning poets against the use of rhyme,
he argues: "When the comforting echo of rhyme is removed,
success or failure in the choice of words, in the sentence structure,
in the order, is at once more apparent. Rhyme removed, the poet
is at once held up to the standards of prose" (*TCC,* 188–89).
Likewise, in a 1936 lecture for the BBC, commenting on Eliot and
on the *éclat* of Eliot's early verse, W. B. Yeats remarks that after
the publication of *Prufrock and Other Observations,* "No romantic
word or sound, nothing reminiscent, nothing in the least like the
painting of Ricketts could be permitted henceforth. Poetry must
resemble prose."[24]

To anticipate a subject that we shall examine in the fifth chapter, the modernists' interest in making poetry more like prose
reflected a desire to obtain not only qualities of the novel, but also
an exactitude comparable to that of scientific discourse. From the
time of the founding of the Royal Society in the seventeenth
century, prose is often associated with scientifically accurate observation, verse with fanciful, figurative speech. In his *History* of
the Royal Society, Thomas Sprat says that the Society's members,
in advocating reforms in English style and usage, aim at "a close,
naked, natural way of speaking, positive expressions, clear senses,
a native easiness, bringing all things as near the Mathematical
plainness as they can." And it is noteworthy that in his *Life and
Writings of Cowley,* Sprat praises Cowley's Pindaric odes and the
ways that their lines of unpredictably varying lengths suggest
prose: "[T]hat for which I think this inequality of number is
chiefly to be preferr'd is its near affinity with Prose . . . which is
certainly the most useful kind of Writing of all others, for it is the
style of all business and conversation."[25] As we shall see, the
experimental poets of the twentieth century wished to write with
scientific precision, and this was an additional reason that they
were drawn to "prosaic" matter and rhythm.

In the context of their desire to rid poetry of vapidity and inflation, the modernists' effort to move verse toward prose is perfectly natural and admirable. Again, as we noted in the first chapter, the modern movement is, in this respect, not unlike earlier literary revolutions. Earlier poets often expressed impatience with dated idiom and a desire for a more natural poetic speech. Yet, historically speaking, there is something unusual in the modern effort. The question for Lyly and Sidney had been whether it was possible to write prose fiction whose vitality would rival that of poetry. The question for Gorgias and Isocrates had been whether it was possible to write prose works from which people would derive a pleasure comparable to that pleasure they derived from metrical compositions. For the leaders of the modern revolution, the question is whether it is possible to write verse which is as vigorous and engaging as good imaginative prose.

3. Poetry Seeking Freedom on the Model of Prose

Modern poetry, then, found itself in an unprecedented position. Modern poets were forced, as earlier reformers were not, to come to grips with an impressive body of prose fiction. They were forced to compare their art, which was metrical and which appeared to be in a state of decline, with an ascendant form of fiction produced without meter. As we saw in the last chapter, conventional metric had become identified with the shortcomings of Victorian verse. In view of these circumstances, perhaps we should not be surprised that the Ford-Pound maxim that "verse must be at least as well written as prose if it is to be poetry" was converted into the idea that verse might profitably be written, as was the novel, without meter.

One sees this conversion in the "formula" that Ford drafted in the nineties, when he began experimenting with *vers libre*. In the

first chapter, this formula was cited, and it may be remembered
that its individual articles were:

> that a poem must be compounded of observation of the everyday life
> that surrounded us; that it must be written in exactly the same
> vocabulary as that which one used for one's prose; that, if it were to be
> in verse, it must attack some subject that needed a slightly more
> marmoreal treatment than is expedient for the paragraph of a novel;
> that, if it were to be rhymed, the rhyme must never lead to the
> introduction of unnecessary thought; and, lastly, that no exigency of
> metre must interfere with the personal cadence of the writer's mind
> or the pressure of the recorded emotion.
>
> (TTR, 206–07)

Beginning with the notion that poetry should address real life and
should be written in the same vocabulary as that which one would
use if one were writing prose, Ford ends with the idea that meter
must not be allowed to interfere with poetry.

If verse is not metrical, a question arises as to how it can be
defined in compositional terms. Does free verse represent a species of what has been traditionally regarded as prose? This question cannot be definitively answered. Nevertheless, one can say
the following. On the one hand, free verse is certainly verse,
insofar as it has been accepted as verse by custom in this century.
On the other hand, free verse is prose, insofar as the principles
with which the leaders of the modern movement explain free
verse are principles customarily elaborated to explain prose. We
can best appreciate this latter aspect of free verse by scrutinizing
several of these principles.

The most common and comprehensive principle the modernists advance is that free verse is, though not metrical, rhythmical.
It is significant that the earliest popular work of what we now call
free verse, Tupper's *Proverbial Philosophy* (First Series, 1838), was
designated by its author as "Rhythmics."[26] Similarly, a poet
whom Ford cites (*TTR,* 198) as a distinguished precursor of his
own brand of *vers libre,* William Ernest Henley, describes the

touching free verse-like poems he composed in the 1870s during a long period of illness as "those unrhyming rhythms in which I had tried to quintessentialize, as (I believe) one scarce can do in rhyme, my impressions of the Old Edinburgh Infirmary."[27] Ford himself reflects this aspect of free verse theory when, in the "Vers Libre" chapter of *Thus to Revisit,* he constructs a linear diagram, one extreme of which is represented by the factual prose of civil service documents and the other extreme of which is represented by highly rhetorical and musical verse, such as the *Marseillaise*— the intermediate area being occupied by forms of prose and verse that are increasingly "creative" as they verge towards the mid-point and each other. Ford writes of the diagram:

> And so the case for *Vers Libre* is made.
>
> It is made for even the least intelligent reader. For who in his senses will deny that, between the entrenched lines of Prosaists and Versificators lies a No Man's Land that is the territory of Neither-Prose-Nor-Verse? And few who have given the matter any attention will deny that this is the oldest, the most primitive, the least sophisticate form of all literature. It is the form of incised writing, of marmoreal inscription, of the prophets—rhythm!
>
> (*TTR,* 194–95)

In essence, Ford is defining rhythm in terms of the opposition Isocrates uses when he says, in a surviving fragment of what is evidently a lost *Art of Rhetoric:* "[P]rose must not be merely prose, or it will be dry; nor metrical, or its art will be undisguised; but it should be compounded with every sort of rhythm."[28] Isocrates is defining, in other words, the same No Man's Land that Ford is defining, and for Isocrates, as for Ford, this territory is "rhythm." Yet for Isocrates, the territory is occupied by artistic prose. For Ford, it is occupied by *vers libre.*

If free verse generally embodies rhythm rather than meter, free verse embodies particular principles that earlier periods have associated with prose. One of these is the principle of suggesting meter, while at the same time avoiding it. With regard to free verse, this principle is most clearly expressed by Eliot:

> [T]he most interesting verse which has yet been written in our language has been done either by taking a very simple form, like the iambic pentameter, and constantly withdrawing from it, or taking no form at all, and constantly approximating to a very simple one. It is this contrast between fixity and flux, this unperceived evasion of monotony, which is the very life of verse.
>
> (*TCC,* 185)

To illustrate his remarks, Eliot quotes Hulme's "The Embankment" and a passage from Pound's "Near Perigord," and comments: "It is obvious that the charm of these lines could not be, without the constant suggestion and the skilful evasion of iambic pentameter" (*TCC,* 186).

These observations resemble those that Demetrius makes when he says (183) of Plato's prose: "Plato in many passages owes his elegance directly to the rhythm. . . . His members seem to glide along and to be neither altogether metrical nor unmetrical." Eliot's observations also resemble those Cicero makes when he urges (*Orator,* 198) that "in spoken prose, a passage is regarded as rhythmical not when it is composed entirely of metrical forms, but when it comes very close to being so." Furthermore, Eliot's argument that, in writing free verse, the poet should move between affirmations and denials of metrical expectation recalls Quintilian's suggestion (9.4.144) that in prose, "It will therefore be desirable from time to time that in certain passages the rhythm should be deliberately dissolved." With respect to this last point, one might remind oneself that Latin in its stress is different from English; thus, it would be wrong to suggest that the aural effect of rhythmical dissolution in an oration would be exactly the same as the effect in an English free verse poem. The principle, however, is very similar.

Another principle advanced by leaders of the modern movement is that in free verse, the poet is concerned with the overall movement of the poem rather than the metrical structure of the individual lines. In free verse, this argument runs, conventional versification is sacrificed in the interests of broader rhythmical arrangement. Pound succinctly expresses this principle when he states, "Prosody is the articulation of the total sound of a poem," and when he subsequently remarks, "There is undoubtedly a sense of music that takes count of the 'shape' of the rhythm in a melody rather than of bar divisions" (*LE,* 421). Eliot expresses this principle when he contends that "the music of verse is not a line by line matter, but a question of the whole poem. Only with this in mind can we approach the vexed question of formal pattern and free verse" (*OPP,* 36). The principle can also be traced in William Carlos Williams' argument that some of Milton's work resembles modern free verse because Milton, like the modern experimentalists, exhibits a "tendency to make the verse paragraph rather than the line his basic unit."[29]

Again, the principle thus expounded is one earlier expounded with respect to prose. It is in fact that principle with which Quintilian distinguishes (9.4.50; 115–16) prose from verse: "[R]hythm has unlimited space over which it may range, whereas the spaces of meter are confined. . . . Further it is not so important for us to consider [in prose] the actual feet as the general rhythmical effect of the period. . . . Therefore rhythmical structure will hold the same place in prose that is held by versification in poetry." In other words, just as some of the modern experimentalists suggest substituting, in prosodic theory, *rhythmos* (rhythm in a broad sense) for *metron* (metrical arrangement in particular), so they suggest substituting, in actual practice, *compositio* (the putting together of words in some generally orderly fashion) for *versificatio* (the specific making of verses).

Another concept sometimes advanced by free verse poets is that it is possible to establish, in free verse, an indeterminate unit of versification. This concept is anticipated by Gerard Manley

Hopkins in his Preface to his *Poems (1876–89)*, in which he discusses "Sprung Rhythm," saying that it involves "feet from one to four syllables, regularly, and for particular effects any number of slack or weak syllables." It is interesting that Hopkins cites the "First Paeon" as being particularly appropriate to Sprung Rhythm and that, in discussing the nature of Sprung Rhythm, he urges first of all that it is prosaically free of affectation: "Sprung Rhythm is the most natural of things. For (1) it is the rhythm of common speech and of written prose, when rhythm is perceived in them." [30] In practice, Hopkins' verse, with its heavily accentual quality, its frequently insistent alliteration, and its rhyme, seems in some ways remote from the work of the twentieth-century free versers; Hopkins himself compares his procedures to those of the older purely accentual tradition of *Piers Plowman*. Yet, insofar as his theory of Sprung Rhythm appeals to prose rhythm and proposes an expandable metrical foot, a foot that can accommodate "for particular effects any number of slack or weak syllables," he prefigures certain modern experimentalists.

Robert Bridges, who was Hopkins' friend and who edited and published in 1918 Hopkins' poems and preface, developed along different lines, ideas like those Hopkins pursued. Yet the best-known exponent of an indeterminate metrical unit is Williams, who, late in his career, developed a theory of what he termed "the variable foot." Though Poe invented this term in his "Rationale of Verse" (*ER,* 50), Poe's "variable foot" involves "caesuras" as much as it does feet (Poe's nomenclature is somewhat murky); Williams appears merely to have adopted the term for his own purposes, without being influenced conceptually by Poe's use of it. Indeed, in Williams' discussion of the variable foot in the *Princeton Encyclopedia,* he does not mention Poe, nor does he include Poe's essay in the bibliography attached to the discussion. [31]

Williams' variable foot is a sort of prosodic accordion. One can squeeze it down to a syllable or two, or draw it out to eight or nine or more syllables. Williams sees in Hopkins a suggestion of this new type of poetic foot. "Hopkins, in a constipated way with his 'sprung' measures, half realized it but not freely enough," says Williams in a 1953 letter to Richard Eberhart (*SL,* 321). And in a 1954 letter to Eberhart, Williams discusses his theory, citing the following lines:

(1) The smell of the heat is boxwood
   (2) when rousing us
      (3) a movement of the air
(4) stirs our thoughts
   (5) that had no life in them
      (6) to a life, a life in which . . .

and then commenting: "Count a single beat to each numeral. You may not agree with my ear, but that is the way I count the line" (*SL,* 326, 327). We have here, that is, six successive feet, which ostensibly possess metrical equivalence to each other (their equivalence consisting of their each having one beat), yet which are also variable (their variability consisting of their accommodating different numbers of unstressed syllables).

An interesting feature of Williams' variable feet, and of indeterminate units of versification generally, is that they recall ancient paeonic feet and *clausulae.* In both modern and ancient cases, we have units that are longer than normal poetic feet, and, in both cases, we find writers exploring such units for the same reason: the units have no association with conventional meters. But the comparison does not extend beyond a certain point. Even the champions of the paeon seem to have believed that paeonic rhythm was applicable only to the beginnings and ends of clauses and periods—and *clausulae* simply marked grammatical pauses—whereas a poet writing in indeterminate feet uses them throughout his poem. Furthermore, even the *clausulae* were relatively well defined and appear to have been recognizable to the ear, whereas the modern variable measures are just what they are said to be—variable—and they discourage perception of any but the roughest proportional relationships. One can assert that a foot of two syllables is prosodically the same as a foot of seven or eight syllables. But the most sensitive listener or reader may well be at a loss to determine a similarity, much less an identity, between such feet.

Several other interesting resemblances between ancient critics of prose and modern free verse theorists should be mentioned. Both often contend that the writer must avoid meter to avoid seeming artificial. Quintilian says (9.4.147) of prose rhythm, "Above all it is necéssary to conceal the care expended upon it so that our rhythms may seem to possess a spontaneous flow, not to have been the result of elaborate search or compulsion." It is on the same grounds that modern critics warn poets to go in fear of metrical regularity. For instance, Ford says that "the worst of verse forms is that they lead almost inevitably to imitation and almost inevitably to insincerity" (*CW*, 161). More generally, the fear of many modern poets that they will be convicted of affectation if they write metrically is much like the fear among ancient orators that they will lose persuasiveness if, in forsenic debate, they do not appear sufficiently spontaneous.

Another interesting circumstance is that just as some ancient orators argue that their art is more demanding than verse, so some advocates of modern free verse contend that their art is more taxing than metrical composition. In both cases, the argument turns on the same idea: the poet working in meter has a pattern to assist him in organizing his material, while the writer not working in meter must create his structure *ex nihilo*. As Isocrates puts it (*Evagoras*, 10),[32] prose is more difficult than verse because "the poets compose all their works with metre and rhythm, while the orators do not share in any of these advantages; and these lend such charm that even though the poets may be deficient in style and thoughts, yet by the very spell of their rhythm and harmony they bewitch their listeners." Cicero takes the same position when he urges (*Orator*, 198) that "prose is harder to write than verse, because in the latter there is a definite and fixed law which must be followed. In a speech, however, there is no rule except that the style must not be straggling or cramped or loose or chaotic."

Similarly, as we will see in the next chapter, Eliot contrasts the straightforwardness of meaning and metric in a poet like Kipling with a poetry based on "a musical pattern of emotional overtones" (*OPP*, 244); Eliot suggests that poetry which is metrically direct is merely "verse," while poetry which is musically elusive in structure is more genuinely "poetry." A related idea informs his view of rhyme: "The rejection of rhyme is not a leap at facility; on the contrary, it imposes a much severer strain upon the language" (*TCC*, 188). In brief, it is as if the age-old debate about the relative difficulty of the two literary arts—poetry with the constraints of meter and at the same time the support and sensuous appeal of meter, prose with the freedom from order and at the same time the need to approximate order—is transposed in the modern period into a debate about the relative difficulty of metrical as opposed to free verse.

There is another interesting feature of the situation we have been examining. If in antiquity and the earlier Middle Ages there existed the idea of a single *ars dictaminis*—an art of discourse which embraced both poetry and prose—that art involved, to some extent, the study of metrical and rhythmical arrangement. At times in this century, there seems a single art discourse, an art based, however, on the absence of such arrangement. For instance, Williams remarks, referring to his use of prose passages in his verse and to Wallace Stevens' statement (in his preface to Williams' *Collected Poems 1921–1931*) that Williams had a "passion for the antipoetic":

> It is *not* an antipoetic device, the repeating of which piece of miscalculation makes me want to puke. It *is* that prose and verse are both *writing*, both a matter of the words and an interrelation between words for the purpose of exposition, or other better defined purpose

of *the art*. Please do not stress other "meanings." I want to say that prose and verse are to me the same thing.

(SL, 263)

And discussing the presence of prose correspondence in Book One of *Paterson,* Williams says:

> The purpose of the long letter at the end is partly ironic, partly "writing" to make it plain that even poetry is writing and nothing else—so that there's a logical continuity in the art, prose, verse: an identity.
>
> Frankly I'm sick of the constant aping of the Stevens' dictum that I resort to the antipoetic as a heightening device. That's plain crap—and everyone copies it. . . . The truth is that there's an *identity* between prose and verse, not an antithesis. It all rests on the same time base, the same measure.

(SL, 265)

Many earlier writers would have agreed with Williams' contention that prose and verse are related. They would probably have taken up that relationship, however, from the side of poetry and its metrical order. For Williams, the relationship seems to involve first and foremost prose and the freedom of its rhythms.

The modern appropriation, for theories of verse, of ideas traditionally associated with prose seems to have been unconscious. In his late article on free verse for the *Princeton Encyclopedia,* Williams refers to Norden's *Antike Kunstprosa,* which was a seminal study (originally published in 1898) of ancient prose rhythm and which was by that time in its fifth edition.[33] Otherwise, there is no evidence that the experimentalists realized the sources of their ideas. Perhaps this should not surprise us because most of the early scholarship about ancient prose rhythm was in German. Nevertheless, Saintsbury's *History of English Prose Rhythm,* which was published in 1912, makes note of the German work,[34] though Saintsbury himself is more concerned with the development of English prose than with matters related to prose rhythm in general. Moreover, most of the relevant classical texts were available, in their original languages and in translations; one would think that Eliot and Pound, both of whom expressed interest in classical literature, might have known some of the material. As it is, their not knowing the material would not matter, except that there is an important point made throughout earlier discussions of meter and rhythm, a point that is clear from Aristotle forward and that is crucially pertinent to any kind of poetry, formal or free. The point is this: speech can be ordered generally by rhythm, particularly by meter; take away meter, and you have nothing left but rhythm.

Equally important is the point, stressed even by those ancient writers who believed prose to be superior to verse, that rhythmical organization has meaning only with reference to a literary context in which meter is practiced. Meters are specific types of the more general quality of rhythm, and one cannot do much in the way of discussing general rhythmical effects except against the backdrop of the more particular structure of meter. Interestingly enough, Eliot makes this point with reference to free verse when he says that "the ghost of some simple metre should lurk behind the arras in even the 'freest' verse: to advance menacingly as we doze, and withdraw as we rouse" (*TCC,* 187). The problem is that the poet may draw his sword and with the cry of "How now? A rat? Dead for a ducat, dead!" make a pass through the arras, and finish off meter once and for all. This is in fact what has happened with much verse since the triumph of the modern revolution. Many poets cease to "withdraw" meter. They appear simply to ignore the question of poetic structure entirely.

There is a related development that must be mentioned. When the experimentalists abandoned meter in hopes of emulating qualities of prose fiction, they did so, as we have seen, in response to a particular literary situation. Poetry had fallen on hard times; the novel was flourishing. Maybe the experiment of writing poetry without meter had to be tried. What has since happened, however, is this: many poets, following the modernists' proce-dures, yet remote from the context of the modernists' revolt, have taken the view that if one tries to work in meter and has trouble expressing what one wants to express, one should as a matter of course turn to free verse, rather than trying patiently to improve and broaden one's skills in conventional versification.

An example of this attitude is provided by one of the most influential poets of the second half of this century, Robert Lowell. Though he wrote his early verse in meter, he became dissatisfied with it because, as he says in an interview in the *Paris Review* in the sixties, "I couldn't get any experience into tight metrical forms. . . . I felt that the meter plastered difficulties and man-nerisms on what I was trying to say to such an extent that it terribly hampered me." This feeling was related to another feel-ing, namely, that "Prose is in many ways better off than po-etry. . . . [O]n the whole prose is less cut off from life than poetry is." Lowell remarks that he attempted for a time to write in prose but "I found it got awfully tedious working out transitions and putting in things that didn't seem very important but were neces-sary to the prose continuity." Faced with these problems, Lowell moved into free verse and into what he terms "breaking forms."[35]

One appreciates Lowell's feeling. At the same time, one cannot help imagining Homer telling the *Chios Quarterly*, "When I be-gan the *Iliad*, I had this crazy notion that I would write it in hexameters. Can you believe that? Well, I soon learned that there was no way I was going to fit the passions of Achilles and Hector into those rigid six-feet lines. The only thing to do, I realized, was to break down my forms." Dionysius says (20) of Homer's com-position, "This is the practice of Homer, that surpassing genius, although he has but one metre and few rhythms. Within these limits, nevertheless, he is continually producing new effects and artistic refinements, so that actually to see the incidents taking place would give no advantage over our having them thus de-scribed." One could apply similar tribute to Dante or Shakespeare or Emily Dickinson or almost any excellent poet. We admire them in part because they write distinctively and vitally in meter.

There is a related issue. Lowell may well feel, as he says in his interview, "It's quite hard to think of a young poet who has the vitality, say, of Salinger or Saul Bellow."[36] Yet, in making this statement, Lowell might have recalled that Salinger's and Bellow's fictions move and entertain us partly because Salinger and Bellow were willing to undertake the "awfully tedious working out of transitions and putting in things that didn't seem very important but were necessary to the prose continuity." An unfortunate aspect of Lowell's attitude is that it entails dispensing with something of great value—poetic meter—without securing in return the discipline of prose fiction. It leaves poetry awkwardly between verse and prose, offering the poet the challenges of neither art, and the reader the appeals of neither. And this is not the end that Ford, Pound, and Eliot had in mind when they initially insisted that poetry should become more like the novel.

Urging that Wordsworth's emphasis on "real language" required qualification, Coleridge observed in the eighteenth chapter of his *Biographia Literaria* that it is one thing for a poet to employ words drawn from common language. It is another matter to suggest that poets should write in the haphazard manner that people use in conversation. One might make a comparable observation about the modernists' interest in prose fiction. It is one thing to say that poets should, if they wish, try to incorporate features of the novel into verse. It is another matter to say that, to do this, they should write in the loose rhythms of prose.[37]

In most respects, prose is more favorably situated than verse. Prose is the more accommodating medium. It is more fluid and variable; it more readily tolerates different kinds of expression. Nonetheless, throughout most of literary history, readers and listeners have loved and venerated verse more, and verse has served as the primary literary art. Its primacy has derived from meter. The intellectual and aural beauty of fine metrical arrangement has, by itself, outweighed the manifold advantages of prose. In concluding this chapter, one can do no better than to cite Dr. Johnson's observations on this point:

> [V]ersification, or the art of modulating his numbers, is indispensably necessary to a poet. Every other power by which the understanding is enlightened or the imagination enchanted may be exercised in prose. But the poet has this peculiar superiority, that to all the powers which the perfection of every other composition can require he adds the faculty of joining music with reason, and of acting at once upon the senses and the passions. I suppose there are few who do not feel themselves touched by poetical melody, and who will not confess that they are more or less moved by the same thoughts as they are conveyed by different sounds, and more affected by the same words in one order than in another. The perception of harmony is indeed conferred upon men in degrees very unequal, but there are none who do not perceive it or to whom a regular series of proportionate sounds cannot give delight.[38]

CHAPTER 3

The Reverses of Time:
The Origin and History of the
Distinction between Verse and Poetry

Modern critics of literature often distinguish "verse" from "poetry." The nuances of this distinction may vary from critic to critic, but its significance is fairly constant. "Verse" indicates composition that, though metrically proficient, lacks more fundamental properties of poetic art. "Poetry," in contrast, indicates writing that, though possibly deficient in conventional versification, nevertheless possesses essential aesthetic qualities absent from "verse."

To clarify this distinction at the outset and to indicate uses to which it is put by modern and contemporary critics, one may cite several cases of its practical application. Eliot, for instance, opens his essay on Rudyard Kipling by asking "whether Kipling's verse really is poetry," and he subsequently suggests that most of Kipling's verse is not poetry, since it represents, among other things, "craft" rather than "art" (*OPP*, 228, 235). In his *Purity of Diction in English Verse*, Donald Davie identifies "verse" with "diction," meaning by this latter term an artificial restriction of poetic speech; he identifies "poetry," in contrast, with a fuller and freer use of "language." Though Davie urges that "verse" has valid uses, he remarks, "We cannot help feeling that verse is somehow less important and splendid than poetry, just as diction is less splendid than language."[1] And Calvin Bedient, in an essay on Davie, approvingly cites the first part of this sentence and, perhaps recalling Eliot's discussion of Kipling and of "art" and "craft," elaborates: "The fact is that, where poetry is an art but not a craft, verse is a craft but not an art. . . . Committed to the notional though it may be, verse betrays, by the very fact that it *is* verse, an impotent, a half-hearted desire for beauty. Verse clings to the *form* of poetry as a prelate clings to a mistress."[2]

In one respect, the verse-poetry distinction incorporates a feeling that many readers of different eras and tastes have shared. Fine poetry involves something much more than technical expertise. It involves a richness of feeling, a startling justness of perception, or an impressive exposition of incident or idea. In contrasting verse and poetry, modern critics are partly voicing sentiments that earlier critics have expressed in different ways and terms. For example, Socrates argues in *Phaedrus* 245A[3] that if a poet is to produce great works, *technē* alone will not suffice; he must have *mania* as well. So, too, Horace observes in *Satires* 1.4.40–44 that it is not enough for a writer, if he wishes to be considered a poet, just to round off a verse, *concludere versum;* he must display in addition native genius, *ingenium,* divine spirit, *mens divina,* and a tongue of great eloquence, *os magna sonaturum.* And "Longinus" contends in *On the Sublime* 33–36 that greatness (*megethos*), even if slightly flawed, is to be preferred to mere correctness (*aptaistos*).

In other respects, however, the modern distinction between verse and poetry differs significantly from earlier formulations of the idea that fine poetry requires more than technique. To be sure, earlier critics argue that great poetry involves qualities attributable only to inspiration. Yet they argue as well that such qualities are compatible with—and indeed require the support of—conventional craft and metrical technique. Modern critics, in contrast, sometimes use the verse-poetry distinction to depreciate traditional versification and to elevate "free verse" over verse composed in meter. As we shall see, this is especially true of Eliot, who suggests that poems written in conventional meters and stanzas are less admirable than poems which embody more "difficult" structural properties and which thereby "revolutionize" the art of poetry.

Because the verse-poetry distinction has significantly contributed to the distrust of meter characteristic of poetic theory and practice in our time, we might well attempt to determine how the distinction originated and how it assumed its present function. Tracing this distinction seems especially needful now, since many poets and critics today appear to believe not only that the distinction embodies a self-evident truth, but also that writers have always subscribed to the distinction.

The distinction is foreign to ancient criticism. Its sources, however, are to be found in several ancient texts. Moreover, though it did not acquire its current meaning until recently, the distinction was formed and focussed in the sixteenth century. In the wake of the recovery and diffusion of the *Poetics* at that time, Aristotle's remarks about imitation were debated with reference to the question of whether it was legitimate to use prose as a medium for fiction. During this debate, his remarks were combined and "harmonized" with observations of other ancient authorities. In consequence, there arose a clear distinction between verse and poetry, a distinction which did not exist in any of the ancient texts, but which emerged as a result of their conflation.

Overall, the distinction between verse and poetry involves the transformation of the ancient idea that poetry is something *more than* meter into the modern idea that poetry may be something *other than* or even *opposed to* meter. In a related sense, the verse-poetry distinction reflects a difference between earlier literature and the literature of our time. In earlier periods, there is an abundance of metrical composition, not all of which is considered poetry. In our time, there is an abundance of composition that is considered poetry, much of which is not in meter.

1. The Ancient Sources of the Modern Distinction

If the Greeks do not distinguish between "verse" and "poetry," it is partly because the terms are not, strictly speaking, Greek. "Verse" derives from the classical Latin, *versus*. And though "poetry" evidently derives from *poiētria*, in ancient Greek the word is simply the feminine of *poiētēs*, "poet" or "maker," and means (as it later means in Latin) "poetess." Not until the Middle Ages does *poetria* indicate poetic writing in general. Though our modern term "poetry" is suggested by *poiēsis* and *poiētikē*, the words imply not just poetry but productive activity at large.[4]

When the Greeks refer to "verse," they use the term *metron*, sometimes combining it with *poiēma*, *poiēsis*, or *poiētēs*, in formulations like "in the meter of poems," *ton meta metrou poiēmatōn* (Isocrates, *Antidosis*, 45).[5] The Greeks also use the term *melos* in speaking of choric and lyric verse designed for musical accompaniment and arranged by strophic pattern rather than by a single repeating unit like the hexameter. *Metron*, in addition to denoting poetic verses, more broadly imports "measure," a fact with which Aristophanes has fun in *The Clouds* 635ff where Socrates endeavors to explain prosody to the farmer Strepsiades, who can grasp its terms only in relation to measures of commercial exchange.

In one sense, poetry is for the Greeks metrical composition. "All poetry (*poiēsin*) I consider and define as words having metre (*logon echonta metron*)," Gorgias comments (*Helen,* 9).[6] "I will state it without metre (*aneu metrou*) for I am not a poet (*poiētikos*)," says Socrates (*Republic,* 393D),[7] while introducing a prose paraphrase of *Iliad* 1.12–42. "[P]rose must have rhythm (*rhythmon*), but not meter (*metron*), otherwise it will be a poem (*poiēma*)," remarks Aristotle in his discussion of prose rhythm (*Rhetoric,* 3.8.2).[8] It should be added that the ability to compose in meter is, for the Greeks, more than a technical acquirement, for meter is itself intimately connected with poetic inspiration. Indeed, one of the signs of *enthousiasmos* or *mania* is the gift of speaking in measure. Even before Pythagoras' discovery of the arithmetic relationship between the intervals of the musical scale, the musico-poetical arts are associated with number and harmony, and poets, rhapsodes, and musicians are believed to receive from the muses the measures that they embody. What is more, measure indicates an order of spirit inspired in the poet by the muse or muses. When, for instance, Solon in his *Hymn* petitions the muse for "the perfect measure (*metron*) of amiable wisdom,"[9] he is asking for aid not simply in perfecting his poem, but in achieving a fullness and intelligence of spirit to guide him in life.

Yet the Greek view of poetry is dual. If the Greeks regard poetry as metrical composition, they also regard it as *mimesis,* imitation. The early history of this term is not clear, though Gerald F. Else has provided a remarkable analysis of the available evidence.[10] The earliest meaning of the word is apparently suggested by the *mim*-root, which indicates "miming" and "impersonation." In time, however, the word acquired a variety of complex associations. When used in connection with poetry, the word eventually came to indicate imitation of human action (*praxis*).

This concept seems to have developed in large part as a response to the triumph of dramatic literature in the fifth and early fourth century, B.C. It is Plato who gives this concept its essential formulation, though he was distrustful of mimetic qualities in poetry and disturbed by the vogue of dramatic literature in his day. Plato nowhere urges that *all* poetry is mimetic. He stresses, however, that the representation of human action is central to much poetic art. In the third book of the *Republic*, he uses (392D–98B) the concept of imitation as a device to classify the three major types of poetry: pure imitation (i.e., drama, in which the characters and chorus in the play entirely carry the discourse); mixed imitation-and-narration (i.e., epic, in which the characters sometimes engage in dialogue with each other, while at other times the author himself speaks of events that befall and thoughts that occur to his characters); and pure narration (i.e., a wide range of dithyrambic and lyric verse, in which the author directly addresses, so to speak, his or her audience).

As is often pointed out, Plato believed that the more imitative the poetry, the more harmful its intellectual and moral effect on its audience; thus, in the tenth book of the *Republic*, purely imitative and imitative-narrative poets are provisionally banished from the ideal state. Yet, in identifying imitation as the central feature of much poetry and in classifying different types of poetry according to the extent to which they are mimetic, Plato suggests a discrimination between the poet's metrical and mimetic functions.[11]

Developing the terms of Plato's discussion, Aristotle makes this discrimination explicit in his *Poetics*. Aristotle regards imitation more positively than Plato had, and in fact inverts Plato's conclusions so as to elevate tragedy over less imitative poetic genres. And Aristotle says in two key passages that the mimetic element is more characteristic of poetry than is its metrical element. Our modern distinction between verse and poetry ultimately derives from these passages.

The passages are well known. In the first, which appears in the *Poetics'* opening chapter, Aristotle objects to the custom of defining poets with respect to their meters (and of calling anyone who writes in hexameters an "epic" poet, or anyone who writes in elegiac couplets an "elegiac" one) rather than with respect to their mimetic function. Speaking of the term "poet," Aristotle observes:

> [P]eople do link up poetic composition with verse (*metrō*) and speak of "elegiac poets," "epic poets," not treating them as poets by virtue of their imitation (*mimēsin*), but employing the term as a common appellation going along with the use of verse (*metron*). And in fact the name is also applied to anyone who treats a medical or scientific topic in verses (*metron*), yet Homer and Empedocles actually have nothing in common except their verse (*metron*); hence the proper term for the one is "poet" (*poiētēn*), for the other "science-writer" (*physiologon*).[12]
>
> (1447b13–20)

The second passage occurs in the *Poetics'* ninth chapter, where Aristotle distinguishes between history and poetry:

> Thus the difference between the historian and the poet is not in their utterances being in verse or prose (*emmetra legein ē ametra*) (it would be quite possible for Herodotus' work to be translated into verse (*metra*), and it would not be any the less a history with verse than it is without it); the difference lies in the fact that the historian speaks of what has happened, the poet of the kind of thing that *can* happen. Hence also poetry is a more philosophical and serious business than history; for poetry speaks more of universals, history of particulars. "Universal" in this case is what kind of person is likely to do or say certain kinds of things, according to probability or necessity.
>
> (1451a38–b5)

Before proceeding, we should establish, as far as possible, Aristotle's own intentions in these two passages. In the first, he is in part attempting to clarify the subject matter proper to poetry. This issue was confused in his day, primarily because of the existence of a vast body of didactic literature in verse. There was versified cosmology (e.g., Parmenides), moral philosophy (e.g., Theognis), political science (e.g., Solon), martial exhortation (e.g., Tyrtaeus), agricultural science (e.g., Hesiod), and medicine (e.g., Aristotle's own pupil Menon). The popular practice of identifying poets with the verse measure in which they wrote further confused the issue. In this regard, we must remember that although the popular view always tends to identify poetry with meter, the identification is more specific in Greek literature than in English literature, for the reason that Greek poets often concentrate on one poetic genre and one type of verse. When, for instance, Theognis is referred to as *elegeiopoios,* "an elegiac poet," the term is a literal indication of the meter—the elegiac couplet, the hexameter-and-pentameter distich—in which Theognis writes.

Aristotle's aim is revealed in his choice of Empedocles to illustrate poetry that is not truly poetic. Aristotle greatly admires Empedocles. Homer and Plato are the only authors Aristotle cites more frequently, and, in a surviving fragment of the lost dialogue *On Poets* (Diogenes Laertius, *Lives,* 8.2.3), he again compares Empedocles to Homer, but this time in order to praise him: "Empedocles was a man of Homeric genius, and endowed with great power of language, and a great master of metaphor, and a man who had employed all the successful artifices of poetry." Aristotle does not apply to Empedocles, as will sixteenth-century commentators, a disparaging term such as "versifier." He simply calls Empedocles a "science-writer," a *physiologos.* In other words, Aristotle mentions Empedocles not to belittle him but to emphasize the importance of imitation. In essence, Aristotle is saying that even a writer as gifted as Empedocles cannot be considered a complete poet if he does not imitate.

If Aristotle contrasts Empedocles with Homer to clarify the subject matter proper to poetry, he contrasts history with poetry for a similar reason: to explain the unique capabilities of poetry as an imitative art and to explain the functions that it can fulfill which no other intellectual discipline can. History is for Aristotle an especially illuminating foil to poetry because in his time, and in later antiquity, these two arts—both of which examine and chronicle human experience—were closely associated, and it was commonly suggested that the metricality of poetry and the non-metricality of history constituted their chief difference.[13] Strabo illustrates this view when, discussing the origins of historical writing, he remarks (*Geography,* 1.2.6): "[P]oetry, as an art, first came upon the scene and was first to win approval. Then came Cadmus, Pherecydes, Hecataeus, and their followers, with prose writings in which they imitated the poetic art, abandoning the use of metre (*metron*) but in other respects preserving the qualities of poetry."[14] In a related fashion, Quintilian calls (10.1.31) history *quodammodo carmen solutum,* "in a certain way a prose poem," echoing the common term for "prose," *oratio soluta;* and Lucian speaks (*How to Write History* 8) of some types of historical writing as *pezē poiētikē,* "prose poetry."[15]

Yet the key difference between poetry and history is not, Aristotle insists, that the one is metrical and the other is not. It is rather that poetry is not tied to the particularities of literal fact. Indeed, poetry's freedom in this respect is, according to Aristotle, the source of its greatest value as an art. Though he never claims that poetry has access to absolute truth, he believes that poetry can present a vision of life informed by a sense of "probability or necessity." Expanding the concept of *mimēsis* beyond the idea of mere copying (a development that Plato anticipates in remarks about visual art in *Sophist* 234B–36c), Aristotle urges that poetic imitation can comprehensively illuminate human experience. A poet can present a story which has all the vividness of real events, but which is free from the random qualities that often characterize history. He can tell a story in which events are plausibly knit together. The historian, on the other hand, tells a story which is, in Aristotle's words (1459a22–24), "not of a single action but of a single period, including everything that happened during that time to individuals or groups—of which events each has only chance relationships to the others."

This idea underlies Aristotle's repeated insistence that a poet should not construct his drama or epic in the manner of a historian, but rather should focus, as Homer does, on a single action which is complete in itself and which has a logically related beginning, middle, and end. This idea also underlies Aristotle's argument that plot is the most important element in tragedy and his contention (1451b27–29) that "it is evident that the poet should be a maker of his plots (*mython*) more than of his verses (*metron*), insofar as he is a poet by virtue of his imitations (*mimēsin*) and what he imitates is actions (*praxeis*)." For it is by creating a coherent plot, a plot depicting human action in terms of causes and effects, that the poet is most able to reveal an order in, or a typology of, human experience.

Aristotle chooses Herodotus—as opposed, say, to Thucydides—to exemplify history for the reason that his *Histories* are the most poetic of all historical writings, both in the fabulous character of much of the work and in its engrossing narrative. (Aristotle cites Herodotus not only in the ninth chapter of the *Poetics,* in his contrast between poetry and history, but also in the twenty-third chapter in a more specific contrast between epic and history. On this latter occasion, Aristotle refers to *Histories* 7.167 and to Herodotus' statement that the Sicilian victory over the Carthaginians and the Greek victory over the Persians at Salamis were said to have occurred on the same day. These events had no causal relationship, and the recording of them typifies, in Aristotle's opinion, the inevitably jumbled and haphazard elements of historical reporting.) Aristotle understands perfectly why people might think that the only reason Herodotus is not a poet is that he does not write in meter, just as he understands perfectly why Empedocles is commonly thought to be a poet because he does. But the real point, Aristotle argues, is that neither of these writers fulfills the most important function of a poet. Neither makes an imitation which is unified and complete in itself and which is governed by narrative or dramatic causality.[16]

One should stress that Aristotle never suggests that meter is not an integral part of poetry. He does not say, as will sixteenth-century students of the *Poetics,* that if a versified Herodotus would not be poetic, a prosified Sophocles or Homer would be. Aristotle emphasizes the importance of meter at various points in the *Poetics* (e.g., 1449a 2–28; 1449b24–31). Though he does speak in the treatise's first chapter about nonmetrical imitations such as mime and Socratic dialogue, referring (1447a28–29) to them with the term *logois psilois,* "speeches bare [of music]," he is at this juncture discussing imitation in general, including instrumental music, dancing, and the like. Once he embarks on his discussion of poetic imitation specifically, he drops entirely the issue of prose imitations. In addition, Diogenes Laertius records the more focussed remark which Aristotle evidently made about Plato's Socratic dialogues, "Aristotle says that the form of his [Plato's] writings was in between poetry and prose,"[17] and this remark would seem to indicate that Aristotle did not intend to assert that dialogues were poetry, at least not in the full sense of the word. Lastly, as has been noted, in the third book of his *Rhetoric,* Aristotle identifies general rhythmical arrangement with prose and the specific rhythmical arrangement of meter with poetry.

A final point to make about the *Poetics* is that it is incomplete. What survives is mostly devoted to Tragedy; a second book on Comedy was evidently lost early in the text's history.[18] Moreover, the *Poetics* is incomplete in the sense that Aristotle appears to ignore a good deal of poetic art. Early in his treatise (1448a19–24), he adopts Plato's tripartite scheme of poetic types and acknowledges the lyric forms by implication. However, Aristotle's subsequent insistence on the preeminence of dramatic imitation—and his insistence that poetic imitation is imitation of human action—leaves the status of lyric verse ambiguous. Admittedly, all Greek genres endeavored to be dramatic to some degree. Even so, one has difficulty applying Aristotle's analysis as broadly as he seems to have intended it to be applied. In other works, he refers to lyric poets and indicates an appreciation of lyric. The second book of the *Poetics* or the dialogue *On Poets* may have explained this discrepancy. As things stand, Aristotle's treatise is a wonderful defense of fiction, especially drama. But there is much poetry for which it cannot account.

This situation is significant. When the *Poetics,* after having been lost to the West for nearly eighteen hundred years, was recovered in the Renaissance, Aristotle's ideas on poetry, however stimulating, were not fully suited to a literary environment in which short forms like the sonnet and expository or allegorical poems like those of Dante, Fracastoro, and Spenser figure prominently. It is one of the curiosities of literary history—and maybe not one of the happier curiosities—that the *Poetics* should have had so little circulation in the literary culture it addressed and so much authority in a literary culture whose poetic forms and preferences ill match the terms of Aristotle's discussion.

Though Aristotle does not, in a verbal sense, suggest distinction between verse and poetry, Quintilian makes a remark that foreshadows the distinction. This remark appears in the *Institutes,* in the course of Quintilian's survey (10.1.46–131) of ancient literature. Quintilian discusses Greek authors first, taking up in turn: (1) hexameter poets, (2) elegiac, iambic, and lyric poets, (3) dramatic poets, (4) historians, (5) orators, and (6) philosophers. He then addresses Latin writers in the same order. With regard to Roman hexameter poets, he awards top honors to Virgil and then devotes a paragraph to a consideration of runners-up:

> I must keep to the same order in dealing with Roman writers also. With us Virgil—like Homer with the Greeks—may provide the most auspicious opening; indeed, of all poets of that genre in either language he undoubtedly comes nearest to Homer. . . . And perhaps we make up by Virgil's good general level for the inferiority our champion shows to Homer's heights.
>
> All the rest will be found to follow far behind. Macer and Lucretius are worth reading—but not for any ability to provide the style that is the stuff of eloquence; each shows elegance on his own subject, but the one is unambitious, the other difficult. Varro Atacinus made

his name as a translator of another's work; he is not to be despised, but he is hardly rich enough to increase an orator's powers. Ennius we must venerate as we do groves whose age makes them holy, full of great oaks that nowadays have less beauty than sanctity. Others are closer to us, and more useful for the matter in question. Ovid is as frivolous in his hexameters as elsewhere: he is too much in love with his own talents, but deserves praise in parts. Cornelius Severus, even though a better versifier than poet (*versificator quam poeta melior*), could lay good claim to the second place if (as has been said) he had completed his *Sicilian War* to the standard of his first book. [There follow comments about poets whose works are largely lost, and then Quintilian mentions Lucan and his unfinished historical epic, the so-called *Pharsalia,* about the war between Caesar and Pompey.] . . . Lucan is passionate, spirited, full of brilliant thoughts: indeed, to be frank, a better model for orators than poets (*magis oratoribus quam poetis imitandus*).

(10.1.85–90)[19]

The key matter is Quintilian's remark about Severus, though, as we will see, scarcely less crucial is the comment about Lucan; and the whole passage is significant. What does Quintilian mean when he speaks of Severus as being a better versifier than a poet? And what does he mean by the term *versificator?*

There are no clear answers to these questions. *Versificator* is a post-Augustan coinage.[20] Quintilian seems to be the earliest notable writer to use it, and he uses it just this once. Because Severus' poem on the Civil War survives in fragments only, it is hard to find in his writing a clue to Quintilian's meaning. It initially appears censorious. Yet Severus is in good company, and having applied the term to him, Quintilian proceeds to rate his talents highly. Furthermore, other distinguished judges also praise Severus. Ovid, who dedicates to Severus one of the *Black Sea Epistles* (4.2), expresses considerable esteem for his work. Seneca the Elder cites (*Suasoriae,* 6.26–27) Severus' lines on Cicero's death as models of eloquent lamentation.

Quintilian may have in mind the Greek term *poiētēs,* and he may be connecting by implication the noun *poeta,* meaning "maker," with the verb *facere,* "to make." In other words, Quintilian may be indicating that Severus excelled in his specific ability "to make verses" (*versus/facio* > *versificare:* hence "maker of verses," *versificator*), but that he was less excellent as a "maker" in the sense in which Quintilian is measuring him against Virgil— this is, as a *poeta epicus* or *poeta herous,* "a maker of an epic or heroic poem." In any case, it would seem misguided to see strong disparagement in Quintilian's remark.

Furthermore, for subsequent ancient writers (e.g., Justin, 6.9.2–5; Terentianus Maurus, *Of Letters, Syllables, Feet, and Meters,* 1011–12),[21] *versificator* means simply "writer of verses." It is only in the later Middle Ages and the Renaissance that the contrast that Quintilian draws between the versifier and poet acquires great pejorative force; and it is only when, in the sixteenth century, Quintilian's remarks are conflated with Aristotle's comments about Empedocles and history that *versificator* acquires a clear and pointed definition. The definition which emerged may be rendered as follows: "a writer who composes verses, but who fails to imitate and thus is not a real poet." It should be added that *versificator* also retains, into modern times, the vaguer and more neutral meaning of "writer of verses," as we will see when, in the third section of this chapter, we look at Dryden's appropriations from Quintilian's discussion of epic.

Setting aside the question of Quintilian's intention in using the word *versificator,* we should note that Quintilian is not, in using the term, indicating that he feels verse is less than essential to poetry. Indeed, the ninth book of the *Institutes,* like the third book of Aristotle's *Rhetoric,* is based on the idea that poetry is metrical and prose rhythmical. And though Quintilian's remark indicates that he, like Aristotle, expects more of poetry than meter alone, Quintilian did not know the *Poetics* and in no way reflects the Aristotelian belief that poetry ought to be mimetic. In fact, in his survey Quintilian does exactly the thing to which Aristotle objects in the first chapter of the *Poetics.* Quintilian classifies poets according to the verse measure in which they write, a classification that results in a hexametric philosophical writer like Lucretius and hexametric historical writers like Severus and Lucan being grouped with Virgil, who is—at least in the *Aeneid* and certain of the *Eclogues*—a genuine "poet-imitator" in the Aristotelian sense.

Furthermore, when Quintilian refers, in *Institutes* 1.4.4, specifically to Empedocles' poetry, he makes clear that he assumes that philosophical material is legitimately poetic and that Empedocles is a legitimate poet. Discussing the importance of giving students a broad literary education, Quintilian urges: "Nor can such training be regarded as complete if it stop short of music, for the teacher of literature has to speak of metre and rhythm. . . . Ignorance of philosophy is an equal drawback, since there are numerous passages in almost every poem based on the most intricate questions of natural philosophy, while among the Greeks we have Empedocles and among our poets Varro and Lucretius, all of whom have expounded their philosophy in verse (*praecepta sapientiae versibus tradiderunt*)."

Yet sixteenth-century readers will look to Quintilian for illumination about Aristotle's remarks in the first and ninth chapter of the *Poetics,* and they will look to Quintilian even when they recognize—as does, for instance, Lodovico Castelvetro in his translation of the *Poetics*—that Aristotle and Quintilian take different views of Empedocles. And there is a reason readers will do this. Though Quintilian assumes positions diametrically opposed to Aristotle's, Quintilian's argument looks, from a certain angle, analogous to Aristotle's. Quintilian appears to be doing, in an orderly fashion, for Latin hexameter poets what Aristotle does, in a more elliptical fashion, for Greek hexameter poets. Furthermore, the steps of the two arguments are strikingly alike.

In effect, Aristotle says: In hexameter verse, our genuine great poet is Homer. In effect, Quintilian says: In hexameter verse, our genuine great poet is Virgil. Aristotle suggests: In hexameter verse, the lesser poets are Empedocles and hexametrified Herodotus (hexameter would have been the measure for Herodotus had he worked in verse: in *Poetics* 1459b32–60a5, shortly after comparing epic and history, Aristotle identifies long narrative poetry with the hexameter). Quintilian says: In hexameter verse, the lesser poets are (to cite the two poets who will be crucial for sixteenth century readers) Lucretius and Lucan. Empedocles and Herodotus represent philosophical-scientific work and historical work respectively. Likewise, Lucretius and Lucan (and Severus) represent philosophical-scientific work and historical work respectively.

A great deal happens to Quintilian's text before it gets conflated with the *Poetics* in the sixteenth century, and what happens partly prepares the way for the conflation. Though the *Institutes* is never wholly lost in the West, as is the *Poetics,* and though later writers like Cassiodorus and Julius Victor draw on Quintilian, the *Institutes* appears to have received little attention in later antiquity and the early Middle Ages. For at least several centuries, the text seems to have been available only in mutilated versions. In the eleventh century, *Institutes* 10.1.46–131 is extracted and circulated as a kind of prototype for the *accessus ad auctores,* a pedagogic tool which is popular in the later Middle Ages and which consists of a list and description for school curricula of authors to be read. It is not, however, until after the time of Poggio Bracciolini's discovery, at St. Gaul in 1416, of a complete copy of the *Institutes* that the full work returns to circulation.[22]

By the time Quintilian returns to circulation, many of the texts of the hexametric poets he discusses in 10.1.87–90 are long since lost. And writers, quarrying or copying the *Institutes,* apply Quintilian's remark about Severus to a variety of hexametric poets whose poems are thought to be unworthy of study or whose poems have simply, like Severus', vanished. Quintilian's remark about Severus thus becomes generalized. As an example of this generalization, one may cite Aeneas Silvius' *On Liberal Education* of 1450. Following Quintilian's pattern of discussing in sequence hexametric, lyric (and satiric and elegiac), and dramatic poetry, and following Quintilian's remarks about Latin hexameter poets, Aeneas applies the term *versificator* to a whole class of poets who fall below the runners-up-to-Virgil category rather than to a single poet within that category as Quintilian had done:

> Among the epic poets let him [the teacher of poetry] prefer before all Vergil, whose eloquence, whose reputation, is so great that it can be augmented by no praise, diminished by no censure. . . . Lucan, a distinguished author of history, and Statius, who is quite polished, should not be neglected. Ovid is everywhere concise, everywhere delightful, but in many places too wanton; yet his most famous work, to which he gave the name *Metamorphoses,* ought in no wise to be cast aside, as the knowledge of this on account of the skill displayed in the stories is of no small profit. Others who write in heroic verse are far inferior to these and ought to be called versifiers rather than poets (*versificatorumque magis quam poetarum*).[23]

Not only has Quintilian's judgment about Severus been broadened to include a whole class of poets, but the *quam . . . melior,* "better than," that Quintilian applied to Severus has become the *magis quam,* "rather than," that he applied to Lucan. (Further evidence of this verbal confusion will be examined shortly.) The change represented is thus a shift not merely from a particular to a general statement, but also from a comparative ("a better versifier than poet") to an antithetical ("versifiers rather than poets") statement.

A similarly general and antithetical character informs a contention made by Thomas Elyot in his educational treatise of 1531, *The Governour.* In a section in which he also cites Quintilian's statement, from the first chapter of *Institutes* 10, that judicious students may derive profit from virtually all authors who have stood the test of time, Elyot argues: "Semblably they that make verses, expressynge therby none other lernynge but the craft of versifyeng, be nat of auncient writers named poetes, but onely called versifyers."[24] Like Aeneas Silvius, Elyot shows that, at a time shortly before the *Poetics* enters wide circulation, Quintilian's remark about Severus had been broadened in such a way as to make it serviceable for readers who would endeavor to interpret the first and ninth chapters of the *Poetics*.

Two other ancient authors make observations important to the modern verse-poetry distinction. The first is Plutarch, who evidently received indirect knowledge of the *Poetics*. In his own "How to Study Poetry," Plutarch offers a garbled version of an analogy that Aristotle makes with respect to the relative importance of plot and character in tragedy (1450a39–b3): "So plot is the basic principle, the heart and soul, as it were, of tragedy, and the characters come second. It is much the same case as with painting: the most beautiful pigments smeared on at random will not give as much pleasure as a black-and-white outline picture." Plutarch's remarks run as follows:

> For not metre (*metron*) nor figure of speech (*tropos*) nor loftiness of diction (*lexeōs onkos*) nor aptness of metaphor (*eukairia metaphoras*) nor unity of composition (*synthesis*) has so much allurement and charm, as a clever interweaving of fabulous narrative (*mythologias*). But, just as in pictures, colour is more stimulating than line-drawing because it is life-like, and creates an illusion, so in poetry falsehood combined with plausiblity is more striking and gives more satisfaction, than the work which is elaborate in metre (*metron*) and diction (*lexin*), but devoid of myth and fiction (*amythou kai aplastou*).
>
> (*Moralia*, 16b–c)

It has often been noted that Plutarch reverses the terms of Aristotle's painting metaphor and identifies color rather than line with plot. What has not been sufficiently appreciated is that Plutarch uses the metaphor itself, which Aristotle had used to contrast *mythos* and *ethos,* plot and character, to contrast *mythos* and *metron* (and the related qualities of trope and diction and metaphor and verbal arrangement).

Plutarch reinforces his substitution of *metron* for *ethos* by proceeding to expound an idea that appears based, if at several removes, on the first chapter of the *Poetics*. And just as he earlier substitutes *metron* for *ethos,* so he substitutes here *mythos* for *mimēsis,* thus achieving a synthesis and simplification of two different, if related, concepts in Aristotle. That is, the two groupings in Aristotle—*mythos-ethos* and *mimēsis-metron*—are transformed by Plutarch into a single *mythos-metron* contrast. Though this contrast is suggested in the *Poetics'* ninth chapter, where Aristotle discusses meter in connection with plot, he also pointedly brings imitation back into the discussion. In any case, in Plutarch's observations, Empedocles figures just as prominently as he does in the first chapter of the *Poetics;* Plutarch also mentions two other pre-Aristotelian philosophical poets, Parmenides and Theognis, as well as the post-Aristotelian toxicological poet Nicander:

> It is true that we know of sacrifices without dancing or flute, but we do not know of any poetic composition without fable or without falsehood (*amython oud' apseudē*). The verses of Empedocles and of Parmenides, the *Antidotes against Poisons* of Nicander, and the maxims of Theognis, are merely compositions which have borrowed from poetic art (*poiētikēs*) its metre (*metron*) and lofty style (*onkon*) as a vehicle in order to avoid plodding along in prose (*pezon*).
>
> *(Moralia,* 16c)

Though Plutarch's alterations of originally Aristotelian ideas are small, they will lead some Renaissance interpreters of the *Poetics* to direct Aristotle's emphasis on plot against meter, whereas in the treatise itself this emphasis is directed more against character.

The final ancient writer who contributes to the modern distinction between verse and poetry is Servius, the grammarian of the late fourth and early fifth century, who wrote an extensive commentary on Virgil, and who is also remembered as one of the characters in Macrobius' *Saturnalia*. If later writers see Aristotle through Plutarch and Quintilian, they see Quintilian through

Servius, or rather through a single remark of Servius. This remark occurs when Servius is discussing *Aeneid* 1.382. At this point in Virgil's poem, Aeneas, having been shipwrecked near Carthage, starts to explore the country. His mother Venus appears to him in disguise. Who are you and how do you come here? she asks with feigned surprise. In response, Aeneas tells her his name and says that he fled westward from Troy after its fall, adding *matre dea monstrante viam,* "my divine mother showed the way."

Virgil, Servius suggests, could have told the whole legendary story, which had been chronicled by Varro, of how Aeneas literally followed Venus, the morning star, until he came to Italy, where the star disappeared, signifying to Aeneas that he had reached the land fated for him. Virgil, however, merely touches on this story, because, according to Servius, it is historical in nature and would not be appropriate for elaboration "according to the rules of poetic art." Then Servius delivers a sentence that was to achieve wide diffusion: *Lucanus namque ideo in numero poetarum esse non meruit, quia videtur historiam composuisse, non poema.* "Lucan for this reason does not deserve to be counted among the poets, because he appears to have composed a history, not a poem."[25]

It is unlikely that, in making this remark about Lucan, Servius had in mind Quintilian's statement that Lucan was a better model for orators than poets. Though Servius refers to the *Major Declamations* that late antiquity attributed to Quintilian, he does not refer to the *Institutes.* It is more likely that Servius was drawing on what was by his time a long tradition of controversy surrounding Lucan's *Pharsalia,* which was commonly taken to task for being a history rather than a proper epic. In view of its lurid and fantastical elements, readers today may find far-fetched the opinion that the poem is historical. Nonetheless, for readers of Lucan's time, epic meant a tale involving, among other things, the mythological gods; and because Lucan consciously violated tradition on this point, excluding the customary deities from active participation in his poem, the *Pharsalia* was often characterized as history.[26]

However Servius came by his judgment of Lucan, the judgment itself is echoed by subsequent writers, among them Isidore (*Etymologiae*, 8.7.10), the compiler of the *Commenta Bernensia* (*On Pharsalia* i.1), and Rabanus (*De Universo*, 15.2: Migne, *Patrologiae Cursus Completus*, 111.419). John of Salisbury refers (*Policraticus*, 2.19) to Lucan as *poeta doctissimus*, "a most learned poet," but wonders "if one can speak of someone as a poet who by his true narration of events more closely approaches the historians" (*si tamen poeta dicendus est, qui uera narratione rerum ad historicos magis accedit*).[27] Similarly, alluding to Horace's suggestion that poets should begin their works *in medias res*, Boccaccio remarks (*Genealogy of the Gods*, 14.13): "For poets are not like historians, who begin their account at some convenient beginning and describe events in the unbroken order of their occurrence to the end. Such, we observe, was Lucan's method, wherefore many think of him rather as a metrical historian than a poet (*potius metricum hystoriographum quam poetam*)."[28]

Such judgments are noteworthy because sixteenth-century readers fuse Servius' and Quintilian's assessments of Lucan with Quintilian's remark that Severus is a better versifier than a poet. Readers associate Severus and Lucan because, though the former's work was lost, it was known that he had, like Lucan, written a "historical" epic about the Roman civil wars. Servius' bluntly dismissive *in numero poetarum esse non meruit* ([He] does not deserve to be counted among the poets) gets mixed and confused with Quintilian's restrained and cautionary *magis oratoribus quam poetis imitandus* ([He is] a better model for orators than poets), with the result that Quintilian is made to say that Lucan is not a poet and that historical poets are only versifiers. A version of this confusion is evident in the passage from Aeneas Silvius cited earlier. Aeneas conflates the two comparative phrases that Quintilian uses—the *versificator quam poeta melior* that applies to Severus and the *magis oratoribus quam poetis imitandus* that applies to Lucan—into a single comparative *versificatorumque magis quam poetarum* that applies to a whole class of poets.

This confusion reinforces the conflation of Quintilian with Aristotle, because the confusion encourages readers to think that Quintilian, who seems to have had no bias against historical poetry, endorses Aristotle's contrast between poetry and history.

Furthermore, when the *Institutes* returns to general circulation, certain early printed texts give 10.1.90 as *magis oratoribus quam poetis numerandus* (or *annumerandus*). This variant is accommodated by the generality of the ablative case, which allows Quintilian's statement that Lucan may be more suitably imitated *by* orators to be transformed, with no grammatical strain, into the statement that he may be more suitably numbered *with* orators. Modern scholars do not even consider this other reading to merit note as a variant, and it does not fit Quintilian's context (he devotes a separate section to orators). How it crept into some editions of the *Institutes* is a matter I have been unable to determine. I would like to believe that the reading reflects an infusion of Severus' *in numero poetarum esse non meruit* into *magis oratoribus quam poetis imitandus*. It is possible, however, that the abbreviated script commonly employed by scribes in the Middle Ages and earlier Renaissance contributed to the confusion, since *numerandus* and *imitandus* are similar to begin with. It is also possible that there is some other explanation altogether.[29]

An additional observation about Servius is in order. So commonplace does the judgment that Lucan is a historian become that Servius himself is rarely explicitly referred to in later discussions of Lucan. One sees this not only in sixteenth-century students of poetry, but also in late medieval and early Renaissance writers like John of Salisbury and Boccaccio, both of whom drew on Servius' *Commentary,* but neither of whom cite him in connection with Lucan. Indeed, when John returns to Lucan in *Policraticus* 8.23 and again offers and qualifies a compliment to Lucan, it is to Quintilian, not Servius, that John refers. Here John calls Lucan *hoc poeta grauissimus,* "this most serious poet," but adds, "if with Quintilian you think it more correct to say orator, I do not object" (*si iuxta Quintilianum rectius dicere malueris oratorem, non repugno*). Similarly, though in *Genealogy* 6.53 Boccaccio specifically cites *ad Aeneid* 1.382, he does not allude to Servius when in *Genealogy* 14.13 he says that some people consider Lucan a metrical historian. It is as if writers at some point ceased to identify Servius with what he had said about Lucan, probably because what he had said was also available from other distinguished authors in almost the same wording.

These, then, are the critical ideas that come together to form the verse-poetry distinction when, in the sixteenth century, the *Poetics* is revived. There is Aristotle. There is Plutarch evidently commenting on Aristotle. There is Quintilian using the term *versificator,* evidently to comment on Aristotle or to do something analogous to what Aristotle had done. There is Servius (and the medieval grammatical tradition) evidently commenting on or with Quintilian.

2. *The Renaissance Conflation of Aristotle, Quintilian, Plutarch, and Servius*

Before examining the Renaissance conflation that produced an explicit distinction between verse and poetry, we should briefly review the steps involved in the recovery of Aristotle's *Poetics.* The late Middle Ages and early Renaissance knew of the *Poetics* through Hermannus Alemannus' Latin translation, in 1256, of a paraphrase in Arabic by Averroës. Though Averroës' paraphrase, which dates from the twelfth century, is interesting in its own right, Averroës was unacquainted with the Homeric epics and classical drama, and the text of the *Poetics* on which he relied was a tenth century Arabic translation (through Syriac) that substantially altered the ideas of the original. Because of these factors, Averroës' hold on Aristotle's text was insecure. In particular, he gave short shrift to Aristotle's discussion of *mimēsis,* contending instead that Aristotle's thesis was that poetic art praises good people and blames bad. Aristotle does remark (1448a1ff.) that poets imitate the actions of either men who are good or important (*spoudaios*) or men who are bad or of no account (*phaulos*); he says as well (1448b25ff.) that the earliest poems were encomia of noble people or lampoons of ignoble people. This, however, is hardly the crux of his argument. And, in general, Averroës' view of Aristotle is only tenuously related to Aristotle himself.

William of Moerbeke's Latin translation of the *Poetics* in 1278, a translation based on the Greek text, received virtually no notice. Only with Valla's (1498) and Pazzi's (1536) Latin translations and with Aldus' *editio princeps* of the Greek text of 1508, does the treatise, written some eighteen centuries earlier, gradually enter circulation. The flood of commentaries on and imitations of the treatise begins in the second third of the sixteenth century; by the end of the century, the *Poetics* is established as arguably the primary document of literary criticism in the West.[30]

When the *Poetics* is recovered, readers "harmonize" Aristotle with other ancient critics. They do so partly out of a desire better to understand Aristotle's thorny text, and partly out of a desire to extract from ancient criticism in general a coherent set of principles to serve contemporary literary practice. The main harmonization, which has long been noted and analyzed, involves the systematic reconciliation of the ideas in Horace's *Art of Poetry* with those in Aristotle's treatise. The harmonization of the first and ninth chapters of the *Poetics* with Quintilian, Plutarch, and Servius is much more particular; perhaps it has been overlooked precisely because of its specialized character. All the same, this harmonization is no less endemic to criticism in the second half of the sixteenth century than the harmonization of Aristotle with Horace, and its effects on subsequent poetic theory and practice have proved no less important.

In presenting evidence of the harmonization, one must do so

with reference to its specific elements as well as with reference to chronology. The crucial thing is to see the different components of the harmonization expressed by different writers in different countries in the second half of the sixteenth century. Hence, for this section of the chapter, we will move back and forth in the period as different points arise, though with each point, chronology will be followed so far as possible. This approach may slightly blur the specific stages in the development of the harmonization. Yet this development itself was so rapid as to have been blurry, and to trace it in a strictly chronological fashion would involve issues (e.g., the diffusion of J. C. Scaliger's and Castelvetro's works) that are subsidiary to the matters at hand.

Let us first consider a text which explicitly fuses Aristotle's contrast between Homer and Empedocles with Plutarch's censure of didactic poets and which, having made this fusion, supports it by implicitly referring to Quintilian and Servius. The text is Bernardino Partenio's *On Poetic Imitation* of 1560. Partenio initially speaks of the first chapter of the *Poetics* and of *Moralia* 16c, saying: "He who does not imitate cannot call himself a Poet, . . . Thus Plutarch does not believe that Nicander merits the name, though the vulgar use the name of Poets for all those who write in verse." Partenio then goes on to quote in Greek Aristotle's remark that "people do link up poetic composition with verse and speak of 'elegiac poets,' 'epic poets,' not treating them as poets by virtue of their imitation, but employing the term as a common appellation going along with the use of verse." Then, commenting on Aristotle's judgment that Empedocles is not a poet as Homer is, Partenio says:

> Nor is Lucretius a poet in the same way that Virgil deserves the name, not having anything more in common with that poet than verse alone (*non hauendo altro di comune con quello, che' l verso solo*). Therefore Homer and Virgil are Poets. Empedocles and Lucretius are Philosophers more than Poets. Thus Lucan is a historian, never a Poet (*Cosi Lucano historico, Poeta non mai*).[31]

Partenio, that is, having quoted Aristotle's remark about the popular practice of identifying poets with their meters, appropriates Aristotle's follow-up remark about Homer and Empedocles having "nothing in common . . . except the verse." Then he applies the remark to a Quintilianic comparison of Virgil and Lucretius, tacking on shortly afterwards the Servian testimony against Lucan.

The ascription to non-imitators of the term "versifier," as well as the conflation of Aristotle with Quintilian and Servius and Plutarch, may be seen in Castelvetro's 1570 edition of and commentary on the *Poetics*. Like many readers in the second half of the sixteenth century, Castelvetro treats Aristotle and Quintilian as if they made the same argument, and also as if they shared the same vocabulary. Quintilian's *versificator* becomes part of Aristotle's text. For example, Castelvetro translates the passage in which Aristotle objects to identifying poets with their meters, and then comments:

> [H]e who only covers with poetic language those subjects of science or art which have been discovered or written about by others and of which it may be said that their history has already been composed, has no part of that by which he can boast of being a poet. Therefore it is not surprising if those versifiers (*versificatori*), Empedocles, Lucretius, Nicander, Serenus, Girolamo Fracastoro in his *Syphilis,* Aratus, Manilius, Giovanni Pontano in his *Urania,* Hesiod, and Virgil in his *Georgics* are not numbered among poets.[32]

And glossing Aristotle's observation that it would be more sensible to call Empedocles a science-writer than a poet, Castelvetro says: "The vulgar believe that versifiers (*versificatori*), those who take art and science as subjects, not only are poets (*poeti*), but also that they take the name of poets according to the manner of their verse; but Aristotle holds the opinion that they cannot be poets who do not take imitation (*rassomiglianza*) as their subject."[33]

Castelvetro subsequently criticizes Lucan and Dante on the grounds that their works contain abstruse astrological references.

Also censuring Lucan in particular for rhetorical excesses harmful to verisimilitude, and reading *annumerandus* for *imitandus* in *Institutes* 10.1.90, Castelvetro says:

> Therefore Quintilian removes Lucan from the ranks of the poets for no other reason than that he employs the rhetorical manner, saying, "Lucan is ardent and tumultuous and full of brilliant thoughts, but, to say what I feel, he is to be numbered rather with the orators than with the poets (*Laonde Quintiliano rimouve dalla schiera de' poeti Lucano non per alto se non perché usa la sentenzia ritoricamente, dicendo: "Lucanus ardens et concitatus et sententiis clarissimus et, ut dicam quod sentio, magis oratoribus quam poetis annumerandus"*).[34]

Arguments similar to Castelvetro's are made by Pierre Ronsard in his preface to his unfinished *Franciade* (ca. 1572), where he insists: "There is as much difference between a Poet (*Poëte*) and a versifier (*versificateur*) as there is between a plough-horse and a noble Neopolitan courser." Defending this position by referring to the *Poetics'* ninth chapter and to Horace's idea that a poet should begin his work *in medias res,* Ronsard contends that the true poet "takes as the indispensable law in his art, never to follow step by step the truth, but the verisimilar and the possible (*la vraysemblance, & le possible*). And on the possible and on what it is possible to do, he bases his work, leaving the narration of the truth to the Historians."[35]

Ronsard emphasizes this point, in Quintilianic fashion, by recommending Virgil to the reader and placing other Roman poets in a second-class category. Ronsard also makes use of the idea, partly derived from the *Poetics'* first chapter and partly derived from the ninth, that true poets should not be confused with writers in verse who do not produce works according to verisimilitude and possibility. In the process, Ronsard dismisses Lucretius, albeit somewhat reluctantly, from the company of poets:

> And do not search out others [other poets], Reader, in the Roman language, except for the gifted Lucretius: but because he wrote his frenzies, which he thought to be true according to his sect [Epicu-

reanism], and because he did not base his work on the verisimilar and on the possible (*sur la vray-semblance & sur le possible*), I would remove from him entirely the name of Poet (*je luy oste du tout le nom de Poëte*), even though some of his verses are not only excellent, but divine. The rest of the Latin poets are only footmen compared to Virgil, first Captain of the Muses.[36]

Shortly afterwards, Lucan and Silius Italicus (the author of the *Punica,* a historical epic which dates from the second half of the first century A.D. and the subject of which is the Second Punic War) are judged to be historians who imprudently chose to write in verse and who thus unfortunately realized Aristotle's hypothetical hexametric Herodotus: "The other ancient Roman Poets, like Lucan and Silius Italicus, covered history with the mantle of Poetry: they would have done better in my opinion, in some places to have written in prose (*ils eussent mieux fait à mon avis, en quelques endroits d'escrire en prose*).[37] Ronsard also sounds the same notes in his earlier (1565) *Epitome of the Art of French Poetry,* in which he once more joins Aristotle's ideas with Quintilian's vocabulary, and urges: "[T]he fable and fiction is the subject of good poets (*la fable et fiction est le sujet des bon poëtes*), . . . and verses are merely the goal of the ignorant versifier (*et les vers sont seulement le but de l'ignorant versificateur*)."[38]

In his *Discourses on the Heroic Poem,* first published in 1594, Torquato Tasso similarly conflates the ninth chapter of the *Poetics* with *Institutes* 10.1.90 and (indirectly) with Servius' idea that Lucan is a historian and not a poet. Quintilian's and Servius' judgments of Lucan are thus injected into Aristotle's contrast between History and Poetry, and Lucan is substituted for the hypothetical Herodotus in verse. In arguing that poetry should be based on the verisimilar or the possible, Tasso cites Aristotle and adds: "But if Lucan is not a poet, this is because he ties himself to the truth of particulars, and has not so much regard for the universal: [and] as it seems to Quintilian, is more like an orator than a poet" (*Ma se Lucano non è poeta, ciò aviene perché s'obliga alla verita de' particolari, e non ha tanto risguardo all'universale: come pare a Quintiliano, è più simile all'oratore ch'al poeta).*[39]

The first and ninth chapters of the *Poetics,* Plutarch, and Quintilian-refracted-through-Servius all are explicitly conflated in *The Ancient Philosophy of Poetry* (1596?) of Alonso López Pinciano. Here one of the characters in the dialogue remarks that Aristotle "in his *Poetics* says, it is not prose (*la prosa*) and meter (*el metro*) that make the difference between History and Poetry, but rather imitation and nothing else." Another character in the dialogue adds: "Also this is confirmed by Plutarch when he says of Nicander that he is not a poet in his *Theriaca.* And the same is said by Quintilian when he counts Lucan among the historians and not the poets (*Y lo mismo Quintiliano, quando a Lucano cuenta entre los históricos, y no entre poetas*); because, in truth, the spirit of poetry is plot (*fábula*)." Plato's statement that some poets are not imitators is then mentioned, but only to be refuted with the argument that "those he calls poets, because they have verse without imitation (*metros sin imitación*), are nothing but versifiers (*metrificadores*)."[40]

Even sixteenth-century readers who disagree with the differentiation of verse from poetry fuse Aristotle's emphasis on mimesis with Quintilian's terminology, and they read the *Poetics* in light of Quintilian's *versificator* remark, in light of Plutarch's contrast of plot and meter, and in light of criticisms of Lucan. Even these readers, who favor identifying verse with poetry, do not urge that Aristotle's ideas are being misinterpreted by being conflated with ideas foreign to them; nor, generally, do they point out that Aristotle never said verse was not essential to poetry. Instead, these pro-verse readers accept the conflations, arguing that Aristotle was wrong to have condemned certain poets as versifiers and to have said that verse was not essential to poetry. When J. C. Scaliger, for instance, in his 1561 *Poetics,* insists that verse is the distinguishing feature of poetry, he connects—no less than do those advocating the opposite view—criticisms of Lucan with Aristotle's criticism of Empedocles, and he suggests that

Aristotle had in effect used the term *versificator* in speaking of
Empedocles:

> Was Lucan a poet? Surely he was. As usual, the grammarians deny
> this, and object that he wrote history. Well now! Produce a pure
> history. Lucan must differ from Livy, and the difference is verse
> (*versu*). Verse is the property of the poet. . . . Moreover, although
> Aristotle exercised this censure [that those who do not imitate are not
> poets] so severely that he would refuse the name of poet to versifiers
> (*versificatores*), yet in practice he speaks differently, and says: "As
> Empedocles poetically wrote" (ὡς ἐποίησεν) so he even calls Em-
> pedocles, who feigned not at all a poet (ποιητήν).[41]

To appreciate better the conflation of Quintilian and Plutarch
and Servius with Aristotle, and to appreciate better how the
distinction between verse and poetry originated, we should list
the second-level or imperfect poets whom the relevant four ancient critics mention, though we need not include all the poets
mentioned by Quintilian, but simply those known by sixteenth-
century readers. All these second-level figures are, it should be
borne in mind, hexameter poets, with the exception of Theognis
(and at times Ovid), who wrote in elegiac couplets. It should also
be borne in mind that because Severus' epic had vanished, Quintilian's *versificator* remark had thus lost its anchor of specific
reference. Therefore, readers applied the remark not only to
Lucan and to historical poets, but also to hexametric poets whose
works were in general felt to be deficient. We should remember
also how criticisms of Lucan seem to confirm observations in the
Poetics' ninth chapter. Finally, we should note how Aristotle's
general proscription of scientific/philosophical and historical poetry appears to receive detailed confirmation in the names of poets
cited by Quintilian and Plutarch and special-case confirmation in
the Servian dismissal of Lucan:

Aristotle	*Quintilian*	*Plutarch*	*Servius*
Empedocles	Lucretius	Empedocles	Lucan
Herodotus	Lucan	Parmenides	
in hexameters			

138

Quintilian	Plutarch
Severus	Theognis
Varro Atacinus	Nicander
Ovid	

Sixteenth-century commentators, interpreting Aristotle's remarks about imitation, customarily illustrate their interpretations
by referring to a mixture of ancient authors in this table. They
occasionally supplement the mixture with references to other
relevant ancient non-imitators like Manilius and Silius Italicus
and relevant modern non-imitators like Dante and Fracastoro.
This is not to say that, in every case of this sort, the commentator
has at his fingertips the ancient sources and the examples they
cited. In some instances, commentators appear merely to adopt
the harmonization of Aristotle, Plutarch, Quintilian, and Servius
as the cliché it had become and to avail themselves of the commonplace illustrations of it.

When, for example, Giovanni Pietro Capriano, in his *On True
Poetry* of 1555, excludes Empedocles, Lucretius, and Lucan from
the ranks of *poeti perfetti* and then goes on to distinguish between
poets and "lowly and inept versifiers, or to put it better, simple
metricians" (*versificatori bassi & inettissimi, o per meglio dire, met-
rici semplicissimi*),[42] one can see, from the authors cited as well as
from the vocabulary, that Capriano has mixed Aristotle with
Quintilian, even though Capriano cites Aristotle alone in defense
of his judgment.

Something similar occurs in Antonio Minturno's 1564 *Art of
Poetry* dialogue:

> I shall never affirm that there is epic poetry in these works [Minturno
> says to his friend Vespasiano, referring to the *Metamorphoses* and the
> *Fasti* and the lost non-Homeric epics that Aristotle criticizes in *Poet-
> ics* 1451a16ff. for being linear and episodic rather than unified, as
> were Homer's epics, by a single action]; why then are their authors to
> be called poets? I will explain to you. It is both because the common
> people attribute the name to all those who write in verse, whether
> they treat of agriculture, as Vergil [in the *Georgics*] and Hesiod, or of

139

astrology, as Aratus, Manilius, and Pontanus, or of medicine, as Nicander, or of things done in war, as Quintus Calaber, . . . Silius Italicus, and Lucan, and because they adorn them with poetic splendors and add to them things feigned.[43]

Minturno does not mention Aristotle (though his friend has mentioned him earlier), Quintilian, or Plutarch, nor does he directly echo Servius. But once one is aware of this nexus of source materials, one feels its presence here as clearly as one does in writers who explicitly cite the sources.

Philip Sidney deserves special mention here. He is one of the most interesting sixteenth-century writers to make use of the *Poetics,* and his *Apologie for Poetrie* of 1583 contains many of the same interpretations of the treatise that are found elsewhere in the period. For example, when he says, "Poesie therefore is an arte of imitation, for so *Aristotle* termeth it in his word *Mimesis*"[44] and then excludes from the number of "right Poets" Lucretius and Lucan (among others), one can see that Sidney is fusing Aristotle's definition with an idea ultimately derived from Quintilian. Yet there is an additional element in Sidney that requires comment. For, having cited Aristotle's definition of poetry as an art of imitation, Sidney goes on to discuss the popular custom of identifying poets with "the sorts of verses they liked best to write in"; and, in the course of this discussion, he remarks:

> [I]ndeede the greatest part of Poets have apparelled their poeticall inventions in that numbrous kinde of writing which is called verse: indeed but apparelled, verse being but an ornament and no cause to Poetry, sith there have beene many most excellent Poets that never versified, and now swarme many versifiers that neede never aunswere to the name of Poets.[45]

An important feature of these remarks is that in fusing Aristotle's idea with Quintilian's terminology, Sidney does more than urge that not all who write verse are poets. He also speaks of "verse being but an ornament and no cause to Poetry." Sidney gives, briefly and explicitly, a distinction between "verse" and

"Poetry." The distinction is not a contrast, as it will become in later writers like Eliot. But the distinction has been made.

Sidney does something else. Thinking of authors of prose romances like Heliodorus and of Xenophon's fictional-historical *Cyropedia*, he states that some who have never written verse are nevertheless poets: "many most excellent Poets . . . never versified." And he later reinforces this statement by remarking: "It is already sayde (and, as I think, trulie sayde) it is not ryming and versing that maketh Poesie. One may bee a Poet without versing, and a versifier without Poetry."[46]

This last idea commonly appears in sixteenth-century readers of Aristotle, and it is in fact often attributed to him. For instance, in discussing the ninth chapter of the *Poetics,* Castelvetro glosses 1451b1−4 by saying: "[J]ust as the history of Herodotus composed in verse would remain history, not become poetry, so on the other hand the *Electra* of Sophocles, put into prose, would remain poetry, not diverge into history." (*[C]ome l'istori d'Erodoto composta in verso resta istoria, né diviene poesia, così dall'altra parte l'* Elettra *di Sofocle, se fosse composta in prosa, resterebbe poesia, né diverrebbe istoria.*) Not surprisingly, in his next sentence Castelvetro brings Lucan into the discussion: "And therefore one, proceeding further, may say that Lucan, Silius Italicus, and Girolamo Fracastoro in his *Joseph* are historians. . . . And by the same token, Lucian in many of his *Dialogues,* and Boccaccio in his *Decameron* and *Filopono,* are poets."[47]

In the same way, one of the characters in López's dialogue observes with respect to *Poetics* 1451b1−4: "[I]f the work of Herodotus were put into meter, and that of Homer into prose, one could not for that reason say that the one was a poet and the other a historian." (*[S]i la obra de Herodoto se pusiesse en metro, y la de Homero en prosa, no por esso dexaría de ser éste poeta y auqél histórico.*) Then another character (López himself actually) adds that "many Italian comedies in prose are poems and seem very excellent" (*también las comedias italianas en prosa son poemas y parecen muy bien*).[48]

Advocates of imitation tend ultimately to argue that though imitation is the essence of poetry, and though poetry can exist without verse, the best poetry is imitation *with* verse. This position is represented alike by Castelvetro, Sidney, and López. Having suggested that a prose *Electra* would still be poetry and that the *Decameron* is poetry, Castelvetro quickly adds that although "verse and prose do not constitute the essential difference between poetry and history, nevertheless verse accompanies and adorns poetry, and prose history, as their most fitting vestments. Neither can history without censure don verse, nor poetry don prose than can a woman don men's clothing or men the clothing of women."[49] Sidney uses a similar metaphor to make the same point. After arguing that verse is "no cause to Poetry," he says that nevertheless "the Senate of Poets have chosen verse as their fittest rayment, meaning, as in matter they passed all in all, so in maner to goe beyond them: not speaking (table talke fashion, or like men in a dreame,) words as they chanceably fall from the mouth, but peyzing [weighing] each sillable of each worde by iust proportion according to the dignitie of the subiect."[50]

López's dialogue supplies a good general statement of this line of reasoning. Just after López asserts that some Italian prose comedies are poems, the character of Fadrique, to whom López defers and whose opinions are presented as carrying greater weight than López's, puts in a qualification. Fadrique points out that, according to Horace (scarcely less authoritative a figure than Aristotle), the aim of poetry is delightful teaching; and because meter contributes so greatly to delight, the poet should write in it. Fadrique also makes the point that Aristotle simply says in discussing tragic plot in *Poetics* 1451b27–29, that "the poet is a poet more so for plot and imitation than for meter" (*el poeta más lo es por la fábula y imitación que no por el metro*). Aristotle, Fadrique urges, "thus signifies that meter holds some part in Poetry, even if not in imitation" (*adonde significa que el metro tien alguna parte en la Poética, aunque no en el imitación*). And Fadrique concludes:

Meter is not necessary to the poet, but is something which much ornaments and dresses that lady called poesy (*No es forçoso el metro al poeta, mas es una cosa que atauía y orna mucho a esta dama dicha poesia*), and escorts her with such fitting grace and time that there is great beauty in their kinship; and it is certain, at least, that some species of Poetry cannot exist without meter; and it does not seem to me a bad idea to call imitation with meter perfect poetry and imitation without meter and meter without imitation imperfect poetries (*y no me pareciera mal que a la imitación con metro llamassen poesía perfecta, y, a la imitación sin metro y al metro sin imitación, poesías imperfectas*).[51]

One could cite numerous statements like these from Aristotelians of the second half of the sixteenth century, many of whom wish to establish the primacy of imitation, while at the same time retaining the concept of poetry as metrical composition. Many critics use the clothing metaphor to present this compromise. Other critics employ an analogy according to which imitation is to meter as the soul is to the body. The imitation, the soul, is the most important thing, but the soul, the imitation, requires a body, a metrical framework, if it is to be appreciated by mortal sense. As Agnoli Segni puts it in his *Considerations of Matters Pertinent to Poetry:*

> [P]oetry is a composite of imitation and of verse, in which the imitation is its essence and not the verse; but not for this reason can it be poetry without verse, which is necessary to it as its proper matter, just as a body is necessary to man, and not just any body, but a particular body and a particular matter: but to the soul and to the form corresponds, in poetry, the imitation, just as the language corresponds to the body and to a certain kind of body, and not any language whatsoever but this fixed one, that is, metrical language or language made in verse (*l'orazione metrica, ò fatta in versi*).[52]

The Aristotelian position that imitation and not verse is the essence of poetry is frequently attacked by the Platonists. The Platonists draw ammunition particularly from passages such as *Symposium* 205c and *Gorgias* 502c, in which poetry is identified with meter, and from *Republic* 392D–98B, in which Plato contends not only that there is a whole class of poetry having no imitation, but also that this class of poetry is superior to imitative poetry.

Proclus also supplied Renaissance Platonists with arguments that could be deployed against Aristotelian proponents of mimesis. For Proclus, the highest sort of poetry eschewed imitation and aimed at rendering the Ineffable and the higher truths above or beyond the mere sensory world. In the fourth dissertation of his *Commentary on Plato's Republic* (fifth C. A.D.), Proclus had relegated imitative poetry to a third-class status beneath poetry dealing with divine matters and poetry dealing with moral matters. "[T]his first kind of poetry," Proclus had said of the divine and, in his opinion, highest species, "proceeding from divine inspiration, fills the soul with symmetry, and hence adorns even its least energies with measures and rhythms."[53]

Because so much space has been devoted to Aristotelian arguments about the importance of imitation vis-à-vis verse, it may be only fair to grant a paragraph to the Platonist side of the debate. Giovanni Antonio Viperano evinces Platonic leanings when he writes in his *Three Books on Poetry* of 1579: "[A] poem perfect and complete in all its meters, I call, as Plato does, beautiful (*poema perfectum, & omnibus numeris absolutum cum Platone pulchrum appello*)."[54] Likewise, in his *Inquiry into Poetry* of 1586, Lorenzo Parigiuolo says at the outset of his discussion: "We shall therefore first deny Aristotle's proposition. In addition to this we shall prove that verse makes poetry, not imitation (*il verso fa la poesia non la imitatione*). From this it will follow that writers of verses without imitation are true poets, contrary to Aristotle's deduction."[55] And in what is the most extended and varied Renaissance attack on Aristotelian poetics, Francesco Patrizi's encyclopedic *On Poetry* of 1586, Patrizi argues "that verse is so proper and essential to poetry that it is necessary for it, and that poetry can neither be made nor be without verse" (*ch'il verso alla poesia sì proprio ed essenziale sia, che le sia necessario. E che poesia non possa nè farsi, nè essere senza verso*). In the last paragraph of the tenth and final book of the "Decade of Debate" section of his treatise, Patrizi concludes more generally, "that the most common teachings of Aristotle, and those which are, as it were, the postulated principles of his art, are not true either with respect to its universal origin or with respect to its particular species" (*che gl'insegnamenti aristotelici più communi, e quei che quasi principi presupposti sono dell'arte sua poetica non sono veri, nè quanto all'origine sua universale, nè quanto a di molte spezie particolari*).[56]

One should make clear that Aristotelian critics apply the idea that imitation is the essence of poetry and that poetry may be written in prose in only a restricted fashion. The idea is seen as having reference only to longer forms, principally romance and drama. As was observed in the previous chapter, many regarded the romance as the most distinctive modern contribution to literature. (Though there were romances written in antiquity, the romance never appears to have been considered a major genre and did not really become popular until the second or third century A.D.) Because romances were frequently written in prose, defending achievements of modern writers against those of classical writers involved, in part, defending the use of prose in "poetry," the term meaning here simply "fiction."

Not having considered drama in relation to the question of prose fiction, we should pause for a moment to reflect on the state of dramatic literature when the *Poetics* (which is, after all, mainly concerned with drama) comes into circulation. In the sixteenth century, at least in its earlier stages, the vernacular literatures offered no certain and convenient medium to dramatists. For all practical purposes, serious drama had been in eclipse for centuries; there was little in the way of a living tradition for playwrights to follow. Moreover, versification in the vernaculars was associated with structural rhyme, and whatever advantages rhyme might have in other genres, it was often felt that its effects were unsuitable to drama. This feeling in turn gives rise to suggestions that verse itself might be unsuitable to drama and that plays should be written in prose.

Viable vernacular verse forms for drama develop in the sixteenth century. Giangiorgio Trissino's tragedy of *Sofonisba,* with its pioneering use of unrhymed hendecasyllabics, dates from 1515. When in 1543 Giraldi Cinthio defends his use of verse instead of prose for his tragedy, *Dido,* he states he believes that Trissino has given Italian playwrights a measure as effective as the iambic trimeter (or "senarius") in which dialogue in ancient drama was commonly written:

> It likewise appeared to Signor Trissino that prose was not at all adapted to tragedy. Therefore he composed his *Sofonisba* in that sort of verses which he before anyone else most suitably gave to the stage in place of the iambic which the Greeks and Latins used. For it appeared to him that these verses loosed from the obligation of rhyme carried with them the same reason for being as the senarii, composed of iambics, in the Greek and the Latin tongues, namely, that they are similar to the familiar speech of our times, and fall, like the iambics, from the mouths of speakers (though they do not know it) in common speech.[57]

In England in the last two decades of the sixteenth century and in the first two decades of the seventeenth, a related development occurs. Employing the unrhymed iambic pentameter, Marlowe, Greene, Shakespeare, Jonson, Webster, Beaumont, and Fletcher produce a body of dramatic poetry that not only rivals but, arguably, surpasses any comparable body of dramatic poetry in antiquity. In France in the seventeenth century, in the plays of Corneille and Racine and in those comedies of Molière that are in meter, rhymed vernacular verse achieves a similar triumph. These developments, however, do not resolve the debate about the proper vehicle for drama. Indeed, the contrasting successes of English blank verse and French Alexandrine couplets contribute to variations on and continuations of the debate, a fact to which Dryden's critical writings attest.

More pertinent to the issue at hand, some sixteenth-century dramas, especially comedies (as López indicates in his dialogue), are written in prose. Moreover, one hears, in the arguments in favor of prose drama, notes that will be sounded when, much later, poets begin to advocate free verse. Particularly crucial in this regard is the argument, voiced by various sixteenth-century proponents of prose drama, that meter not only is not to be identified with poetry, but also is detrimental to poetic verisimilitude. This argument is offered in *The Ancient Philosophy of Poetry* when López, just before saying that Italian prose comedies are poems, says that "imitation . . . is based on verisimilitude, and speech in meter has no likeness to truth" (*imitación . . . ésta fundada en la verisimilitud, y el hablar en metro no tiene alguna semejança de verdad*).[58] As a more extended illustration of this argument, we may cite a passage in Paoli Beni's 1596 *Disputation in which it is Shown how to Excel at Comedy and Tragedy Freed of the Chains of Meter:*

> [I]n comedy and in tragedy we imitate human actions properly with prose, less properly—nay, even absurdly—when bound by the limits of verse. Therefore prose is to be practiced, verse rejected, . . . since poetry is an imitation of human actions either as they actually were done or as they should have been done, neither of which can be achieved in comedy and tragedy through an imitation bound down by verse.[59]

To be sure, writers have always realized that it takes talent and training to write naturally in meter; and writers have often observed that if meter is a wonderfully flexible instrument in the hands of the expert poet, the inept or inexperienced author may have great difficulties with the medium. But of meters themselves, it is traditionally recognized (e.g., Aristotle, *Poetics* 1448b20ff.; Cicero, *Orator,* 178; Quintilian, 9.4.114–15) that they get established precisely for the reason that they accommodate, and in some cases even exemplify, naturally and instinctively appreciated patterns of living speech. The argument that meter might be the poet's enemy is foreign to earlier criticism and would seem to be an invention or a result of the Renaissance debate that we have been examining. It is a version of this argument—that meter gets in the way of natural poetic expression—that will later become a central part of the theories of poets such as Lawrence, Pound, and William Carlos Williams.

Though sixteenth-century discussions of imitation generally are as inadequate to deal with lyric verse as the *Poetics* itself is, certain critics attempt to relate lyric verse to discussions of issues involving the more obviously mimetic types of poetry. And there is at least one Renaissance treatise on poetics that does address, however fleetingly, the possibility that lyric poems, as well as plays, might be written without verse. This treatise, which dates from 1592, is Agostino Michele's *Discourse in which it is clearly shown Contrary to the Opinion of All the Most Illustrious Writers on the Art of Poetry that it is possible to write Tragedy and Comedy Perfectly Well in Prose.*

Michele's work is composed in alternating sections. Objections to prose are delivered in short paragraphs and are then refuted in longer ones. The treatise is divided into two larger parts, the first of which concerns almost exclusively tragedy and comedy, the second of which deals with poetic art in general. In the penultimate section of the second part, one sees a ghostly intimation of a poetry from which meter has entirely vanished. Here the objection to prose runs:

> If Comedy and Tragedy can be set forth in Prose, so likewise would it be possible to set forth Epic and Lyric Poems, these being no less poetry than the first; but it is not only far from the truth, but impossible, that an Epic Poem, a Sonnet, or a Madrigal be composed in Prose. (*Se la Comedia, e la Tragedia possono essere spiegate in Prosa potrebbono essere spiegati parimenti i Poemi Epici, e Lirici; essendo non*

men de primi dalla poesia compresi; ma è non pur lontano dal vero, ma impossibile, che un Poema Epico, & un Sonetto, od un Madrigale sia composto in Prosa.) [60]

Like other critics defending the use of prose, Michele wants prose to be used only in certain cases. And having earlier in his treatise contended that, just as imitation is to different degrees appropriate to different types of poetry, so prose is to different degrees suitable to different types of fiction, Michele argues at this point that prose is eminently suited to comedy, less suited to tragedy, not suitable to epic, and utterly unsuitable to lyric. Indeed, with regard to lyric verse, Michele says that it "receives its form more from the number of its verses and the order of its rhymes than from any other intrinsic cause. Therefore it is a ridiculous thing to speak of making a Sonnet or Canzone in Prose and implies a contradiction" (*più dal numero de versi, e dall'ordine delle rime, che da altra cagione intrinseca riceveno cotal forma. Laonde è ridicola cosa il dire di fare un Sonetto, od una Canzone in Prosa, & implica contraditione).* [61]

Though meterless lyric seems a *ridicola cosa* to Michele, it is striking that he suggests its possibility. It is as if he briefly glances down a byway that twentieth century poetry will make into its principal thoroughfare.

3. The Modern Opposition of Verse and Poetry

After the sixteenth century, the debate about the legitimacy of prose fiction dies down, and the doctrine that poetry is imitation falls gradually out of favor. In literary discussions, "imitation" increasingly denotes "emulation of a model" rather than "feigning" or "story-telling." Montaigne anticipates this development. In his remarks about poetry in "On the Education of Children" of 1580, he draws the distinction between the poet and versifier, saying: "I am not one of those who thinks good rhythm makes a good poem. Let him [the poet] lengthen a short syllable, if he wishes; that is of no importance. If the inventions are successful, if intellect and judgment have done their job well, 'Here is a good poet (*bon poëte*),' I will say, 'but a bad versifier (*mauvais versificateur*).'" Yet when Montaigne introduces the concept of imitation into his analysis, he does so not to fortify his poet-versifier argument, but merely to denigrate Ronsard's and Bellay's followers as "lesser men" who lack the excellence of their masters and who "fall very short of imitating (*imiter*) the rich descriptions of the one [Ronsard] and the delicate inventions of the other [Bellay]."[62]

In the seventeenth century, writers increasingly associate poetry with sublimity, a development influenced by the recovery of the treatise on the subject by "Longinus." Indeed, if literary criticism in the sixteenth century is greatly affected by the diffusion of the *Poetics,* criticism in the seventeenth is similarly, if less spectacularly, affected by the diffusion of *On the Sublime.* With the rise, in the eighteenth century, of Romantic theories of art, new elements appear in discussions of poetry, which comes more and more to be regarded as the expression of passion or musicality or organic growth.

Yet the results of harmonization of Aristotle with Quintilian (and with Plutarch and the Servian estimate of Lucan) remain crucial. The distinctions between versifier and poet and between verse and poetry are applied to the newer contexts. As so often happens in literary history, an idea created to deal with a particular situation drifts free of its initial meaning and purpose after the situation passes. Eventually, the idea attaches to other situations and other meanings and purposes, and it is in the process transformed into another idea altogether.

To illustrate the persistence, into the seventeenth century, of the fusion of Aristotle's argument about mimesis with Quintilian's *versificator* remark, one may cite Drummond's reminiscence of Ben Johnson's visit to Scotland in 1618. Drummond reports that Jonson commented about Du Bartas "that he thought not Bartas a Poet but a Verser, because he wrote not Fiction."[63] In a different spirit, Henry Reynolds in his *Mythomystes* [1632?] praises Edmund Spenser and Samuel Daniel but qualifies his praise by treating them as latter-day versions of Empedocles and Lucan: "I must approve the learned Spenser, in the rest of his poems, no less than his *Fairie Queen*, an extract body of ethic doctrine: though some good judgments have wished (and perhaps not without cause) that he had therein been a little freer of his fiction, and not so close-riveted to his moral; no less than many do to Daniel's *Civil Wars*, that it were (though otherwise a commendable work) yet somewhat more than a true chronicle history in rhyme" (*LTSP*, 198). And this last comment recalls Michael Drayton's verse epistle to Reynolds, in which Drayton refers to

> . . . Samuel Daniel, whom if I
> May spake of, but to sensure doe denie,
> Onely have heard some wisemen him rehearse,
> To be too much historian in verse;
> His rimes were smooth, his meeters well did close,
> But yet his maner better fitted prose.[64]

In his preface to his romantic epic *Gondibert* of 1650, William Davenant offers a survey of the "Heroick Poem" from Homer to Spenser, and, after discussing Homer and Virgil, he says of Lucan: "*Lucan*, who chose to write the greatest actions that ever were allowed to be true, . . . did not observe that such an enterprize rather beseem'd an Historian then a Poet." Having made this Servian assessment, Davenant goes on to draw an Aristotelian distinction between the historian and poet: "I would imply that Truth narrative and past is the Idol of Historians, who worship a dead thing, and truth operative, and by effects continually alive, is the Mistris of Poets, who hath not her existence in matter but in reason [i.e., not factually and particularly but generally and plausibly]."[65]

In his "Answer to Davenant's Preface to *Gondibert*," also of 1650, Thomas Hobbes makes a more extended argument that clearly derives from Aristotle and from sixteenth-century interpretations of the *Poetics:*

> They that take for poesy whatsoever is writ in verse will think this division imperfect [Hobbes has said that there exist only six genres of poetry—epic, tragedy, satire, comedy, pastoral, and pastoral comedy], and call in sonnets, epigrams, eclogues, and the like pieces, which are but essays and parts of an entire poem, and reckon Empedocles and Lucretius (natural philosophers) for poets, and the moral precepts of Phocylides, Theognis, and the quatrains of Pybrach and the history of Lucan, and others of that kind amongst poems, bestowing on such writers for honor the name of poets rather than of historians or philosophers. But the subject of a poem is the manners of men, not natural causes; manners presented, not dictated; and manners feigned as the name of poesy imports, not found in men. They that give entrance to fictions writ in prose err not so much.

> (*LTSP,* 213)

In his later "The Virtues of an Heroic Poem" (1675), Hobbes criticizes the *Pharsalia* on the grounds that it is too partisan in spirit. This quality removes the epic from the realm of true poetry, according to Hobbes, who predictably calls in Quintilian in defense of his judgment: "*Lucan* shews himself openly in the *Pompeyan* Faction, inveighing against *Caesar* throughout his Poem, like *Cicero* against *Cataline* or *Marc Antony,* and is therefore justly reckon'd by *Quintilian* as a Rhetorician rather than a Poet."[66]

Dryden's "Discourse Concerning the Original and Progress of Satire" of 1693 is another significant work which seems to lean heavily on Quintilian's analysis of ancient poets. Indeed, discussing satire, Dryden quotes Quintilian's well-known observation (10.1.93) that Roman poets invented the genre: *Satira . . . tota nostra est,* "Satire is entirely ours." When Dryden turns his attention to epic, he appropriates some of Quintilian's remarks about that topic as well, though to Quintilian's observation about Lucan's fiery (*ardens*) quality, Dryden appears to add something of Joseph Scaliger's criticism of Lucan. Scaliger had written: "Lucan's talent was violent and terrible. . . . he didn't know what it was to make a Poem" (*Lucanus violentissimum et terribilissimum ingenium. . . . il n'a sceu que c'estoit que faire un Poëme*). Dryden also seems to make use of Scaliger's characterization of Statius, whom Scaliger had called "the first epic poet after Virgil, and he doesn't rant and rave like Lucan" (*le premier poète epicus après Virgile, et il ne déclame point comme Lucain*).[67] In his remarks about epic, it is interesting that Dryden interprets Quintilian's term *versificator* in a descriptive rather than a pejorative sense:

> Now if it may be permitted me to go back again to the consideration of epic poetry, I have confessed that no man hitherto has reached, or so much as approached, to the excellencies of Homer or Virgil; I must farther add that Statius, the best versificator next to Virgil, knew not how to design after him, though he had the model in his eye; that Lucan is wanting both in design and subject, and is besides too full of heat and affectation.
>
> (*ODP*, 2.82)

Jonson, Reynolds, Drayton, Davenant, Hobbes, and Dryden are, to varying degrees, still arguing in favor of the concept of poetry as imitation. At points in the second half of the seventeenth century, however, Aristotelian ideas come to be deployed to defend sublimity rather than imitation. This phenomenon is illustrated by Edward Phillips, who in his dictionary, *The New World of English Words* (5th ed., 1696), defines "Versifier" as "a maker of Verses, generally taken in an ill sense,"[68] and who in the preface to his 1675 *Theatrum Poetarum*—a preface in which his uncle John Milton may have had a hand—writes of epic poetry:

> [T]he greatness of the argument . . . is that which makes up the perfection of a poet. In other arguments a man may appear a good poet, in the right management of this alone a great poet; for if invention be the grand part of a poet, or maker, and verse the least, then certainly the more sublime the argument the nobler the invention and by consequence the greater the poet. And therefore it is not a mere historical relation spiced over with a little slight fiction, now and then a personated virtue or vice rising out of the ground and uttering a speech, which makes a heroic poem, but it must be rather a brief, obscure, or remote tradition, but of some remarkable piece of story, in which the poet hath an ample field to enlarge by feigning of probable circumstances.[69]

Phillips offers the Aristotelian characterization of the poet as a "maker"; he also asserts that "verse [is] the least" part of poetry and that poetry is not "historical." Yet for Phillips, the poet is the maker no longer of a plausible, coherent plot, but of a sublime argument, involving "a brief, obscure, or remote tradition." Phillips thus prefigures later writers who will similarly elevate the "argument" of a poem—its theme or subject—over its metrical form. Emerson's famous remark that "it is not metres, but a metre-making argument, that makes a poem" (*EL,* 450) illustrates this tendency.

In the eighteenth century, Aristotelian ideas are adapted to the defense of the concept of poetry as passion. An instance of such an adaptation is provided by John Dennis' *Advancement and Reformation of Modern Poetry* of 1701. Echoing chapter one of the *Poetics* and challenging the popular identification of poetry with meter, Dennis writes:

> As poetry is an art, it must be an imitation of nature. That the instrument with which it makes its imitation is speech need not be disputed. That the speech must be musical no one can doubt. . . . That the speech by which poetry makes its imitation must be pathetic is evident, for passion is still more necessary to it than harmony. For

154

harmony only distinguishes its instrument from that of prose, but passion distinguishes its very nature and character. For therefore poetry is poetry, because it is more passionate and sensual than prose. A discourse that is written in very good numbers, if it wants passion, can be but measured prose. But a discourse that is everywhere extremely pathetic, and consequently everywhere bold and figurative, is certainly poetry without numbers.

(LTSP, 273–74)

Dennis takes the Aristotelian position that poetry is imitation and that it is wrong to identify poetry with harmonious speech. For Dennis, however, poetry imitates "nature" rather than human action and is distinguished by passion rather than plot. Whereas some sixteenth-century critics had argued that fiction without meter was poetry, and that meter without fiction was not, Dennis argues that prose with passion and pathos is poetry and that meter ("good numbers") without them is "measured prose."

Another early eighteenth-century instance of the verse-poetry distinction appears in a letter that Alexander Pope writes in 1710. Suggesting that Richard Crashaw was a gifted amateur who "writ like a Gentleman, that is, at leisure hours" and who did not exhibit a professional poet's concern with the larger matters of the art, Pope characterizes "Verse" as being merely part of the "dress" of poetry. Somewhat in the manner of Renaissance Aristotelians, he urges that a poem's soul and body consist of "Design, Form, [and] Fable" and of a unified adjustment or "consent" of parts. Crashaw excelled with respect to verse and ornament, Pope says, but, like other amateurs, was unequipped or uninclined to achieve higher qualities. And referring to a copy of Crashaw's works that he evidently enclosed with his letter, Pope comments:

> All that regards Design, Form, Fable, (which is the Soul of Poetry) all that concerns exactness, or consent of parts, (which is the Body) will probably be wanting; only pretty conceptions, fine metaphors, glitt'ring expressions, and something of a neat cast of Verse, (which are properly the dress, gems, or loose ornaments of Poetry) may be found in these verses. This is indeed the case of most other Poetical

Writers of *Miscellanies;* nor can it well be otherwise, since no man can be a true Poet, who writes for diversion only. These Authors shou'd be consider'd as *Versifiers* and *witty Men,* rather than as *Poets;* and under this head will only fall the Thoughts, the Expression, and the Numbers.[70]

Subsequently, urging that Crashaw still merits admiration regardless of his deficiencies, Pope remarks that "the time consider'd of his writing, he was (ev'n as uncorrect as he is) none of the worst Versificators."[71] (It is interesting that a century later Pope himself would become a victim of the vocabulary that he employs and that critics would come to ask whether he was a genuine poet or merely a writer of versified argumentation.)

In his "Life" of Abraham Cowley, Dr. Johnson refers to the *Poetics'* first chapter and treats the metaphysical poets as Empedoclean writers who express knowledge instead of composing fiction. It is worth observing that Dr. Johnson suggests in passing a more comprehensive and perhaps more useful definition of poetic imitation than does Aristotle:

> The metaphysical poets were men of learning, and to show their learning was their whole endeavor. But, unluckily resolving to show it in rhyme, instead of writing poetry they only wrote verses, and very often such verses as stood the trial of the finger better than of the ear, for the modulation was so imperfect that they were only found to be verses by counting the syllables.
>
> If the father of criticism [Aristotle] has rightly denominated poetry Τέχνη μιμητική, 'an imitative art', these writers will, without great wrong, lose their right to the name of poets for they cannot be said to have imitated anything: they neither copied nature nor life, neither painted the forms of matter nor represented the operations of intellect.[72]

In the Romantic period and after, Aristotle's ideas about poetry are subject to mutations almost too many to number. Several may be mentioned. In the twenty-second chapter of his *Biographia Literaria,* Coleridge cites the *Poetics'* ninth chapter and, through a slight misreading, introduces an interesting reversal of Aristotle's position. Coleridge refers to Aristotle's statement (1451b6–7) that "poetry is a more philosophical and serious business than history" (*philosophōteron kai spoudaioteron poiēsis historias estin*). However, probably quoting from memory, Coleridge speaks of "the essence of poetry, which Aristotle pronounces to be σπουδαιότατον καὶ φιλοσοφώτατον γένος [the most serious and philosophical sort], the most intense, weighty and philosophical product of human art."[73] Coleridge, that is, drops the poetry-history contrast and then alters philosopho*teron* to philosopho*taton,* and spoudaio*teron* to spoudaio*taton,* changing the comparatives into superlatives. In consequence, Aristotle's argument that poetry, like philosophy, can speak in ways that have wide relevance to human experience is transformed into the very un-Aristotelian suggestion that poetry is a species of "philosophical" writing. This suggestion is made explicit when elsewhere Coleridge urges that at least some philosophical works in prose are in fact poems and poems of the "highest kind": "The writings of PLATO, and Bishop TAYLOR, and the Theoria Sacra of BURNET, furnish undeniable proofs that poetry of the highest kind may exist without metre."[74]

If Coleridge interprets Aristotle in such a way as to make him validate, as poetry, philosophical and didactic work like that of Taylor and Burnet and some of Plato, Shelley effects a similar reversal with respect to Aristotle and historical writing. In his *Defense of Poetry* (1821, pub. 1840), Shelley remarks that "the popular division into prose and verse is inadmissible in accurate philosophy" and remarks as well that "[t]he distinction between poets and prose writers is a vulgar error" (*LTSP,* 501). Shelley proceeds to make an argument that is modelled on the ninth chapter of the *Poetics,* though he substitutes "story" for "history," so that, instead of a history-poetry contrast, one finds an opposition between story and poetry:

> A poem is the very image of life expressed in its eternal truth. There is this difference between a story and a poem, that a story is a

catalogue of detached facts, which have no other connection than time, place, circumstance, cause and effect; the other is the creation of actions according to the unchangeable forms of human nature, as existing in the mind of the creator, which is itself the image of all other minds. The one is partial, and applies only to a definite period of time, and a certain combination of events which can never again recur; the other is universal, and contains within itself the germ of a relation to whatever motives or actions have place in the possible varieties of human nature.

(*LTSP,* 502)

Having said this, Shelley concludes "thus all the great historians, Herodotus, Plutarch, Livy, were poets," because their works feature "living images" (*LTSP,* 502). As is the case with Coleridge, Shelley appropriates arguments from Aristotle in order to validate as poetry not only a kind of prose composition, but also a kind of literature that Aristotle himself classified as non-poetic. Shelley also applies the term "versifiers" to bad poets, saying that some intelligent observers have objected to poetry because of a distaste for "certain versifiers; I, like them, confess myself unwilling to be stunned by the Theseids of the hoarse Codri of the day" (*CTSP,* 513). This last statement alludes to Juvenel's criticism (*Satires* 1.2) of Codrus, who evidently composed an inferior epic about Theseus; Juvenal, however, does not use the term "versifier," which seems rather to have come to Shelley from the critical tradition we have been examining.

Another notable feature of Shelley's argument is the following. Whereas sixteenth-century readers argue, on the authority of the *Poetics'* ninth chapter, that prose narrative is poetry, Shelley uses the same text to distinguish poetry from prose fiction. This shift suggests how the rise of the modern novel altered the meaning of "poetry." For the late Middle Ages and the Renaissance, one of its primary meanings was "fiction." With the success of the novel, "poetry" and "fiction," which had long been nearly synonyms, come to be regarded, in many instances, as antonyms.

This shift appears more obviously in John Stuart Mill's 1833 *What Is Poetry?* Referring to the question his essay raises, Mill remarks, "The vulgarest [answer] of all—one with which no person possessed of the faculties to which poetry addresses itself can ever have been satisfied—is that which confounds poetry with metrical composition." Mill urges, "The object of poetry is confessedly to act upon the emotions," and, as does Shelley, he distinguishes poetry from prose fiction rather than from history: "[T]here is a radical distinction between the interest felt in a novel as such, and the interest excited by poetry; for the one is derived from incident, the other from the representation of feeling. . . . The truth of poetry is to paint the human soul truly: the truth of fiction is to give a true picture of life." Mill ends his essay by reinforcing this distinction between poetry and narrative: "All art, therefore, in proportion as it produces its effects by an appeal to the emotions partakes of poetry, unless it partakes of oratory, or of narrative" (*LTSP*, 537, 538, 543).

These last citations raise an interesting point. If sixteenth-century readers, in joining Quintilian, Plutarch, and Servius with Aristotle, at times distort their sources, later writers in a sense distort the Renaissance conflation of the ancient sources. This is especially evident during the free verse movement. George Saintsbury appears to cast a cold eye on the experimental poetry of his day and complains of Sidney's *Apologie:* "Again Sidney commits himself in this same piece to the pestilent heresy of prose-poetry, saying that verse is 'only an ornament of poetry'."[75] Arguing on behalf of free verse, Ford writes:

> I wish I could take for granted the Reader's acceptance of the doctrine that Poetry is a matter of the writer's attitude towards life, and has nothing in the world to do—nothing whatever in the world to do—with whether the lines in which this attitude is put before him be long or short; rhymed or unrhymed; cadenced or interrupted by alliterations or assonances. One cannot expect to dictate the use of words to a race; but it would be of immense service to humanity if the

Anglo-Saxon world could agree that all creative literature is Poetry; that prose is a form as well adapted for the utterance of poetry as verse.

(*TTR*, 185)

Both Saintsbury and Ford are making arguments that recall statements made by sixteenth-century writers. Yet Sidney is not, in his *Apologie,* defending "prose-poetry" in the sense that Saintsbury seems to use the term. (The term itself apparently becomes common only in the second half of the nineteenth century, though the French *poème en prose* can be traced as far back as Fénelon's *Télémaque* (1699) and though the concept of "prose-poetry" is suggested frequently in Renaissance discussions of the *Poetics*. For instance, Patrizi gives the fifth of his *Ten Books of Debate* the interrogative title, "Se Poesia Si Possa Fare In Prosa.") Sidney is just urging that extended prose narratives like the *Arcadia* may rightly be called poems. Nor do sixteenth-century readers, in arguing that prose can be legitimately employed for plays or romances, wish to take the position that Ford takes in arguing that poetry is simply "a matter of the writer's attitude towards life."

It should be noted that during the nineteenth century some poets protest against the increasing disparagement of the technical elements of verse. Possibly the most eloquent of the protesters is, as one might expect, Matthew Arnold. To be sure, in his famous judgment of Dryden and Pope, Arnold reflects the tendency of his time to downplay metrical skill: "Though they may write in verse, though they may in a certain sense be masters of the art of versification, Dryden and Pope are not classics of our poetry, they are classics of our prose."[76] Yet Arnold expresses a very different view in his preface to his *Poems* (1853). Here he cites Goethe's "Notes on Dilettantism" and comments:

Two kinds of *dilettanti,* says Goethe, there are in poetry: he who neglects the indispensable mechanical part, and thinks he has done enough if he shows spirituality and feeling; and he who seeks to arrive at poetry merely by mechanism, in which he can acquire an artisan's readiness, and is without soul and matter. And he adds, that the first does the most harm to Art, and the last to himself. If we must be *dilettanti:* if it is impossible for us, under the circumstances amidst which we live, to think clearly, to feel nobly, and to delineate firmly: if we cannot attain to the mastery of the great artists—let us, at least, have so much respect for our Art as to prefer it to ourselves: let us not bewilder our successors: let us transmit to them the practice of Poetry, with its boundaries and wholesome regulative laws, under which excellent works may again, perhaps, at some future time, be produced, not yet fallen into oblivion through our neglect, not yet condemned and cancelled by the influence of their eternal enemy, Caprice.[77]

With the free verse movement, the Aristotelian notion that poetry is something more than meter sometimes is converted into the notion that poetry is something other than meter. Alluding to Aristotle's idea that the poet should make imitations as well as verses, William Carlos Williams states with reference to the versification of Pound's *Cantos:* "His [Pound's] excellence is that of the maker, not the measurer—I say he *is* a poet. This is in effect to have stepped beyond measure" (*SE,* 108).

The most influential modern exponent of the verse-poetry distinction is Eliot, who makes use of it at length in his essay on Kipling. As was noted earlier, Eliot opens his essay by asking "whether Kipling's verse really is poetry" (*OPP,* 228). Eliot devotes much of the essay to explaining why he believes this question must be answered, for the most part, in the negative.

According to Eliot, there are several reasons that Kipling's compositions are "verse" rather than "poetry." For one thing, they represent "balladry," Eliot argues, and as such are too simply composed to be on the same level as "the more esoteric kinds of poetry" and "the more difficult forms of poetry" (*OPP,* 232). Though Eliot does not explicitly state what he means by the esoteric kinds and difficult forms of poetry, it is clear that his discrimination between balladry/verse and esoteric/difficult poetry is in turn related to another distinction he draws, a distinction between craft and art—the former representing "verse" and the latter "poetry." If it seems that Eliot's terms are slippery and that he elucidates one distinction merely by drawing another, to his credit he acknowledges this problem, saying: "The difference between the craft and the art of poetry is of course as difficult to determine as the difference between poetry and balladry" (*OPP*, 235).

Eliot then draws yet another distinction to clarify the difference between verse and poetry. Verse is straightforward in its purpose—the message it communicates is explicit—and verse possesses a clearly articulated structure. Poetry, on the contrary, communicates indirectly and has a more musically elusive form. Discussing the qualities of true poetry, Eliot appears to refer to poems that do not express, as Kipling's do, directness of structure and intent, but rather express themselves in a more intuitive fashion and grow out of an intuitive sense of a "musical" form:

> For Kipling the poem is something which is intended to *act*—and for the most part his poems are intended to elicit the same response from all readers, and only the response which they can make in common. For other poets—at least, for some other poets—the poem may begin to shape itself in fragments of musical rhythm, and its structure will first appear in terms of something analogous to musical form; and such poets find it expedient to occupy their conscious mind with the craftsman's problems, leaving the deeper meaning to emerge from a lower level. It is a question then of what one chooses to be conscious of, and of how much of the meaning, in a poem, is conveyed direct to the intelligence and how much is conveyed indirectly by the musical impression upon the sensibility.
>
> (*OPP*, 238)

The "poetry" that Eliot contrasts with Kipling's "verse" is thus precisely the kind of poetry that Eliot himself writes. Eliot disarmingly admits this personal connection, saying, shortly before the main section of his argument, that "part of the fascination of this subject is in the exploration of a mind so different from one's own. I am accustomed to the search for form: but Kipling never seems to be searching for form, but only for a particular form for each poem" (*OPP*, 237).

Eliot subsequently returns to the notion that "poetry" is distinguished by musicality by connecting Kipling and Dryden and by arguing that the work of both illustrates the non-musical character of "verse." Again suggesting that "verse" involves straightforwardness of meaning and metric, while "poetry" involves a more musical use of speech and form, Eliot comments: "The question whether Kipling was a poet is not unrelated to the question whether Dryden was a poet. . . . Both were masters of phrase, both employed rather simple rhythms with adroit variations; and by both the medium was employed to convey a simple forceful statement, rather than a musical pattern of emotional overtones" (*OPP*, 243–44).

At the end of his essay, Eliot once more juxtaposes Kipling's conventional "verse" with musical "poetry." In doing this, he returns to the question that opens the essay—"whether Kipling's verse really is poetry"—and gives his fullest statement of why he believes that it is not. This statement brings together earlier arguments. It also introduces a new element in his argument: Kipling is a writer of "verse" because he does not "revolutionize" and because he does not change the "*form*" of English poetry:

> I return to the beginning. The late poems like the late stories with which they belong, are sometimes more obscure, because they are trying to express something more difficult than the early poems. They are the poems of a wiser and more mature writer. But they do not show any movement from 'verse' to 'poetry': they are just as instrumental as the early work, but now instruments for a matured purpose. Kipling could handle, from the beginning to the end, a considerable variety of metres and stanza forms with perfect competence; he introduces remarkable variations of his own; but as a poet he does not revolutionize. He is not one of those writers of whom one

can say, that the *form* of English poetry will always be different from what it would have been if they had not written. What fundamentally differentiates his 'verse' from 'poetry' is the subordination of musical interest.

(*OPP*, 250–51)

In some ways, one sympathizes with Eliot's remarks. Though greatly admiring poems like "The Broken Men" and "Epitaphs of the War," a reader may feel that much of Kipling's work is a shade too pat in conception and execution. Eliot's attempt to distinguish such work from compositions that are more lively, acute, or weighty seems sensible.

Yet Eliot's argument is troubling on several accounts. One pauses, for instance, at his suggestion that Kipling is somehow deficient because he did not engage in "searching for form, but only for a particular form for each poem." Setting aside the question of how one searches for form in the abstract, without reference to a specific poem, one feels that Eliot's remark about searching for form would entail a devaluation of virtually every fine poet from the eighth century B.C. forward. Shakespeare, for instance, wrote thirty-seven five-act plays in iambic pentameter and approximately 150 sonnets in the same line. It is possible that when he was preparing to write *The Tempest* or "Poor soul, the center of my sinful earth," he considered writing in some "experimental" measure. Yet such a scenario seems unlikely.

So, too, Eliot's remarks about "the more difficult forms of poetry" warrant serious consideration. Eliot is right to note that some kinds of poems are relatively undemanding and that, whatever the merits of such poems, the best poetry has a certain richness of meaning that lesser poetry does not have. Is it right, however, to identify this richness with formal difficulty? There's nothing formally "difficult" about the hexameters of Homer or the Alexandrines of Racine. Are these poets then, like Kipling, writing "verse"? Most readers would find this argument hard to accept. The richness of the *Iliad* or *Phèdre* issues not from the poet's having invented some complicated or odd form, but from the poet's having tackled serious subject matter and having written like an angel.

Finally, Eliot's statement, "What fundamentally differentiates his 'verse' from 'poetry' is the subordination of musical interest," requires scrutiny. This remark is telling, because Eliot suggests in his "Music of Poetry" essay, that the salient feature of free verse is that it has a musical rather than a metrical structure: "[T]he music of verse is not a line by line matter, but a question of the whole poem. Only with this in mind can we approach the vexed question of formal pattern and free verse" (*OPP*, 36). In view of this remark, in view of Eliot's additional judgment that Kipling writes "verse" partly because "as a poet he does not revolutionize," and in view of Eliot's association of "verse" with "metres and stanza forms," one is almost forced to this conclusion: Eliot believes that poetry, in the traditional sense of *metron* and *melos,* is not poetry, while revolutionary musical experiment is. Though it is hard to believe that Eliot consciously intended this argument, it is this argument that he presents. And when in the last paragraph of his essay he says, "I make no apology for having used the terms 'verse' and 'poetry' in a loose way" (*OPP*, 251), one cannot help but think that he might have served himself and his audience better had he attempted a greater precision.

Eliot marks the end of a long process. To the extent that we may read the verse-poetry distinction back into ancient literature, we may say the following. The ancient view that the relationship of verse to poetry is that of genus to species (there is a great deal of metrical composition, only a portion of which is genuine poetry) has been transformed into a modern view in which the relationship of verse to poetry is frequently that of two contrasting genera (there is verse, which is metrically orthodox composition, and there is poetry, which is metrically unorthodox and the structure of which is, to use two of Eliot's terms, "musical" or "difficult").

The modern poet and critic in whom the older view most noticeably prevails is the classical scholar, A. E. Housman. In "The Name and Nature of Poetry," his Leslie Stephen lecture at Cambridge in 1933, Housman cautions his audience against using the term "poetry" in too broad a fashion, saying, "It is not bad English to speak of 'prose and poetry' in the sense of 'prose and verse'. But it is wasteful; it squanders a valuable word by stretching it to fit a meaning which is accurately expressed by a wider term." That wider term, according to Housman, is "verse," and he goes on to argue: "Verse may be, like the 'Tale of Sir Thopas' in the judgment of Our Host of the Tabard, 'rym dogerel'; and the name of poetry is generally restricted to verse which can at least be called literature, though it may differ from prose only in its metrical form, and be superior to prose only in the superior comeliness of that form itself, and the superior terseness which usually goes along with it."[78] Housman is saying that poetry must be verse before it is poetry and that poetry is an excellent and special kind of verse. Though Housman's view is more in keeping with earlier attitudes towards poetry, modern criticism and practice have tended to follow the path that Eliot walks.

Aristotle continues to figure in current discussions of "verse" and "poetry." An instance of this continuity is supplied by an article by Marjorie Perloff in an 1980 issue of *PN Review*, the English literary journal. In an anthology entitled *British Poetry since 1970*, two of the magazine's editors, who were also the editors of the anthology, had criticized Professor Perloff's advocacy of David Antin's improvisational "talk poems." Responding to this criticism, Professor Perloff attacks some metrical poems which appeared in the anthology, particularly, "After Haymaking," a short poem by Robert Wells.

> The last bale placed, he stretched out in the hay.
>   Its warmth and his were one.
> He watched the fields beneath the weakening day
> And felt his skin still burning with the sun.

When it was dusk, he moved. Between his skin
And clothes the sweat ran cold.
He trembled as he felt the air begin
To touch and touch for what it could not hold.[79]

Professor Perloff comments that "what is missing here is quite
simply everything that turns a group of words on the page into a
poem."[80] She argues that Professor Antin's poems, extempo-
raneous "lectures" which are delivered into a tape recorder and
subsequently transcribed and lineated for publication, are more
properly poetical. Professor Antin himself summarizes his poetic
method in his prefatory poem to his collection, *talking at the
boundaries:*

> for the last few years ive been working at talks that ive
> been calling "talk poems" because i see all poetry as
> some kind of talking which is some kind of thinking
> and because ive never liked the idea of going into a
> closet to address myself over a typewriter what kind
> of talking is that? ive gotten into the habit of going
> to some particular place with something on my mind
> but no particular words in my mouth looking
> for a particular occasion to talk to particular people in a
> way i hope is valuable for all of us because these
> talks were worked out with no sense of a page in mind
> the texts are not "prose" which is as i see it a kind
> of "concrete poetry with justified margins" while
> these texts are the notations or scores of oral poems[81]

Contending that Professor Antin's work is properly "poetry" and
that the metrical work in the Carcanet anthology is not, Professor
Perloff cites *Poetics* 1447a29–b20 and comments:

> It is one of the great neglected passages in the *Poetics,* for Aristotle
> understood, as have few critics, that what he calls the 'art of language
> alone' (mime, Socratic dialogue, lyric) is related to such modes as

tragedy, comedy, and epic by its intrinsic nature as mimetic speech. The poet, says Aristotle in Chapter IX, is the maker, not of verses (*ton metron*) but of plots (*ton mython*). Plot, 'the first principle and, as it were, the soul of tragedy' is, of course, not simply what happens; it is the arrangement of the incidents (*ton pragmaton systasis*). The word *systasis* is central here: what Aristotle means is that the sine qua non of poetry (whether in prose or verse, whether dramatic, epic, or lyric) is the *arrangement* of the incidents, which is to say the *structuring* of the individual parts into a pleasing whole. By this definition, Antin's talk poems can indeed be considered 'poetry' although they certainly don't belong to the genre 'lyric'. Again by this definition (not, incidentally an invention of post-Structuralism!), some of the texts in the Carcanet anthology are, I contend, barely poetry at all, although they certainly are in verse.[82]

In view of the mountains of commentary earlier centuries have raised on the passage Professor Perloff cites, it is mistaken to describe it as neglected. It may also be questionable to employ Aristotle's concept of plot, which concerns the plausible coordination of narrative cause and effect, to validate intentionally random composition. In addition, Professor Perloff misleadingly cites 1451b27. What Aristotle says is, "*[T]on poiētēn mallon tōn mythōn einai dei poiētēn ē tōn metrōn, hosō poiētēs kata tēn mimēsin estin, mimeitai de tas praxeis.*" ("[T]he poet should be a maker of his plots more than of his verses, insofar as he is a poet by virtue of his imitations and what he imitates is actions.") The construction is not negative. Aristotle never says "the poet is the maker, not of verses"; *mallon* merely means "more than" or "rather than." And the overall statement is qualified by the *hosō* ("in proportion to" or "insofar as") clause.

Nevertheless, Professor Perloff illustrates the way the *Poetics*—and, behind the *Poetics,* Quintilian's remark about Severus, Plutarch's discussion of poetry, and Servius' judgment of Lucan—continue to influence the way we think about poetry. In one sense, it is heartening that critics like Professor Perloff have per-

sisted in discussing the issues raised by Aristotle. Such discussion
testifies to the willingness of writers and readers in our time to
address the question, What is Poetry?—a question for which
there is no absolute answer, but which is no less important for
that fact.

In another sense, it is disappointing to see the *Poetics* put to uses
of which its author probably would not have approved. Aristotle
believed no less firmly than Plato that measure is a fundamental
need of the human spirit and that one of the purposes of poetry is
to answer this need. As Aristotle says in *Rhetoric* 3.8.2–3, "that
which is unlimited is unpleasant and unknowable. Now all things
are limited by number, and the number belonging to the form of
diction is rhythm, of which the metres are divisions." Whether
one agrees or disagrees with Aristotle's contention that poetry can
be properly defined as mimetic, and whether one agrees or disagrees with his contention that it is wrong to identify poetry
simply with meter, one should remember that the rhythms of
prose and the meters of poetry are givens in Aristotle's view of
literary composition. If we forget this in reading the *Poetics,* we do
so to our own confusion.

This last point is important today, when so little poetry is
metrical and when—to judge from contemporary criticism—so
few critics understand the nature and function of meter or why
poets ever wrote in it. This situation not only limits the contemporary practice of poetry; it signals a sharp decline in our ability to
appreciate the poetry of earlier ages.

It may have been with such considerations in mind that J. V.
Cunningham, in his essay "The Quest for the Opal," explained
his reasons for writing his poem, "For My Contemporaries."
Cunningham describes as the subject of the poem "the generally
received distinction between poetry and verse," a distinction
which he characterizes as follows: "Verse is a professional activity,
social and objective, and its methods and standards are those of
craftsmanship. It is a concern of the ordinary human self. . . . But

poetry is amateurish, religious, and eminently unsociable. It dwells in the spiritual life, in the private haunts of theology or voodoo."[83]

Cunningham recognized that we live in an age in which much "poetry" lacks the virtues of "verse." He appreciated (and wrote eloquently about) the irrational factors that often enter into poetic composition. He was, however, disturbed by the narrow, sloppy writing that frequently results from an exclusive devotion to these factors. And because he hoped that poets might recover a respect for "verse" and for skillful and conscientious metrical composition, it is appropriate to close this chapter with his poem:

> How time reverses
> The proud at heart!
> I now make verses
> Who aimed at art.
>
> But I sleep well.
> Ambitious boys
> Who big lines swell
> With spiritual noise,
>
> Despise me not,
> And be not queasy
> To praise somewhat:
> Verse is not easy.
>
> But rage who will.
> Time that procured me
> Good sense and skill
> Of madness cured me.[84]

CHAPTER 4

Free Verse
and Aestheticism

When advocating free verse, the modern movement's leaders sometimes urge that each poem is an autonomous, self-contained entity and that each poem should therefore be free to establish its own individual mode of versification. For example, William Carlos Williams urges, "A poem is a complete little universe. It exists separately"[1]; likewise, discussing versification and his theory of the "variable foot," he suggests that "measure varies with the idiom by which it is employed and the tonality of the individual poem."[2] On occasion this concept is supplemented with the related concept that poetic structure should not be imposed from outside the poem, but should grow organically from within it. Explaining why he and his co-revolutionaries adopted free verse, Eliot states, as was noted earlier, that the medium represented "an insistence upon the inner unity which is unique to every poem, against the outer unity which is typical"; he adds, "The poem comes before the form, in the sense that a form grows out of the attempt of somebody to say something" (*OPP,* 37). And frequently the idea that each poem is its own universe—and may thus have its own measure—is accompanied by the argument that poetic composition should aim for a musical freedom from verbal prosody. Speaking of *vers libre* and suggesting that the resources of conventional meter are too restricted, Pound says, "The movement of poetry is limited only by the nature of syllables and of articulate sound, and by the laws of music, or melodic rhythm" (*LE,* 93).

The preceding statements recall ideas about poetry and art that were first clearly articulated in the eighteenth century. To be more specific, the statements reflect the theory of "Aesthetics" which was invented and elaborated during that crucial period and which held that the fine arts had their own special sphere of activity and that the individual artist composed by means of a freely creative imagination. Obviously, the pioneers of aesthetics, such as Alexander Gottlieb Baumgarten, Kant, Friedrich Schelling, and Coleridge, did not advocate *vers libre.* They elevated poetry and the arts, however, to the status of autonomous pursuits, and they stressed not only the role of the imaginative faculty in the creation of art, but also suggested that the nature of the imagination was essentially subjective and independent of the mind's rational and moral faculties. In addition, they and those who later built on their speculations sometimes suggested that poems and works of art were, at their best, organically or musically independent of mechanical convention. Originally entertained in theory only, these ideas are in the modern movement applied in practice to versification. As a result, rather than versifying with reference to objective principles, many poets approach versification as a subjective matter. This approach is exemplified by Ford, who says in his lecture on *vers libre:* "The only verse-canon . . . of vers libre is to have no other verse canon than that the phrases, the cadences and the paragraphs shall satisfy the intimate ear of the writer himself" (*CW,* 161).

This chapter examines this development. It examines the influence of "Aestheticism" on modern poetry and versification. It may be advisable to stress that the term is intended to indicate here not simply or even principally the doctrine of art for art's sake. The term is meant to indicate the much deeper and more general conviction, shared by many modern writers of otherwise different persuasions, that poetry is a subjective and self-determining enterprise. The term "Romanticism," it should be added, is at once too narrow and too broad for our purposes. It is too narrow because one thinks, rightly or wrongly, of the Romantic movement as having spent its energies by the middle of the nineteenth century, whereas Aestheticism exerts an obvious influence through the modern period. And Romanticism is too broad a term because it denotes a complex phenomenon, of which Aestheticism is only one aspect; indeed, there are other elements in the Romantic movement that could be rightly called anti-aesthetic. Furthermore, aesthetics grows out of a philosophical tradition as much as it does out of the Romantic movement in the arts.

It should also be said that the modern movement is, like the Romantic movement, a complex phenomenon. In challenging Romantic and Victorian predecessors and in adopting free verse, the modern movement's leaders are partly rejecting earlier attitudes towards poetry, including some attitudes shaped by Aestheticism. This chapter does not aim to contend that the modern movement is exclusively "Aesthetic." It aims rather to point out the contributions of the Aesthetic tradition to free verse.

1. The Background of Aestheticism

Aesthetics, the study of Beauty as the special property of the Fine Arts and of Taste as the special faculty which judges their products, is a recent discipline. The term itself was not coined until Baumgarten used it in his *Philosophical Meditations Pertaining to Poetry,* which was Baumgarten's doctoral dissertation for the University of Halle and which was published in 1735. Though derived from *aisthētikos,* the Greek term means merely "sensory" or "perceptual." This meaning is illustrated in *Timaeus* 67, in Socrates' discussion of hearing and sight: "The third organ of perception (*aisthētikon*) within us which we have to describe in our survey is that of hearing. . . . We have still remaining a fourth kind of sensation (*aisthētikon*), which we must divide up seeing that it embraces numerous varieties, which, as a whole, we call 'colours'."

Also recent is perhaps the most basic assumption of aesthetics, namely, that the individual fine arts share characteristics that make it possible to analyze them collectively. One finds comparisons of the arts as early as Simonides' remark (Plutarch, *Moralia,* 346f) that painting is silent poetry and poetry painting that speaks. However, as Paul Oskar Kristeller points out in his brilliant paper "The Modern System of the Arts," a philosophy of the fine arts not only did not exist until the eighteenth century, but probably was not possible until that time.[3] Because the ancients held manual labor in low esteem, the visual arts of sculpture, painting, and architecture did not enjoy consistent prestige in antiquity. This situation extended through the Middle Ages, when the visual arts were excluded from the scheme of the seven liberal arts, which consisted of the mathematical "Quadrivium" arts of arithmetic, astronomy, geometry, and music, and of the literary "Trivium" arts of rhetoric, dialectic, and grammar. Because of its association with mathematics, music was highly prized by the Greeks and remained so later. It was respected primarily, however, for its theoretical and numerical properties rather than for properties related to its performance; indeed, in the medieval classification of the liberal arts, music is placed in the Quadrivium, the division of studies which we today would think of as being more "scientific" than "aesthetic." Poetry is esteemed in antiquity, though it is closely connected with rhetoric and oratory, and poetry is not given, as rhetoric is, full status among the medieval liberal arts. This indicates poetry's sometimes shaky position in the Middle Ages, as does St. Thomas's characterization of poetry (*Summa Theologiae*, 1.1.9) as "the lowest among all intellectual studies" (*infima inter omnes doctrinas*).[4]

With the development of polyphonic music and with the triumphs of the visual arts in the Renaissance, the prestige of what we now call the fine arts increased. Their prestige also increased as a result of invention of the modern concept of genius. Principally developed by Marsilio Ficino and the Florentine Neoplatonists, this concept involved a fusion of the Aristotelian medical concept of melancholia with the Platonic spiritual concept of frenzy. For the ancients, melancholia signified a physiological imbalance, and they regarded frenzy as being produced by an external agency, such as a god or muse. Ficino and others initiated the view that these elements were part of the intrinsic character of the gifted individual. More to the point at hand, genius came to be associated with artistic activity in particular and thus lent special distinction to the artist.[5] In addition, the mechanical aids of printing and engraving and the secularization of music, the performance of which had earlier been tied largely to ceremonial and religious functions, made the arts available to a wider public, and made it possible for that public to think of the arts as related pursuits. By the second half of the eighteenth century, painting, sculpture, architecture, music, and poetry had been gradually grouped together as the fine arts—as arts that, whatever their differences, mutually possessed features that rendered them susceptible to a single comprehensive study.

One must also stress that "aesthetics" grew out of developments in philosophy as much as out of developments in the arts. Baumgarten himself was a student and later a teacher of philosophy (with special interests in poetry and rhetoric), and he used the term to explain a theory of knowledge. Baumgarten took the traditional distinction between thought (*noēsis*) and perception (*aisthēsis*) and argued that the latter had a cognitive value independent of the former and that the sensuous cognition of perception complemented the logical cognition of thought. Baumgarten's intention is clear in his introduction of the term "aesthetics" in the 116th of his *Meditations,* in which he draws a distinction between "*things perceived* [αισθητα] and *things known* [νοητα]" and then comments: "Therefore, *things known* are to be known by the superior faculty as the object of logic; *things perceived* [are to be known by the inferior faculty, as the object] of the science of perception, or aesthetic" (*Sunt ergo* νοητα *cognoscenda facultate superiore obiectum logices,* αισθητα επιστημης αισθητικης *sive AESTHETICAE*).⁶ Baumgarten's *Meditations* and his later *Aesthetica* (1750, 1758) are, to be sure, concerned with art. Yet he conducts his analysis within the context of a larger concern with the nature of knowledge.

This larger philosophical framework is even more crucial in Kant's seminal discussion of aesthetics, which occupies the first half of his *Critique of Judgment* (1790). Kant's arguments about how the mind makes aesthetic judgments are connected with his earlier arguments about how the mind makes sense of the phenomenal world and the moral world. Indeed, the *Critique of Judgment* was conceived partly as a response to a problem raised by his two earlier critiques, the *Critique of Pure Reason* (1781, 2d ed. 1787) and the *Critique of Practical Reason* (1788).

These earlier two critiques endeavor to demonstrate how scientific and moral knowledge are possible independently of an appeal to the speculative metaphysics which had been a central feature of philosophy from St. Thomas's time and the validity of which Kant himself acutely called into question. In his *Critique of Pure Reason*—which is actually more concerned with "Understanding" (*Verstand,* the synthesizing and rational intelligence) than with "Reason" (*Vernunft,* a faculty which is, for Kant, generally more intuitive than logical)—Kant argues that Understanding, aided by the *a priori* concepts of space and time and by categories like quality, quantity, and modality, unifies its perceptions of miscellaneous sensation into a coherent view of the world of Nature. In Kant's view, this world is literally "phenomenal." It is a world of sense appearances, rather than a supersensible "noumenal" world of essential properties. This phenomenal world of Nature can be known and understood, Kant contends, only insofar as it is interpreted according to the law of cause and effect.

In his second critique, the *Critique of Practical Reason,* Kant argues that Reason, by means of "categorical imperatives," relates the mind to noumena that comprise the spiritual substratum of phenomenal nature. These categorical imperatives, such as "Act as if the principle by which you act were about to be turned into a Universal Law of Nature," have no connection with the causal order of the phenomenal world. We cannot logically justify, Kant suggests, categorical imperatives. Reason (here again we must remind ourselves that Kant uses the word, as Coleridge often does, to indicate the mind's intuitive capacity) simply must experience them and assent to their validity. By this means alone, spiritual knowledge and ethical conduct are possible.

The two *Critiques* thus divide the theoretical philosophy that addresses the empirical world of nature from the practical philosophy that addresses the spiritual and ethical world of free will and moral choice. As Kant puts it, "Understanding and reason, therefore, have two distinct jurisdictions over one and the same territory of experience. But neither can interfere with the other. For the concept of freedom just as little disturbs the legislation of nature, as the concept of nature influences legislation through the concept of freedom."[7]

This division implies that moral life has no grounding in empirical Nature and that, conversely, empirical Nature is alien to morality or spirituality. Moreover, the division clouds the status of moral choice: moral choice is meaningful only insofar as it manifests an effect, through the human will, in the phenomenal world. In one respect, then, the two *Critiques* intensify that separation of Mind and Matter, of Subjective Will and Objective World, that had been suggested by Descartes in his *Meditations*.[8]

Kant appreciated this difficulty. And though he had originally intended to write only two *Critiques,* he undertook a third *Critique* designed in part to resolve the problem raised by the first two. In this third work, the *Critique of Judgment,* Kant argues that *Urteilskraft*—"the power of judging," specifically the power of making aesthetic and teleological judgments—mediates between the faculty that deals with the empirical world and the faculty that deals with the moral world. Kant states that "judgement is intermediate between understanding and reason. . . . [I]t will effect a transition from the faculty of pure knowledge, i.e., from the realm of concepts of nature, to that of the concept of freedom, just as in its logical employment it makes possible the transition from understanding to reason" (*CJ,* 17).

Yet Kant's third *Critique* does not so much illustrate the ways in which Judgment mediates between Understanding and Reason as it illustrates the way in which Judgment is in its turn different from those faculties. If the first two *Critiques* left man as, in Kant's formulation, a citizen of two worlds, the third left him as a citizen of three. For just as Kant's first two *Critiques* imply a separation of the Good (Moral Reason) from the True (Scientific Understanding), so his third *Critique* implies a separation of the Beautiful (Judgment) from the True and the Good.

Part of the problem is that Judgment in general and aesthetic

Judgment in particular can claim no philosophical legitimacy. Kant regards philosophy as being comprised of two traditional branches, the theoretical and the practical, and these are occupied respectively by Understanding and Reason. Judgment can mediate between them, but that is all. Similarly—and this is more directly relevant to our concerns—poetry and art can function only in a mediating capacity. According to Kant, they can aid empirical Understanding by diverting, relaxing, and civilizing it. They can aid Moral Reason by creating "symbols" to represent its truths. But the idea that Aristotle, in the ninth chapter of the *Poetics,* so casually and hearteningly advances—the idea that a poem can in its own distinctive manner embody theoretical and practical insight—is not possible for Kant.

The consequences of Kant's view for poetry may be seen in the *Critique of Judgment*'s fifty-third chapter:

> *Poetry* (which owes its origin almost entirely to genius and is least willing to be led by precepts or example) holds the first rank among all the arts. It expands the mind by giving freedom to the imagination. . . . It invigorates the mind by letting it feel its faculty—free, spontaneous, and independent of determination by nature—of regarding and estimating nature as phenomenon in the light of aspects which nature of itself does not afford us in experience, either for sense or understanding, and of employing it accordingly in behalf of, and as a sort of schema for, the supersensible. It plays with semblance, which it produces at will, but not as an instrument of deception; for its avowed purpose is merely one of play.
>
> (*CJ,* 1.191–92)

Though poetry, thus construed, has great liberty, it lacks direct relevance to the world of empirical fact and ethics. Intrinsically it is merely "play" (*spiel*). It involves the spontaneous, and, as Kant says elsewhere, the "self-active" or "self-determining" (*selbsttätig*) Power of Imagination (*Einbildungskraft*).

If poetry is spontaneous play, the question arises: Is the poet at liberty to abandon convention? Or, to phrase the matter in terms related to our subject, is the poet free to abandon meter? Remarkable as it may appear, Kant in 1790 recognizes this implication of aesthetics—that is, of a view that treats art as separate from Understanding and Reason. In the *Critique*'s forty-third chapter, in the course of distinguishing art from handicraft, Kant grapples with this implication. Though art is fundamentally free (*freie*) and involves play, this does not mean, Kant argues, that art may dispense with rules; and he illustrates his opinion by referring to the art of poetry and its rules of metrics. Somewhat in the manner of Renaissance critics who contended that imitation rather than meter was the soul of poetry, but who still urged that meter was the body necessary to the manifestation of the soul's operations, Kant urges that the soul of art must be free, but that the soul still requires technical embodiment and governance to manifest and preserve itself:

> It is not amiss, however, to remind the reader of this: that in all free arts something of a compulsory character is still required, or, as it is called, a *mechanism*, without which the *soul*, which in art must be *free*, and which alone gives life to the work, would be bodyless and evanescent (e.g. in the poetic art [*der Dichtkunst*] there must be correctness and wealth of language, likewise prosody and metre [*die Prosodie und das Silbenmass*, "syllable-measure"]). For not a few leaders of a newer school believe that the best way to promote a free art is to sweep away all restraint, and convert it from labour into mere play (*blosses Spiel*)."
>
> (*CJ*, 1.164)

The difficulty with this argument is that Kant himself pronounces poetry to be a matter of "play." He says this not only in the passage from the fifty-third chapter already cited, but also in another passage in the same chapter of the *Critique*, in which he contrasts the candor and freedom of poetry with the utilitarian calculations of rhetoric, and praises poetry precisely for being *blosses unterhaltendes Spiel*, "mere entertaining play." Kant says,

"In poetry everything is straight and above board. It shows its hand: it desires to carry on a mere entertaining play with the imagination" (*CJ*, 1.193). It is possible to contend that if they are to have meaning, play requires some regulation and poetry requires the legislation of metric. Frost was in effect adopting such a position when he objected that writing free verse was like playing tennis without a net. Kant, however, does not make this argument; in any case, given his emphasis on spontaneity, the argument might not carry the weight it would in a context in which art was regarded as involving normative procedure no less than free expression.

Kant thus elevates and limits poetry. Mixing metaphors, one might say that he crowns it with liberty while painting it into a corner. He can extricate poetry by appealing to its relations with Understanding and Reason. Yet these relations are tenuous; and if they are lost—and if the aesthetic faculty's connections to the mind's other faculties are diminished—poetry is left in utter, if majestic, isolation.

Coleridge is acknowledged to be the writer who, more than any other, brought Kantian aesthetics into poetic theory.[9] Much of Coleridge's thinking about poetry is indebted to Kant, with crucial assistance being supplied as well by Schelling. Schelling is important for this reason: though following Kant in many respects, Schelling rejects in his *System of Transcendental Idealism* (1800) Kant's division of the realms of nature and freedom. He argues instead that all reality is vitally interconnected. There exists both in the external world of nature and in the internal world of free will, Schelling urges, a *natura naturans,* a "naturing nature," whose power allows for the interpenetration and identification of matter and mind. Schelling further urges that it is aesthetic intuition that most securely unites the realms of nature and mind. Though this idea is a variation on Kant's argument that Judgment can mediate between Understanding and Reason, aesthetic intuition is, in Schelling's view, not contingent upon

these other realms, but co-exists with them and, by its very operations, fuses their evidently disparate operations. This view is anticipated and made clear when Schelling says of aesthetic
intuition:

> The postulated intuition [*Anschauung*] should comprehend what
> exists separated in the appearance of freedom and in the intuition of
> the product of nature, namely, *identity of conscious and unconscious in
> the ego* and *consciousness of this identity*. The product of this intuition
> will thus be contiguous on the one side with the product of nature
> and on the other side with the product of freedom, and it will have to
> unite within itself the characteristics of both.[10]

Coleridge adopts Schelling's theory that external Nature and
internal Consciousness are essentially related. Arguing for a more
integrated concept of the mind than Kant could supply, Coleridge
states, in the twelfth chapter of his *Biographia Literaria*: "For as
philosophy is neither a science of the reason or understanding
only, nor merely a science of morals, but the science of BEING
altogether, its primary ground can be neither merely speculative
or merely practical, but both in one."[11] Coleridge suggests, as
Schelling had, that the subjective mind (with its moral and spiritual perceptions) and the objective world of external nature share
a common essence; he suggests as well that the subjective mind, in
moments of "self-intuition," can recognize that this essence is in
fact in itself and a property of itself. "The theory of natural philosophy would . . . be completed," says Coleridge of science,
"when all nature was demonstrated to be identical in essence with
that, which in its highest known power exists in man as intelligence and self-consciousness" (*BL,* 1 : 256). Developing this idea,
Coleridge points out that the fact that we so naturally accept the
reality of the external world—the fact that we accept it as naturally as we accept our own reality—must indicate that the external world partakes of and corresponds to something within us:

> [That] the existence of things without us, which from its nature
> cannot be immediately certain should be received as blindly and as

independently of all grounds as the existence of our own being, the transcendental philosopher can solve only by the supposition, that the former [objective nature] is unconsciously involved in the latter [subjective mind]; that it is not only coherent but identical, and one and the same thing with our own immediate self-consciousness.

(*BL,* 1 : 260)

Though in the *Biographia* Coleridge acutely and confidently argues for a transcendental unity of subject and object and of spirit and matter, in his later "On Poesy or Art" he raises the problem again and, in resolving it, intimates that he is not wholly satisfied with the resolution:

For of all we see, hear, feel and touch the substance is and must be in ourselves; and therefore there is no alternative in reason between the dreary (and thank heaven! almost impossible) belief that every thing around us is but a phantom, or that the life which is in us is in them likewise.[12]

For Coleridge it is the Imagination that insures, confirms, or demonstrates the identification of subjective and objective realms. Like Kant's faculty of Judgment, Coleridge's Imagination mediates between the domain of the spirit and the domain of the external world. But Coleridge's Imagination does more than Kant's Judgment. More like Schelling's aesthetic intuition, it has a fusing and creative capacity of its own. This is most evident in Coleridge's definition, in the *Statesman's Manual,* of the imagination as:

that reconciling and mediatory power, which incorporating reason [i.e., the morally and spiritually intuitive faculty as opposed to the "understanding" which examines phenomenal nature] in images of the sense, and organizing (as it were) the flux of the senses by the permanence and self-circling energies of the reason, gives birth to a system of symbols, harmonious in themselves, and consubstantial with the truths of which they are the conductors.[13]

The same view appears to underlie Coleridge's famous remark, in the thirteenth chapter of the *Biographia,* about the Secondary

Imagination. The Primary Imagination is that instinctive mental faculty that mainly absorbs impressions from various sources and integrates them into a coherent picture of the world; it is "the Living Power and prime Agent of all human Perception." The Secondary Imagination, in contrast, is the more freely active and poetic faculty that creatively mediates and builds and unifies; it is that faculty that "dissolves, diffuses, dissipates, in order to re-create; or where this process is rendered impossible, yet still at all events it struggles to idealize and to unify" (*BL,* 1 : 304).

Coleridge's remarkable attempt to find a way out of the Kantian bind would appear, however, to produce a bind of its own. One is reluctant to criticize so serious and so rich an analysis of such difficult philosophical issues. Yet at the same time one may feel that Coleridge gives objectivity to the processes of the internal mind by subjectifying external nature. In Coleridge's analysis, subject and object are related, but they are related by a process in which the former seems to swallow up the latter. External nature is connected to internal mind, but is connected on the principle that it is basically, to use Coleridge's term, a *"husk"* (*BL,* 1 : 256) that conceals an internal essence that is also a property of the mind.

This idea leads Coleridge to the position that the artist should not so much deal with the phenomenal world as break through to and render the noumenal world. As he puts it in his "On Poesy or Art" essay,

> If the artist copies the mere nature, the *natura naturata,* what idle rivalry! . . . Believe me, you must master the essence, the *natura naturans,* which presupposes a bond between nature in the higher sense and the soul of man. . . . The artist must imitate that which is within the thing, that which is active through form and figure, and discourses to us by symbols—the *Natur-geist,* or spirit of nature.[14]

The task of the mind thus becomes that of piercing through nature to discover the essence within it. It is this task that Ahab

sets himself in *Moby Dick,* and it is the danger of such an enterprise that Melville dramatizes so grippingly. Treating nature as a
cryptic text and believing the whale to be an embodiment of
mystic malignity, Ahab goes mad. Starbuck pleads with him to
entertain the possibility that the animal is merely a "dumb brute,"
but the Captain responds: "Hark ye yet again,—the little lower
layer. All visible objects, man, are but as pasteboard masks. . . . If
a man will strike, strike through the mask!" [15] What Ahab finally
discovers behind the mask is nothingness and death, and his quest
ends in his destruction and that of his whole crew, save Ishmael.
What Coleridge's analysis of the mind and art appears to encourage is a turning away from the common phenomenal world of
external nature to a kind of symbolism or mysticism. And if we
long for a philosophy of mind and of art that supports both an
allegiance to the phenomenal world to which we have access and a
respect for the noumenal realm which we only dimly and imper-
fectly intuit, we may feel that Coleridge's analysis is, for all its
brilliance, imbalanced.

Kant and Coleridge influence much subsequent thinking
about poetry. However, later writers tend to distinguish the aesthetic faculty from the mind's other faculties without realizing, as
had Kant and Coleridge, the dangers of this distinction. If Kant
and Coleridge made the distinction, it was with the awareness
that it was important not to allow the distinction to pass into
outright segregation; it was crucial, they felt, to try to discover
and maintain connections between the aesthetic faculty and the
other faculties. For Kant, and to a great extent for Coleridge, the
study of aesthetics and the Imagination is continually referred to
the larger issue of finding a sound and integrated explanation of
human consciousness and knowledge. Over the course of the
nineteenth century, however, aesthetics is gradually separated
from its philosophical moorings and turned into an independent
theory of creativity. As a result, many poets simply assert the
power of the unfettered poetic imagination without realizing the
assertion's wider implication—that an unfettered imagination

may be a solipsistic imagination and that a poet liberated from normative procedures is possibly a poet cut off from the empirical and ethical world.

In addition, later writers tend to take the idea that the aesthetic faculty mediates between Understanding and Reason to mean that the aesthetic faculty is superior to both. One sees this tendency, for example, in Emerson's "The Poet" (1842–43), in which Emerson argues: "[T]he Universe has three children . . . which we will call here, the Knower, the Doer, and the Sayer. These stand respectively for the love of truth, for the love of good, and for the love of beauty. . . . The poet is the sayer, the namer, and represents beauty. He is a sovereign and stands on the centre" (*EL,* 449). So, too, in "The Poetic Principle" (ca. 1848), Poe states in Kantian fashion that aesthetic taste lies between Understanding and Moral Reason and, in Kantian fashion, he identifies poetry with aesthetic taste. But unlike Kant, he sharply severs the connections between poetry and the empirical and moral realms:

> Just as the Intellect concerns itself with Truth, so Taste informs us of the Beautiful while the Moral Sense is regardful of Duty. . . .
>
> To recapitulate, then:—I would define, in brief, the Poetry of words as *The Rhythmical Creation of Beauty.* Its sole arbiter is Taste. With the Intellect or with the Conscience, it has only collateral relations. Unless incidentally, it has no concern whatever either with Duty or with Truth.
>
> (*ER,* 76, 78)[16]

Similarly, in his preface to *The Renaissance* Walter Pater urges that those who appreciate aesthetic impressions should not worry about relating them to the world of truth or practical experience, since these worlds are irrelevant to aesthetics: "[H]e who experiences these impressions strongly, and drives directly at the discrimination and analysis of them, has no need to trouble himself with the abstract question what beauty is in itself, or what its exact relation to truth or experience—metaphysical questions, as unprofitable as metaphysical questions elsewhere. He may pass them all by as being, answerable or not, of no interest to him." [17] Pater's remark is especially telling because it reveals how aesthetics, which originated in part as a response to metaphysical questions in philosophy, was not only separated from its original context, but also placed in direct opposition to that context.

In much the same spirit, George Santayana in his *Nature of Beauty* (1896), says: "Science is the response to the demand for information, and in it we ask for the whole truth and nothing but the truth. Art is the response to the demand for entertainment, for the stimulation of our senses and imagination, and truth enters into it only as it subserves these ends. . . . Morality has to do with the avoidance of evil and the pursuit of good: aesthetics only with enjoyment" (*CTSP*, 698, 706). A good deal of the aesthetic tradition is summed up by Benedetto Croce, who edited Baumgarten's *Meditations* and *Aesthetica*. Croce's own *Aesthetic as a Science of Expression and General Linguistic* (1902) looks back to Baumgarten and ahead to the associational and imagistic literature of our time:

> Knowledge has two forms: it is either intuitive knowledge or logical knowledge; knowledge obtained through the imagination or knowledge obtained through the intellect; knowledge of the individual or knowledge of the universal; of individual things or of the relations between them: it is, in fact, productive either of images or of concepts.
>
> (*CTSP*, 727)

In general, these juxtapositions comprise, Croce says, "[t]he difference between a scientific work and a work of art, that is, between an intellectual fact and an intuitive fact" (*CTSP*, 727–28).

In many ways, reactions against Aestheticism reinforce its tendencies. This is not as paradoxical as it sounds. Central to much literary theory in earlier periods is the belief that the Good, the

True, and the Beautiful are aspects of a single quality of Being or are qualities capable of being reconciled among themselves. Once Goodness, Truth, and Beauty are separated, however, and once poetry becomes identified with Beauty, those who object to this identification tend to stress poetry's potential connections with Goodness or with Truth, to the exclusion of its connections with Beauty. One reductive view, that is, is attacked with another. The frequency with which this happens in the middle and second half of the nineteenth century will be clear to any student who reads an anthology of the period's literary criticism. On one page, he will find a Marx insisting that the function of imaginative literature is the ethical and utilitarian one of convincing its audience of the legitimacy of "correct" ideology. On another page, he will find a Zola insisting that the function of imaginative literature is the scientific one of embodying documentary truth. On a third page, he will find a Pater insisting that the function of imaginative literature is the formal one of creating objects whose structural harmony will provide intense pleasure to those who contemplate them. Superficially, these approaches are different. At a deeper level, each reflects the same identification of literature exclusively with either the Good or the True or the Beautiful.[18]

2. *Autonomous Poetry,*
Autonomous Poet

For much of literary history, writers argue that poetry requires both native gift and craftsmanly training. This is true even of writers like "Longinus" and Sidney, who stress the indispensability of innate endowment. "Longinus" remarks (2.3) that "the very fact that in literature some effects come of natural genius alone can only be learnt from art"; and, having repeated the proverb that an orator is made, a poet born, Sidney observes,

"Yet confesse I alwayes that, as the firtilest ground must bee manured, so must the highest flying wit have a *Dedalus* to guide him. That *Dedalus,* they say, both in this and in other [arts], hath three wings to beare it selfe up into the ayre of due commendation: that is, Arte, Imitation, and Exercise."[19]

In the last two centuries, however, many writers have urged that the poet is free to write as he pleases, even if this means disregarding the conventions of art, the standards of earlier masterworks, and the precepts of traditional craft. A poem, according to this view, expresses the individual poet and should be judged solely in light of its own properties. What may be most significant is that even modern writers who are impatient with amateurishness (e.g., Pound and Eliot) nevertheless often adopt this view. This circumstance indicates something of the protean and almost hypnotic nature of the aesthetic doctrine of artistic autonomy: the doctrine finds powerful advocates among those who are in many ways not sympathetic to it.

Both Kant and Coleridge endeavor to defend conventional craft, especially metric, while at the same time stressing the freedom of the aesthetic or imaginative faculty. As has been noted, Kant insists that meter is necessary even to aesthetically "free" poetry. Coleridge takes much the same position when, in the *Biographia,* he reflects on "the *origin* of meter" and argues that the poet needs meter to express effectively the passions that are sometimes felt to be opposed to its laws:

> This ["the *origin* of metre"] I would trace to the balance in the mind effected by that spontaneous effort which strives to hold in check the workings of passion. It might be easily explained likewise in what manner this salutary antagonism is assisted by the very state, which it counteracts; and how this balance of antagonists became organized into *metre* (in the usual acceptation of that term) by a supervening act of the will and judgement, consciously and for the foreseen purpose of pleasure.
>
> (*BL,* 2:64)

Arguing that "the *elements* of metre owe their existence to a state of increased excitement," and that meter mediates between impulse and volition, Coleridge continues:

> [T]hese elements are formed into metre *artificially*, by a *voluntary* act, with the design and for the purpose of blending *delight* with emotion, so the traces of present *volition* should throughout the metrical language be proportionally discernible. Now these two conditions must be reconciled and co-present. There must be not only a partnership, but a union; an interpenetration of passion and of will, of *spontaneous* impulse and *voluntary* purpose.
>
> (*BL*, 2:65)

To put the matter in philosophical terms, Coleridge argues that meter beneficially links will (a property of moral reason and choice) with feeling (a property of the aesthetic or Imaginative faculty). Though he defends the independence of genius, he insists that it is meter that enables genius to speak comprehensively.

Other writers in the aesthetic tradition, however, merely assert the autonomy of genius and reject the idea that rules may be valuable aids to genius. For instance, Friedrich Schlegel says, "Romantic poetry is a progressive universal poetry. . . . It alone is infinite, as it alone is free; and as its first law it recognizes that the arbitrariness of the poet endures no law above him."[20] Blake contends that it is foolish to make rules for art because "[e]very eye sees differently. As the eye, such the object," and because the true artist is by definition infallible: "Genius has no error; it is ignorance that is error" (*CTSP*, 403, 408). Emerson asserts that the poet, as the representer of beauty, has an imperial freedom from external standards: "For the world is not painted, or adorned, but is from the beginning beautiful; and God has not made some beautiful things, but Beauty is the creator of the universe. Therefore the poet is not any permissive potentate, but is emperor in his own right" (*EL*, 449).

Leading experimentalists in verse also sound this theme. Walt

Whitman, for example, says of the poet: "He is a seer—he is individual—he is complete in himself. . . . He is not one of the chorus—he does not stop for any regulation—he is the president of regulation."[21] In a more moderate vein, Wallace Stevens comments on his own work, "There is such a complete freedom now-a-days [Stevens writes in 1938] in respect to technique that I am rather inclined to disregard form so long as I am free and can express myself freely."[22] Discussing prosody, Williams offers the observation (which was cited earlier): "I have never been one to write by rule, even by my own rules" (*SL,* 325).

Just as Aestheticism encourages the view that the poet is above rules, so Aestheticism encourages the view that poetry's chief aim should be to escape the constraints of the phenomenal world. Hegel says in his *Philosophy of Fine Art:* "Poetry is, in short, the universal art of the mind, which has become essentially free, and which is not fettered in its realization to an externally sensuous material, but which is creatively active in the space and time belonging to the inner world of ideas and emotion" (*CTSP,* 530). In a similar spirit, Poe praises Tennyson for the reason that the effects of his poems are "at all times, the most ethereal—in other words, the most elevating and the most pure. No poet is so little of the earth, earthy" (*ER,* 92). Finally, Arthur Symons, in his influential *Symbolist Movement in Literature,* characterizes symbolism as "an attempt to spiritualise literature, to evade the old bondage of rhetoric, the old bondage of exteriority."[23]

Though rebelling against the diction and subjects of nineteenth-century verse, the modern movement's leaders stress, no less than do their predecessors, that poetry is autonomous. Sounding surprisingly Paterian, Williams writes: "Let the metaphysical take care of itself, the arts have nothing to do with it" (*SE,* 256). Likewise, Eliot writes, "I have assumed as axiomatic that a creation, a work of art, is autotelic" (*SE 1917–32,* 19). Moreover, his well-known statement, "Poetry is a superior amusement"[24] bears testimony to a line of thought that extends all the way back to the fifty-third-chapter of the *Critique of Judgment,* as does Stevens' remark, "Poetry creates a fictitious existence on an exquisite plane."[25]

To say that poetry exists in a realm of its own is not necessarily to say that meter should be abandoned. Yet meter's rules are not individual but comprehensive: they ask the same obedience and offer the same rewards to all poets. This quality brings meter into conflict with views which stress the self-sufficiency of the individual poet and poem and with views like Williams' which hold that even private legislation is not to interfere with the poet.

3. From Organic Form to Free Verse

Because scholars have explored extensively the emergence in the Romantic movement of an organic theory of poetry, it will suffice for us simply to make several points about the early development of the theory before examining its ramifications in modern poetic practice.[26]

Though organicism is one of the most distinctive features of Romantic and modern criticism, analogies between poems and living organisms appear as early as Plato and Aristotle. After complaining of the cleverly misleading disorder of Lysis' speech on love, Socrates says in *Phaedrus* 264c that "every discourse must be organised, like a living being (*zōon*), with a body of its own, as it were, so as not to be headless or footless, but to have a middle and members, composed in fitting relation to each other and to the whole." Urging that tragic plots should exhibit a well-proportioned unity, Aristotle says in *Poetics* 1450b34ff.: "[S]ince the beautiful, whether a living creature (*zōon*) or anything that is composed of parts, should not only have these in a fixed order to one another but also possess a definite size which does not depend on chance . . . so with plots: they should have length, but such that they are easy to remember."

The Greek words *organon* and *organikos,* from which we derive our word "organic," indicate both natural organs of bodies and crafted implements like surgical and musical instruments. For at least some of the earlier Romantics, "organic" retains its original meaning of "organized" or "instrumental" and denotes that which is constituted in orderly fashion to fulfill a function. As long as this meaning of the term informed organic theories of poetry, and as long as poets remained observant of the fact that nature tends to operate in an orderly fashion and to create according to basic forms and traits, organic theories co-existed with traditional poetic practice.

Goethe illustrates this circumstance. His interest in organicism coincides with his admiration of classical and Renaissance art, precisely for the reason that, in his view, organicism and classical and Renaissance art equally, if differently, confirm the order of the created world. This view directs the analysis which Goethe makes in his *Italian Journal* of Raphael's frescoes in the Vatican and in the Chigi Chapel in Santa Maria della Pace. Goethe discusses in particular those frescoes that are executed in spandrels or in spandrel-like spaces around, beneath, or above arches and doorways, and he urges that the very rigor and skill of the frescoes, fitted to tight and odd spatial requirements, are organically expressive:

> Raphael never let himself become bound by the space left to him by the architect; on the contrary, the fact that he knew how to fill and adorn any kind of space is characteristic of his greatness and of the elegance of his genius. Even the superb paintings of the *Mass at Bolsena,* the *Liberation of St. Peter,* and the *Parnassus* would not have been so indescribably successful without the singular limitation of space. Also here in the *Sibyls* the concealed symmetry, so important in the composition, dominates in the most sublime way; because in the organism of nature (*Organismus der Natur*) as well as in art, the

perfection of expressing the life of life manifests itself within very precise limits.[27]

A further point should be made. Goethe's discussion of art and nature is analogical: nature illuminates art and art nature. The terms are separate. This same separation appears in the influential sixty-fifth chapter of the *Critique of Judgment,* in which Kant examines the similarities between physical organisms and products of human craft. Here Kant argues that, though the products of nature and craft are in some ways similar, works of art are not characterized, as works of nature are, by a reciprocal cause-and-effect relationship of parts and wholes. In natural organisms, parts may be seen as effects contingent on the whole and yet simultaneously as causes producing other parts and contributing to the whole itself. A work of art, on the other hand, is not truly a self-determining end-in-itself. Its creation requires "the causality of the conceptions of external rational agents" (*CJ,* 2.21)—requires, that is, the volitional activity of the artist. Something exterior to the work participates in its creation. Kant summarizes this matter by saying that in a product of nature,

> every part is thought as *owing* its presence to the *agency* of all the remaining parts, and also as existing *for the sake of the others* and of the whole, that is as an instrument (*Werkzeug*), or organ (*Organ*). . . . [T]he part must be an organ *producing* the other parts—each, consequently, reciprocally producing the others. No instrument of art can answer to this description, but only the instrument of that nature from whose resources the materials of every instrument are drawn—even the materials for instruments of art. Only under these conditions and upon these terms can a product be an *organized* and *self-organized being* (*organisiertes und sich selbst organisierendes Wesen*).
>
> (*CJ,* 2.21–22)

In other words, Kant insists that, though nature and art share some qualities, the former involves internal causality and the latter external causality. It is the disappearance of this distinction that accounts for the character of much modern organic verse.

Schelling and Coleridge tend to synthesize the terms that Goethe and Kant distinguish, and thus they prepare the way for modern organic art. Yet Schelling and Coleridge insist, no less than Kant and Goethe do, that nature is formally organized and manifests itself by orderly arrangement. Schelling stresses this point in his discussion, in his *Relation of the Plastic Arts to Nature,* of what we now call organic form:

[I]f form [*Form*] were necessarily restrictive to essence [*Wesen*] it would exist independently of it. But if it exists with and through essence, how could the latter feel restricted by that which it creates itself? Violence might certainly be done to essence by form which was imposed upon it, but never by that which flows out of itself. It is bound rather to rest satisfied in the latter and feel its existence to be autonomous and self-enclosed. Definiteness of form in nature is never a negation but always an affirmation.[28]

The idea that organic expression is formal, and that formal definition is nature-affirming, also appears in Coleridge, most notably in his "Shakespeare's Judgment Equal to his Genius" essay. What is especially interesting in this essay is that Coleridge associates organicism not only with organization in general, but with meter in particular. Shortly before he defines organic form as that which "is innate; it shapes, as it develops, itself from within, and the fullness of its development is one and the same with the perfection of its outward form" (*CTSP,* 462), he says:

The spirit of poetry, like all other living powers, must of necessity circumscribe itself by rules, were it only to unite power with beauty. It must embody in order to reveal itself; but a living body is of necessity an organized one; and what is organization but the connection of parts in and for a whole, so that each part is at once end and means? This is the discovery of criticism; it is a necessity of the human mind; and all nations have felt and obeyed it, in the invention of meter, and measured sounds, as the vehicle and *involucrum* [covering] of poetry, itself a fellow-growth from the same life, even as the bark is to the tree!

(*CTSP,* 462)

For poets like Coleridge and Goethe (and Wordsworth), metrical organization and organic expression do not conflict. Rather, they are part and parcel of the same natural law. Later poets, however, abandon the idea that meter reflects natural order; they also abandon the idea that they are agents of conscious intelligence who produce "naturally" insofar as their works, like nature's, are orderly. Instead many poets see themselves as agents of unconscious generation who produce "naturally" in the sense of expressing mysterious interior processes of growth. The last notion, it perhaps goes without saying, develops partly from the aesthetic concern with subjective, noumenal essences.

Coleridge prepares the shift in organic theory towards subjectivity. For, after having in his Shakespeare essay connected organicism and meter, he continues:

> No work of true genius dares want its appropriate form, neither indeed is there any danger of this. As it must not, so genius cannot, be lawless: for it is even this that constitutes it genius—that of acting creatively under laws of its own origination.

> (*CTSP*, 462)

By associating genius with "living power" and "organic form" (*CTSP*, 462) and in characterizing genius as "acting creatively under laws of its own origination," Coleridge commits himself to a crucial confusion. Natural organisms do not "originate" their own laws. Though they develop from "within," they do not create the principles of that development. These are created by God or a First Cause or a Principle of Matter and Life. An aspen, for instance, does not freely elect, when a seedling, to grow up to be a medium-sized tree with a smooth, light-colored trunk and fine-toothed leaves. To say that the poet originates his own laws is not to connect him with nature, but to abstract him from it. This is in fact what increasingly transpires in later literary theory. Even as poets are praised as being children of nature, they are transformed from natural mortal beings into, in Emerson's phrase, "liberating gods" (*EL,* 462). Nor is it surprising that such a transformation should occur. Once poets are thought to create their own laws, instead of receiving them from the Muses, poets become Muses themselves.

By the middle of the nineteenth century, organicism is often opposed to meter. Emerson's "The Poet" illustrates this opposition. In defining his topic, Emerson says: "For we do not speak now of men of poetical talents, or of industry and skill in metre, but of the true poet" (*EL,* 450). Then Emerson explicitly contrasts organic form with meter:

> For it is not metres, but a metre-making argument, that makes a poem,—a thought so passionate and alive, that, like the spirit of a plant or an animal, it has an architecture of its own, and adorns nature with a new thing.
>
> (*EL,* 450)

Emerson later adds that just as nature is self-sufficient, so is poetry. "This expression, or naming," says Emerson of poetry, "is not art, but a second nature, grown out of the first, as a leaf out of a tree. What we call nature, is a certain self-regulated motion, or change; and nature does all things by her own hands, and does not leave another to baptise her, but baptises herself" (*EL,* 457).

Such arguments recall Keats's observation to John Taylor that "if poetry comes not as naturally as the leaves to a tree it had better not come at all" (*CTSP,* 474). But whereas Keats is objecting to overwrought or labored composition, Emerson is stressing the autonomy of poetic composition, and his remarks have an explicitly anti-metrical slant.

In Whitman, who received the aesthetic tradition through Emerson's essays and Emersonian transcendentalism, one sees organic theory pursued in a prosodic context. In his preface to *Leaves of Grass,* Whitman remarks that the poet's goal is to express himself as nature does: "[T]o speak in literature with the perfect rectitude and insouciance of the movements of animals, and the unimpeachableness of the sentiment of trees in the woods and grass by the roadside, is the flawless triumph of art" (*CPSP,* 577). In the next paragraph, Whitman urges that poets are freely expressive and that "new free forms" are justified because true genius creates its own conventions:

> The old red blood and stainless gentility of great poets will be proved by their unconstraint. A heroic person walks at his ease through and out of that custom or precedent or authority that suits him not. Of the traits of the brotherhood of first-class writers, savans, musicians, inventors and artists, nothing is finer than silent defiance advancing from new free forms. . . . The cleanest expression is that which finds no sphere worthy of itself, and makes one.
>
> (*CPSP,* 578)

The versification of *Leaves of Grass* is anticipated by that of Tupper's *Proverbial Philosophy,* and it is interesting that Tupper refers his compositional procedures to spontaneous organicism. In the fourth and final series of *Proverbial Philosophy* (1876), Tupper casts a retrospective gaze over his "Rhythmics," and he says (writing at this point mostly in fourteeners and not in the looser line that characterizes much of the work):

> They have grown in unpremeditated guise, these weeds
> of my mind's garden,
> Were cut and stored at random, and uncarefully got
> in . . .
> Let truths be frankly spoken, whether critics blame
> or praise;
> These fallows of my brain are rank with thoughts
> uncultured;
> Self-sowing, after many days they yield a bounteous
> crop,
> And ever grow spontaneously, of uninvited impulse,
> Spontaneously, not idly, nor void of earnest
> purpose.[29]

Organicism supports subsequent free verse in several ways. Free verse poets often employ the concept of organic form to indicate that just as some objects in nature grow or flow this way and that, so some poems grow or flow this way and that. Pound, for instance, writes in his "Retrospect" essay:

> I think there is a 'fluid' as well as a 'solid' content, that some poems may have form as a tree has form, some as water poured into a vase. That most symmetrical forms have certain uses. That a vast number of subjects cannot be precisely, and therefore not properly rendered in symmetrical forms.
>
> (*LE,* 9)

A more specific way in which organicism is deployed in defense of free verse is illustrated by D. H. Lawrence's introduction to the American edition of his *New Poems* (1918). Speaking of the free verse poems of which this collection is comprised, Lawrence distinguishes between "gem-like lyrics" and verse of "the immediate present."[30] Identifying free verse with the latter, Lawrence explains:

> There are no gems of the living plasm. The living plasm vibrates unspeakably, it inhales the future, it exhales the past, it is the quick of both, and yet it is neither. . . . The perfect rose is only a running flame, emerging and flowing off, and never in any sense at rest, static, finished. Herein lies its transcendent loveliness.[31]

Because he is writing in 1918, Lawrence is addressing a literary community in which free verse has become common. And his sharpest remarks are directed not against traditional poets but against contemporary free versers who, in his opinion, are mere violators of conventional metric and who fail to appreciate that "in free verse we look for the insurgent naked throb of the instant moment":

> They do not know that free verse has its own *nature,* that it is neither star nor pearl, but instantaneous like plasm. It has no goal in either eternity [i.e. past or future]. It has no finish. It has no satisfying

stability, satisfying to those who like the immutable. None of this. It is the instant; the quick; the very jetting source of all will-be and has-been. The utterance is like a spasm, naked contact with all influences at once. It does not want to get anywhere. It just takes place.[32]

In his belief that poetry should be immediate, Lawrence recalls Kant's emphasis on that quality. In his belief that poetry embodies organic energy, Lawrence recalls Coleridge's statement that the poet deals "in life-producing ideas . . . essentially one with the germinal forces of nature."[33] Much, however, has happened since the time of those earlier writers. Missing from Lawrence is Kant's insistence that, though poetry's effects should be immediate, the poet should obey the laws of meter. Also missing is Coleridge's belief that poetry, though expressing the vitality of nature, nevertheless reveals itself in form.

As Lawrence's remarks indicate, organicism could be employed to validate not only plasmatic free verse in particular, but automatic verse in general. In this respect, one could perhaps pursue this matter as far back as Blake's *Milton,* which Blake professed to have written "from immediate Dictation"[34] and parts of which exhibit no discernible metrical structure. More relevant to our concerns, however, are the systematic programs for automatic free verse that various modern authors have constructed. One such program is André Breton's surrealism, which Breton defines as "[p]ure psychic automatism, by which it is intended to express, verbally, in writing, or by other means, the real process of thought. Thought's dictation, in the absence of all control by the reason and outside all aesthetic or moral preoccupations."[35] If Lawrence's interest in automatic writing is with plasmatically organic processes, Breton's is more with neurologically organic processes. His concern is psychological, and in rushing free verse poems like the title poem of his collection, *L'Union Libre,* he attempts to display the processes of the mind in a freely associational state; for the most part, the varying lengths of the individual associations supply the lengths or "measures" of the individual verses. These differences aside, Lawrence and Breton are working from much the same basis.

Connections between organicism and free verse are also to be found in Williams, who argues that whatever expresses unconscious movement or respiration provides a measure for poetry. Williams writes of the versification of Pound's *Draft of XXX Cantos:* "The measure is an inevitability, an unavoidable accessory after the fact. If one move, if one run, if one seize up material—it cannot avoid having a measure, it cannot avoid a movement which clings to it—as the movement of a horse becomes a part of the rider also" (*SE,* 108). And hailing Vazakas as having discovered a new measure, Williams says of him: "He writes as he breathes" (*TN,* x). Such a theory accords well with the aesthetic doctrine of the autonomous poem. If measure is "an unavoidable accessory after the fact," every utterance will create—indeed will be—its own measure. Such a theory also accords well with the concept of the autonomous poet. If measure is "an inevitability," the poet need not submit to laws of versification. Instead, versification will chase in his wake, so to speak, veering now this way and now that to suit his speech at any given moment.

The notion that free verse expresses breath patterns informs the theory of "COMPOSITION BY FIELD" that Charles Olson develops, in part following Williams and Pound. Olson argues that the poet can precisely register his breath patterns by using the spacebar of his typewriter and the typographic layout of his page, thus informing the reader of the way the poem should be read. Olson says, "It is the advantage of the typewriter that, due to its rigidity and its space precisions, it can, for a poet, indicate exactly the breath, the pauses, the suspensions even of syllables, the juxtapositions even of parts of phrases, which he intends." Significantly, this typewriter-poetry is, as Olson explains it, a kind of automatic writing, and he refers to the typewriter itself as "the personal and instantaneous recorder of the poet's work."[36]

Olson, in addition, voices the aesthetic doctrine that poetry should be organic and autonomous. Indeed, the value of the free

verse poems that result from "COMPOSITION BY FIELD" or "PRO-
JECTIVE VERSE" is, Olson contends, that they possess a spontaneously and autonomously vegetable character:

> The objects which occur at every given moment of composition (of
> recognition, we can call it) are, can be, must be treated exactly as they
> do occur therein and not by any ideas or preconceptions from outside
> the poem, must be handled as a series of objects in field in such a way
> that a series of tensions (which they also are) are made to *hold,* and to
> hold exactly inside the content and the context of the poem which has
> forced itself, through the poet and them, into being.
>
> . . . Let me just throw in this. It is my impression that *all* parts of
> speech suddenly, in composition by field, are fresh for both sound
> and percussive use, spring up like unknown, unnamed vegetables in
> the patch, when you work it, come spring." [37]

According to Olson, "ideas or preconceptions from outside the
poem" cannot be allowed to enter into the poetic process, and the
poet himself is not so much the poem's creator as the passive agent
through which its generative force operates. As for "*all* parts of
speech," they "spring up" into being and assume forms by means
of their own internal laws.

Olson's analysis is interesting and attractive to the extent that it
elucidates the dynamic power of language itself. The analysis also,
however, indicates a logical difficulty in organic theory, at least as
one finds it in some modern writers. Even the most "organic"
literary composition involves volition. The surrealist poet has to
obtain paper and pencil and set the latter to the former before he
can record the psychic processes of his subconscious. The projec-
tivist poet must obtain and sit down at a typewriter before it can
serve as "the personal and instantaneous recorder" of his work.
There is no comparable act of will in the formation and growth of
an orange. The poet who claims to be composing organically thus
misconstrues, at least in one sense, composition and nature alike.

There is another logical difficulty with much free verse organicism. It is related to a matter discussed earlier. Nature does
not produce in free-form fashion. Its products exhibit definite and

predictable formal characteristics. An apple tree tends to have a certain size and shape, and its fruits are quite similar. If the poet is like a tree whose fruits are poems (or like a gardener whose tomatoes, cabbages, and carrots are poems), he presumably more resembles Wyatt writing sonnets, epigrams, and songs than Olson composing *The Maximus Poems*. This is not to criticize Olson or *The Maximus Poems:* while desiring that verse should have a natural rightness or grace, one should perhaps be wary of the idea that poems grow in the way that fruits or vegetables do. Nevertheless, if a poet proposes to follow an organic model, he is naturally compelled, one would think, to some degree of regularity.

Olson also argues that PROJECTIVE VERSE is musical and that the space bar of the poet's typewriter allows the poet to create a kind of musical score that supplies the function formerly supplied by traditional meter. Similarly, Williams contends that the new breath line of Vazakas is musical: "And what neither Whitman nor anyone else envisioned—the poetic line annihilated—Vazakas has invented: a workable expedient to replace it. He has found a *measure* based not upon convention, but upon music for his reliance" (*TN,* xiv).

If, then, Olson and Williams show how organic form has promoted free verse, their remarks also suggest that another component of aestheticism has contributed to the development of a poetry free of conventional metric. This component is the idea that music is the primary art and that all arts should be musically expressive.

4. *The Rise of Music, the Fall of Poetry*

It is understandable that many writers in the aesthetic tradition view music as the primary art. If one regards autonomy as the principal characteristic of art, one will particularly prize music: of all the arts, it is the most autonomous. It is most pure, the most free of extra-aesthetic associations. Poetry, due to its verbal nature, is affiliated with statement. The visual arts traditionally represent external objects. Yet music, especially instrumental music, can elude exterior subject matter. Commenting on the esteem accorded music in the modern period, Sidney Lanier, who urged that versification should be treated in terms of musical notation, says: "[M]usic is the characteristic art-form of the modern time. . . . For music, freed from the stern exactions of the intellect, is also freed from the terrible responsibilities of realism."[38] A similar point is made by Paul Valéry, who, however, distrusts music's influence on the other arts: "Music [is] metapoetry—a projection beyond articulate thought." And speaking of the effect of music on the listener, Valéry adds, "It is this indetermination that is the key of this prestige." (*Musique—métapoésie—dépassement de la pensée articulée. . . . C'est cette indétermination qui est la clef de ce prestige*).[39]

For early writers on aesthetics, poetry rather than music is usually the primary art. However, the relevance of music to the very concept of aesthetics is appreciated readily and, on occasion, uneasily. Kant's comments about music are especially revealing. Assessing the comparative worth of the fine arts, Kant disparages music in such a way as to suggest that he anticipates the manner in which an independent aesthetics might lead to a tyranny of music over the other arts. Because he wishes to relate the fine arts, even as he stresses their independence, to Science and Morals, music assumes for him an equivocal character. On the one hand, Kant recognizes that music possesses, to a singular degree, the aesthetic qualities of immediacy and intensity. "For though it speaks," he says of music, "by means of mere sensations without concepts, and so does not, like poetry, leave behind it any food for reflection, still it moves the mind more diversely, and, although with transient, still with intenser effect" (*CJ,* 1.193–94). On the other hand, Kant realizes that this intense effect cannot be related to the other mental faculties in the way that the effects of poetry and painting can be, and, for this reason, he judges music to have less aesthetic value than poetry and painting.

Kant defends this judgment by appealing to a distinction between two kinds of delight that the arts can produce: a lower delight provided by what is "agreeable" and a higher delight provided by what is "beautiful." Kant urges that music, by its agreeability, "gratifies" our senses. In contrast, poetry and the visual arts, by their beauty, "please" our disinterested observation. About music, Kant concludes:

> It is certainly, however, more a matter of enjoyment than of culture—the play of thought incidentally excited by it being merely the effect of a more or less mechanical association—and it possesses less worth in the eyes of reason than any other of the fine arts. . . . [If] we estimate the worth of the fine arts by the culture they supply to the mind, and adopt for our standard the expansion of the faculties whose confluence, in judgement, is necessary for cognition, music, then, since it plays merely with sensations, has the lowest place among the fine arts—just as it has perhaps the highest among those valued at the same time for their agreeableness.
>
> (*CJ*, 1.194,195)

This discussion suffers from an awkwardness related to that which one meets in Kant's argument that prosodic law is necessary to poetry. If one urges that poetry is spontaneously playful, it is hard to see how one can contend that metric is of more than ancillary significance to it. If one urges that art is nonconceptually immediate, it is hard to see how one can avoid the conclusion that music is the most artistic of the arts. Even if one concedes the point that music is mainly "sensational," the fact remains that music is less obligated to phenomenal appearance—is less obliged to depict a world of substance and action or to examine the objects and agents involved in that world—than either poetry or painting. And even if, in Kant's terms, music only minimally partakes of the Reason which apprehends noumena, music nevertheless suggests noumenal experience more than do its sister arts, a point that Schopenhauer will perceive and stress.

In fairness to Kant, one must say that his position is sustainable as long as aesthetics is seen as one aspect of an integral study of the mind. When aesthetics becomes an independent theory of creativity, however, it becomes increasingly difficult to defend poetry and the visual arts against the assertion that the freer art of music is their superior and that they should emulate it.

Subsequent writers on aesthetics elevate music to preeminence among the arts. Friedrich Schiller and Hegel represent a midpoint in this process. Both value music more than Kant does, though neither argues for its primacy. In the twenty-second of his *Letters on the Aesthetic Education of Man* (1795), Schiller writes, apparently recalling Kant's contention that music too much appeals to the senses: "[T]he most ethereal music has, by virtue of its material, an even greater affinity with the senses than true aesthetic freedom really allows." A few sentences later, however, Schiller suggests that music is the most purely formal of the arts and gives it a central position among the arts: "Music, at its most sublime, must become sheer form and affect us with the serene power of antiquity. The plastic arts, at their most perfect, must become music and move us by the immediacy of their sensuous presence. Poetry, when most fully developed, must grip us powerfully as music does, but at the same time, like the plastic arts, surround us with serene clarity" (*CTSP*, 428–29).

Hegel in his *Philosophy of Fine Art* makes more specific claims for music. Arguing for the ideality of art, he remarks that in music, "sound liberates the ideal content from its fetters in the material substance" (*CTSP*, 529). Furthermore, he pronounces music to be one of the three "subjective" arts, along with poetry and painting, which have ascendency over the inferior "external" art of architecture and the intermediate "objective" art of sculpture. Hegel does not grant music preeminence. In the triad of the superior "subjective" arts, music is above painting but below poetry; poetry is superior in Hegel's view because it more fully allows for the outward manifestion of inward self-consciousness.

Nevertheless, with Hegel music arrives near the top of the scale of the arts.

In the fifty-second chapter of Schopenhauer's *World as Will and Idea* (1819), music achieves preeminence among the arts. For Schopenhauer, music is the art in which Will completely escapes from the world of Idea (the phenomenal world governed by the principle of sufficient reason) and experiences transcendent freedom. Schopenhauer argues that, whereas the other arts are committed to phenomenal appearances, music manifests the underlying noumenal reality of creation:

> [Music] is entirely independent of the phenomenal world, ignores it altogether, could to a certain extent exist if there was no world at all, which cannot be said of the other arts. Music is as *direct* an objectification and copy of the whole *will* as the world itself, nay, even as the Ideas, whose multiplied manifestation constitutes the world of individual things. Music is thus by no means like the other arts, the copy of the Ideas, but the *copy of the will itself,* whose objectivity the Ideas are. This is why the effect of music is so much more powerful and penetrating than that of the other arts, for they speak only of shadows, but it speaks of the thing itself.[40]

And a little later, Schopenhauer reasserts that music "never expresses the phenomenon, but only the inner nature, the in-itself of all phenomena, the will itself."[41]

A great admirer of Schopenhauer, Richard Wagner applies in his operas principles developed by Schopenhauer and other writers in the aesthetic tradition. In Wagnerian "music drama," poetry and visual spectacle are drawn into a super-art under the aegis of music. Wagner's influence on modern poetry is considerable. This influence is indicated by Mallarmé's enthusiastic "Richard Wagner, Revery of French Poet," which appears in Mallarmé's *Divagations*. The influence is indicated as well by Mallarmé's remark in his "Crisis of Verse" essay, also in *Divagations:* "[M]usic meets Verse to form, since Wagner, Poetry" (*la Musique rejoint le Vers pour former, depuis Wagner, la Poésie*).[42]

Wagner's own *Letter on Music* addresses the relationship of poetry and music in a way that prefigures later discussions of the topic. The following passage, which Baudelaire admired and quoted, is especially relevant:

> The rhythmical arrangement and the embellishment (nearly musical) of the rhyme are for the poet the means of guaranteeing the verse, the phrase, a power which captivates as by a charm and governs at its pleasure the sentiment. Essential to the poet, this tendency conducts him to the limit of his art, a limit that touches immediately on music, and, in consequence, the poet's most complete work ought to be that one which, in its final achievement, would be a perfect music.[43]

Wagner's *Letter* calls to mind Pater's famous statement, in his essay on the School of Giorgione, about the place of music in the modern system of the arts: *"All art constantly aspires towards the condition of music."* Several paragraphs later, comparing music and poetry, Pater adds:

> In music, then, rather than in poetry, is to be found the true type or measure of perfected art. Therefore, although each art has its uncommunicable element, its untranslatable order of impressions, its unique mode of reaching the "imaginative reason," yet the arts may be represented as continually struggling after the law or principle of music, to a condition which music alone completely realises.[44]

Music is, according to Pater, not simply the highest art, but art itself. As for verse, it is, in Poe's phrase, "an inferior or less capable Music" (*ER,* 34).

Pater concludes the transition from Kant's position that poetry, in its ability to connect the Aesthetic faculty to Empirical Understanding and Moral Reason, is superior to music, to the position that music, in its ability to free itself of those other faculties, is superior to poetry. And though he is not interested specifically in versification, Pater prefigures indirectly developments in modern poetry in which para-musical structure replaces metrical structure.

5. *Versification as Musical Form*

The belief that music is the primary art, and the art to whose condition poetry should aspire, manifests itself in several ways that affect prosodic practice. At one level, poets desiring musicality seek to make poetry "indefinite" in the way that music is indefinite. Initially, indefiniteness of meaning alone is sought; gradually, however, indefiniteness of measure is sought as well. At another level, poets desiring musicality seek to appropriate for poetic structure the principles of musical notation. Poets urge that words and syllables may be treated as if they were musical notes and that, just as different combinations and numbers of notes may be found in musical bars governed by the same time signature, different combinations and numbers of syllables should be allowed to appear in "identical" poetic feet or lines. At yet another level, poets desiring musicality seek to suggest, by the devices of modern typography, the visual effects of a musical score. Poets dispose letters about the page in such a way as to make their poems look like sheet music. This procedure recalls, in some respects, ancient and Renaissance experiments with pattern or shaped poetry. Yet, as was noted in the introduction, earlier poems that produced visual impressions were also metrical. In contrast, modern poets who attempt to create poems that look like musical scores (or objects such as flowers or neckties) tend to avoid conventional versification.

Before examining these matters more extensively, one should mention two points. First, when certain modern poets seek musicality, their model is customarily instrumental music. These poets want to escape not only from meter, but from the discursive quality of words as words. Second, when the model is not purely instrumental, it is Wagnerian, in the sense that music dominates the words. Modern free verse is thus different from earlier musico-poetical traditions, like that of Greek lyric, in which the verse prosody largely governs or is independent of the rhythm of the music.[45] In modern musical poetry, "music" or "musical measure" is seen as a substitute for poetic meter rather than a complement to it. This is true even when the "music" is purely metaphorical and no actual score accompanies the poetic text.

Many writers in the nineteenth and twentieth century assert that poetry should exhibit musically indefinite meaning. For example, Poe says of Tennyson's "fantasy-pieces" like "The Lady of Shalott":

> If the author did not deliberately propose to himself a suggestive indefinitiveness of meaning, with the view of bringing about a definitiveness of vague and therefore of spiritual *effect*—this, at least, arose from the silent analytical promptings of that poetic genius which, in its supreme development, embodies all orders of intellectual capacity.
>
> I *know* that indefiniteness is an element of the true music—I mean of the true musical expression. Give to it any undue decision— imbue it with any very determinate tone—and you deprive it, at once, of its ethereal, its ideal, its intrinsic and essential character.
>
> (*ER,* 1331)

In a related manner, Pater pronounces "lyrical" verse the most poetic of poetic forms, in virtue of its musical indefiniteness: "[L]yrical poetry, precisely because in it we are least able to detach the matter from the form, without a deduction of something from that matter itself, is, at least artistically, the highest and most complete form of poetry. And the very perfection of such poetry often appears to depend, in part, on a certain suppression or vagueness of mere subject, so that the meaning reaches us through ways not distinctly traceable by the understanding."[46] Defending the obscurity in his own poems, Whitman says in his preface to the two-volume Centennial Edition of *Leaves of Grass* and *Two Rivulets:*

> In certain parts in these flights, or attempting to depict or suggest them, I have not been afraid of the charge of obscurity, in either of my

two volumes—because human thought, poetry or melody, must leave dim escapes and outlets—must possess a certain fluid, aerial character, akin to space itself, obscure to those of little or no imagination, but indispensable to the highest purposes. Poetic style, when address'd to the soul, is less definite form, outline, sculpture, and becomes vista, music, half-tints, and even less than half-tints.

(CPSP, 735)

Similar ideas inform Paul Verlaine's *Art Poétique,* the first stanza of which asserts that poetry should be musical and that its musicality should be *vague* and *soluble:*

> Music's required before all else,
> And for this choose the uneven kind
> That in the air indefinitely melts,
> With nothing that might weigh or bind.[47]

The same thought informs Mallarmé's "Mystery in Literature," in which Mallarmé argues that mystery, the ethereal absence of meaning, "is said to be music's domain. But the written word also lays claim to it. . . . Thus the invisible air, or song, beneath the words leads our divining eye from word to music; and thus, like a motif, invisibly it inscribes its fleuron and pendant there" (*CTSP,* 694). And in his essay on Mallarmé, Symons praises *L'Après-midi d'un Faune* and *Hérodiade* for their suggestiveness, saying that "every word is a jewel, scattering and recapturing sudden fire, every image is a symbol, and the whole poem is visible music."[48]

The same emphasis on musically indefinite meaning is evident in the critical statements of twentieth century poets. For instance, in his "Music of Poetry" essay, Eliot urges that "the poet is occupied with frontiers of consciousness beyond which words fail, though meanings still exist" (*OPP,* 30). An elevation of musical sound over discursive sense may also be observed in Williams, who insists: "By its *music* shall the best of modern verse be known and the *resources* of the music. The refinement of the poem, its

211

subtlety, is not to be known by the elevation of the words but—
the words don't so much matter—by the resources of the *music*"
(*SL,* 326). More recently, John Ashbery has said of his aims in
writing his often opaque poems: "What I like about music is its
ability of being convincing, of carrying an argument through
successfully to the finish, though the terms of this argument
remain unknown quantities. What remains is the structure, the
architecture of the argument, scene or story. I would like to do
this in poetry."[49]

Here it should be noted that the Kantian division of phenomena from noumena has had the effect of leading many poets to a
concern with expressing the inexpressible. Extreme examples of
this concern may be seen in the "sound poetry" of the Dadaists,
that "Verse Without Words,"[50] as Hugo Ball calls it. In such verse,
as in Ball's poem beginning "gadji beri bimba,"[51] speech with-
draws into mysticism. Of Kurt Schwitters' *Ursonata* (a sound
poem which, like Ball's, consists of nonsense syllables and the title
of which conveys its aspiration to primitive musical form), Lazlo
Moholy-Nagy comments: "The words used do not exist in any
language; they have no logical, only an emotional context."[52]
Composition of this type does not refer to the phenomenal world,
but is devoted wholly to noumenal essence. Schwitters himself
remarks of art in general: "Today the striving for expression in a
work of art also seems to me injurious to art. Art is a primordial
concept, exalted as the godhead, inexplicable as life, undefinable
and without purpose."[53]

Though hardly a Dadaist, Eliot also expresses interest in poetry which eludes meaning. In his concluding Norton Lecture,
for instance, Eliot compares meaning in a poem to meat that a
burglar uses, while robbing a house, to distract the watchdog—
the burglar representing the poet and the watchdog the reader.
Eliot suggests that the poet has to give the reader some meaning
so the reader will not raise a ruckus. The meaning keeps "his
mind diverted and quiet" while, according to Eliot, the poem
works deeper effects on him. Eliot adds, however, that some poets

"become impatient of this 'meaning' which seems superfluous, and perceive possibilities of intensity through its elimination."[54] This idea would seem to be related to Eliot's feeling, explored in the previous chapter, that poems which "convey a simple forceful statement" (*OPP*, 244) are not "poetry" but "verse." Indeed, much of Eliot's criticism appears predicated on the belief that the more a poem escapes meaning, the more poetic it is. That this belief should co-exist with Eliot's emphasis on colloquial speech and unmannered communication perhaps testifies to the sometimes contradictory impulses that influenced him and the other leaders of the modern movement.

Modern poets eventually seek not only musically indefinite meaning but musically indefinite form. Mallarmé is illustrative of this development. In his preface to *A Roll of the Dice Will Never Abolish Chance* (1897), he indicates that the poem's ambiguously fragmented and suspended syntax—its 'prismatic subdivisions of the Idea"—reflect its musical character. He says of his composition: "Today or without presuming upon the future which will come out of this, nothing or almost an art, let us readily acknowledge that the endeavor has an unforeseen part in activities peculiar and dear to our time, free verse and the poem in prose. They are being brought together under an influence which, I know, is foreign, that of Music heard in concert." Specifically discussing the poem's versification, Mallarmé speaks of "the counter-point of this prosody," and suggests that the "genre" of the poem may be likened to "the symphony . . . beside personal song."[55]

Ford also associates musical suggestiveness of meaning and musical suggestiveness of form. In his preface to his 1911 *Collected Poems,* for example, he refers to prose as "that conscious and workable medium" (*CP,* 324) and contrasts it to poetry, which for him is a matter of vague musical intuition and spontaneity:

> But with verse I just do not know: I do not know anything at all. As far as I am concerned, it just comes. I hear in my head a vague rhythm:

and presently a line will present itself.

(*CP*, 325)

Williams as well connects musically indefinite meaning with prosodic indefiniteness. This connection is clear in a letter that Williams writes to Pound in 1932:

> I've been playing with a theory that the inexplicitness of modern verse as compared with, let us say, the *Iliad,* and our increasingly difficult music in the verse as compared with the more or less down-rightness of their line forms—have been the result of a clearly understandable revolution in poetic attitude. Whereas formerly the music which accompanied the words amplified, certified and released them, today the words we write, failing a patent music, have become the music itself, and the understanding of the individual (presumed) is now that which used to be the words.
>
> (*SL,* 125–26)

According to Williams, that is, meter formerly provided poetry with music, and words provided poetry with meaning; now, however, meter has been abandoned, and words, merely in their capacity as words, must serve the function that meter once served. (This argument is related to the conflation of diction and metric discussed in the first chapter, to the extent that Williams seems to be urging that diction, by itself, has the capacity somehow to supply measure to speech which has abandoned measure.) Furthermore, because words must abandon meaning to become music, meaning can no longer be supplied by the poet writing the words. Meaning must be imposed on the words by an individual reader, who will, in perusing the unmeaning verbal music of the text, establish an interpretation for it. Referring to the complexities of this arrangement—the vaguenesses of the poetic measure and the shifting, from the poet to the reader, of the task of supplying meaning—Williams adopts a position much like Eliot's: "difficulty" in a poem, at least in a modern poem, makes it more poetic, whereas formal "downrightness" is the sign of a mere versifier. "This blasts out of existence forever," says Williams of the new poet-reader relationship, "all the puerilities of the dum te dum versifiers and puts it up to the reader to be a man" (*SL,* 126).[56]

Connections between musically elusive meaning and musically elusive form appear especially often in Eliot's criticism. As was noted in the previous chapter, Eliot repeatedly identifies "poetry" with music rather than meter. When Eliot appeals to music, he appeals, as does Mallarmé, to instrumental music. This explains what might otherwise seem to be inexplicable features of Eliot's estimate of Kipling. Eliot classifies Kipling's poems as "verse" because of their "subordination of musical interest," and at the same time, he classifies them as "verse" because they are "balladry." At first reading, this seems to be an odd argument, since the musical interest in the ballad is more pronounced than it is in most other poetic forms. Eliot's judgment that "metres and stanza forms" are unmusical may seem even odder, for these are in fact much more immediately musical, much more "melic," than what he calls "the more difficult forms of poetry." Yet Eliot's apparent contradictions vanish when one realizes that, in talking of musical meaning and form, he is not referring to any of the traditional associations between poetic speech and melody. He is referring to modern instrumental music.

This point emerges in the final paragraph of his "Music of Verse," in which Eliot suggests that in times to come poets will discover, in the forms of instrumental music, conventions that will supply the deficiency caused by the overthrow of traditional metric:

> [W]hen we reach a point at which the poetic idiom can be stabilized, then a period of musical elaboration can follow. I think a poet may

gain much from the study of music: how much technical knowledge of musical form is desirable I do not know, for I have not that technical knowledge myself. But I believe that the properties in which music concerns the poet most nearly, are the sense of rhythm and the sense of structure. . . . The use of recurrent themes is as natural to poetry as to music. There are possibilities for verse which bear some analogy to the development of a theme by different groups of instruments; there are possibilities of transitions in a poem comparable to the different movements of a symphony or a quartet; there are possibilities of contrapuntal arrangement of subject-matter. It is in the concert room, rather than in the opera house, that the germ of a poem may be quickened.

(OPP, 38)

Aside from the relevance of these remarks to Eliot's *Four Quartets,* which Eliot evidently saw as structurally analogous to Beethoven's late string quartets, the remarks are revealing in that it is music unrelated to words or song that Eliot holds up as a model for poetry. It is "in the concert room, rather than in the opera house" that the poet is encouraged to look for structure for his work. One should note, too, Eliot's reference to the "contrapuntal arrangement of subject-matter." He suggests, that is, that the poet's presentation of his material might well involve musical counterpoint rather than logical exposition or plausible narrative. Both meaning and form are construed in the terminology of instrumental music.

Modern prosodic practice is also greatly affected by the belief that poetry might profitably seek a complexity of rhythm comparable to that represented by modern musical notation. In principle, verse form is simple. There are in poetry basically four metrical systems—the syllabic (e.g., much poetry of the Far East and of the modern Romance languages), the accentual (e.g., the poetry of the old Germanic tradition), the quantitative (e.g., classical Greek and Latin), and the accentual-syllabic (e.g., modern English, German, and Russian). In syllabic or accentual measures, a fixed number of syllables or a fixed number of accents determines the poetic line. In quantitative or accentual-syllabic measures, the line has as its basis a fixed number of long and short, or accented and unaccented, syllables. Even complex strophic or stanzaic forms like those of a Pindar or a Hardy—forms which mix lines of different lengths and may use different kinds of feet—are still construable in terms of long and short or accented and unaccented syllables. In such forms, the stanzaic units repeat or answer one another, and the line sequences within those units match, from stanza to stanza (or from strophe to antistrophe and epode to epode), the line sequences in corresponding units. In other words, meters involve, for purposes of mere description, a maximum of two factors: long syllables and short syllables or accented syllables and unaccented syllables.

This bare description is misleading, since it hardly accounts for the great variety of stress or duration in the words and syllables of a language or the great variety of rhythmical contour that a poet may strike within the context of a given metrical line.[57] It is precisely this quality of metrical composition that provides such endlessly diverse challenges and pleasures to the poet writing in meter. As was pointed out in the first chapter, however, the modern movement's leaders identified metrical practice with scansion and with scansion's necessarily crude if useful descriptions of lines. One consequence of this was that some poets came to believe that all metrically "accented" syllables were rhythmically identical, that all metrically "unaccented" syllables were rhythmically identical, and that conventional metric was thus hopelessly limited. (In certain cases, such as Pound's, this belief was reinforced by the historical dominance in English poetry of iambic measures. This circumstance made it seem not only that conventional meters were limited in general, but also that English meter particularly was restricted.)

In this context, modern musical notation appealed to experimental poets. Composers have at their disposal not only whole notes and halfnotes, but quarter, eighth, sixteenth, thirty-second, and sixty-fourth notes, as well as a corresponding series of rests. The use of dots above or below or after notes offers a further source of variation. What if, some poets wondered, we treated syllables and words as musical notes? Perhaps poetry would acquire a whole new arsenal of effects.

Pound exemplifies this development. In his "Tradition" essay, for instance, he argues that free verse represents a realization, in verbal art, of the principles of musical notation:

> No one is so foolish as to suppose that a musician using 'four-four' time is compelled to use always four quarter notes in each bar, or in 'seven-eighths' time to use seven eighth notes uniformly in each bar. He may use one 1/2, one 1/4 and one 1/8 rest, or any such combination as he may happen to choose or find fitting.
>
> To apply this musical truism to verse is to employ *vers libre*.
>
> (*LE*, 93)

It is difficult to see how this idea can be practically adapted to versification. In English especially, there are problems with such a procedure, because the duration of vowels is largely a phonetic rather than a phonemic matter, not to mention the fact that stress plays a major role in English speech and that stress is determined by syntactic context as well as by phonetic and phonemic considerations. As a result, vowels and syllables cannot be assigned the invariable abstract values of musical notes, unless one had an infinite number of notes. If it is entertained in a vague way, however, this idea is useful to a free verse poet: it may allow him to put, say, twelve syllables in one line and four in another and still feel that he is writing lines that are rhythmically equivalent. It lends metrical legitimacy to a poem like Pound's musically titled "Coda":

> O my songs,
> Why do you look so eagerly and so curiously into people's
>   faces,
> Will you find your lost dead among them? [58]

218

There seems to be no measure in this poem. But Pound may have felt that the *O* that begins the first line is so long, and that the word *songs* is so long, that the line itself is "equal" to the two other lines, whose syllables may be, in Pound's way of thinking, much shorter and possibly analogous to thirty-second and sixty-fourth notes. Or Pound may have felt that the initial line represents a radically abridged version of the second line and that the length of the third line constitutes a balancing compromise between the first two. It is also possible, of course, that Pound wrote the lines without giving much thought to their relationship.

Like Pound, Williams sometimes explains free verse as composition according to musical bars. For example, in examining Vazakas's free verse, Williams says:

> The thing to notice about this more or less accidental discovery of Vazakas, is that it has a very definite regularity resembling, however vaguely, a musical bar. A bar, definitely, since it is not related to grammar, but to *time,* as Vazakas uses it. The clause, the sentence, and the paragraph are ignored, and the progression goes over into the next bar as much as the musical necessity requires . . . [Williams' ellipsis] a sequence of musical bars arranged vertically on the page, and capable of infinite modulation.
>
> (*TN,* xii)

As with Williams' other comments about musical verse, this one is significant partly for the reason that it exhibits an attempt to escape not merely from meter to music, but from conventional grammar and discursive meaning into a kind of extra-verbal liberty.

If experimental poets have seen in musical notation a justification for free verse, so they have frequently found the printed musical score to be a useful device to which to refer free verse. Modern poets, that is, often speak of free verse poems as visual equivalents of musical scores. On occasion, this idea includes the idea that free verse poems are not only like musical scores but like objects of visual art. This additional idea reflects not simply a

concern with making poetry musical, but also the broader aesthetic concern with synthesizing the arts.

In his *A Roll of the Dice* preface, Mallarmé characterizes the
poem as *une partition,* a musical score. Writing of his placing of
individual words here and there over the poem's pages, and of the
interplay of typefaces in the text, he says:

> The literary advantage, if I may so call it, of this reenacted distance
> which mentally separates groups of words or the words from each
> other, seems at times to speed up or to slow down the movement,
> marking it, even conveying it in terms of seeing the Page all at once:
> the latter being taken as a unit as is elsewhere the Verse or rounded
> line. . . . Add that this unadorned use of thought with doublings
> back, goings on, runnings away, or the very portrayal of it, results, for
> who will read aloud, in a musical score. The different type-faces
> between the principal motif, a secondary and adjacent ones, dictate
> their importance to oral delivery and the pitch on the page, middle,
> high or low, will notate whether intonation rises or falls.[59]

Guillaume Apollinaire gives a similar account of free verse and
draws other connections between free verse, lyricality, and sheet
music. "Up to now the literary field has been kept within narrow
limits," Apollinaire remarks. "One wrote in prose or one wrote in
verse. . . . As for [French] poetry, rimed versification was the only
rule. . . . Free verse gave wings to lyricism." And Apollinaire
suggests that free verse offers the prospect of a synthesis of the
arts, the effects of which will be orchestral:

> Typographical artifices worked out with great audacity have the
> advantage of bringing to life a visual lyricism which was almost
> unknown before our age. These artifices can still go much further
> and achieve the synthesis of the arts, of music, painting, and litera-
> ture. . . . One should not be astonished if, with only the means they
> [poets] have now at their disposal, they set themselves to preparing
> this new art (vaster than the plain art of words) in which, like
> conductors of a orchestra of unbelievable scope, they will have at
> their disposition the entire world, its noises and its appearances, the

thought and language of man, song, dance, all the arts and all the artifices, still more mirages than Morgane could summon up on the hill of Gibel, with which to compose the visible and unfolded book of the future.[60]

Related notions appear in more recent explanations of non-metrical poetry. For instance, discussing poetry and music and the role of the typewriter in projective verse, Olson remarks: "For the first time the poet has the stave and the bar a musician has had. For the first time he can, without the convention of rime and meter, record the listening he has done to his own speech and by that one act indicate how he would want any reader, silently or otherwise, to voice his work."[61]

To the extent that the displacement of meter by music enabled poets to explore ideas about their art that they might not have otherwise explored, one can sympathize with their enterprise. However, one may be troubled by theories of musical versification in the same way one is troubled by theories of organic form. In both cases, certain aspects of the theories seem based on misunderstandings of the topics to which they appeal. As was observed earlier, words and syllables are not musical notes. They do not have the mathematically exact relations that musical notes have. This is particularly true in English, in which speech stress plays so central a role. A system of versification founded on duration or musical time would appear doomed to excessive artificiality.[62] Furthermore, when it is said of certain poems that they visually resemble a musical score, one might point out that it is not the visual effect of the score that makes us prize a Mozart piano concerto or a symphony by Schubert. Rather, we prize the bringing to life of the score by wonderful musicians. A score-like poem cannot produce melodies and harmonies in the manner that an orchestra or chamber ensemble can, nor can poems with contrapuntal subject matter please the ear or mind the way a composition by Bach or Haydn does.

On a related note, one might make the following observations about the various species of modern shaped and concrete poetry.

It is one thing to write a shaped poem like Herbert's "Easter Wings," which aims at a visual effect but which also retains conventional metricality. In such a case, the poetic effect is clear, and the visual effect is a bonus. It is another matter to instruct a typographer to rain letters down a page or arrange them in the shape of a stop sign. A visual effect undeniably results from this procedure. The effect, however, may well seem mechanical and uninteresting compared to the effects that a fine artist can achieve with brush and paint. Though sharing certain general aims, the different arts involve different media. Without relinquishing a lively interest in the other arts, poets might well remember this difference and remember Goethe's comment: "One of the most striking signs of the decay of art is when we see its separate forms jumbled together."[63]

A further matter deserves mention. Much of the verse of our time that aims at non-mechanical musicality in fact leans heavily on the mechanics of typography. Olson defines "NON-Projective" verse (meaning evidently metrical verse) as "what a French critic calls 'closed' verse, that verse which print bred and which is pretty much what we have had, in English & American, and have still got, despite the work of Pound & Williams."[64] In reality, metrical verse grew out of oral traditions and still connects us with those traditions, at least insofar as we still memorize poems that we love and recite them to others to whom we wish to communicate our enthusiasm. On the other hand, *The Maximus Poems* and the *Cantos* are not, for the most part, suited to oral delivery. One has to see the printed pages of Olson's work to know where the white spaces are that mark the breath pauses. Many of the abrupt changes in diction, subject, and tone in the *Cantos* are simply bewildering unless one has the page before one, and can see that Pound is now quoting a letter from someone or other, now introducing a few Chinese characters, or now presenting a series of musical notes.

In defense of poets writing autonomously musical or organic free verse, one should say that a serious desperation informs their practice. Much modern poetry expresses the anxiety that all the great poems have been written, and that there is nothing more for poets to do. The aesthetic elevation of music is thus important in another way, for it contributes to this anxiety. Though, in the nineteenth century, music became the primary art, the wealth of music produced during the period led eventually to the speculation that the possibilities of conventional harmony were being played out. And even as it became a symbol of aesthetic expression, music also became a symbol of aesthetic exhaustion.

The idea that music is mortally ill and that the other arts are dying, too, is voiced by Wyndham Lewis in *Blasting & Bombardiering,* published in 1937. Surveying the arts, Lewis says:

> As far as Opera is concerned, and for what that form of art is worth, the best Operas date from the last century. There will be no more Wagner, much less Mozart. And as to the supreme orchestral compositions, they all seem to have been written, too. There are no more Bachs or Beethovens just as there were no more Leonardos and Michelangelos after the Renaissance, only hasty reminders of what artists once excelled in doing, or despairing jokes, or jazzed-up echoes of perfection.
>
> These are not lost arts—much music is still written and very intelligent music, and the dying struggle of the visual arts is often impressive. But something has occurred in the world that has long ago caused the greatest creations to stop being born. No more will come.
>
> Literature, or rather language, is a hardier material. But that it will shortly be quite impossible to imagine a book of a very high order of excellence being written any more—and we may soon have reached that stage—is no more inconceivable, than it is inconceivable to anticipate the appearance at any moment of a new Beethoven.[65]

These are words of despair. In our next and last chapter, we will examine how this despair contributed to the desire to make modern poetry prosodically "experimental" and "scientific," in the hope that poetry might thereby be revitalized and might claim, as science was claiming, central importance in the modern world.

CHAPTER 5

Sciences of Sentiment:
The Crisis of
Experimental Poetry

Discussing the early days of the modern movement, Wyndham Lewis observes that its leaders hoped that a new age of scientifically accurate art was dawning: "The natural sciences which had been responsible for the Industrial Age had acquired maturity, it seemed, and the human mind was to indulge, once more, its imagination. Scientific still, essentially, it was to go over from the techniques of the sciences into the field of art."[1]

Lewis's reminiscence reminds us that modern poets have aspired to the condition not only of music but of science. This latter aspiration is reflected in the vocabulary that the modern movement's leaders employ in discussing the qualities that they seek in their poems. Williams, for instance, contends that poems should have the efficiency of machinery: "A poem is a small (or large) machine made of words. When I say there's nothing sentimental about a poem I mean that there can be no part, as in any other machine, that is redundant" (*SE,* 256). In addition, poets often describe their procedures as "experimental" and suggest that the poet himself should seek a "depersonalization" that is characteristic of a scientist in a laboratory. Furthermore, some of the modern movement's leaders assert that their experiments represent scientific advances over older techniques. For example, when Pound derives, from Ernest Fenollosa's *The Chinese Written Character as a Medium for Poetry,* a new way of writing poems, he describes the procedure as "THE IDEOGRAMMIC METHOD OR THE METHOD OF SCIENCE" (*ABC,* 26); and he urges that it stands in relation to former poetics as modern science stands in relation to medieval philosophy.[2]

At first, the scientific proclivities of modern poets may seem at odds with their aesthetic tendencies. This is not, however, the case. For the science advocated by the experimentalists involves two things. First, it involves a Baconian mistrust of generalization and of conventional ways of examining experience. Second, it involves an interest in quasi-mathematical procedures designed to produce a feeling or image which is instantaneously persuasive and which, like a geometrical demonstration, does not require the mediation of concepts extrinsic to its presentation. A "science" of this type is nonconceptual and nondiscursive, and it harmonizes with Aestheticism.

Something similar may be said about the "scientific" poet. In his depersonalization, he is impartial and skeptical. He is unlikely to commit what Poe calls "the heresy of *The Didactic*" (*ER,* 75) or to write the sort of poetry that Eliot disparages as "instrumental" (*OPP,* 250). If he appears to trespass into the un-aesthetic realm of scientific understanding, he still fulfills the aesthetic requirement of being independent of moral reason.

Modern attempts to make poetry scientific, and to assert that poetic experimentality produces advances in poetry in the same way that scientific experimentality produces advances in science, reflect the anxiety that poetry and art are dying. This anxiety results, in part, from the increasing prominence of science and technology in our culture in recent centuries. If, in the Middle Ages and the Renaissance, art and religion centrally engaged the energies of men, in the modern period science has moved to the fore. To many writers, it has seemed that poetry is no longer as important as it was. Williams comments, "Where then will you find the only true belief in our day? Only in science" (*SE,* 262). Poets have sometimes felt, moreover, that the intellectual prestige once enjoyed by their art has been transferred to science. They have experienced in consequence a sense of inferiority to the scientific investigator. "When I find myself in the company of scientists," W. H. Auden gloomily remarks, "I feel like a shabby curate who has strayed by mistake into a drawing room full of dukes."[3]

Given the anxiety that poetry is dying and science is progressing, one should not be surprised that modern poets have attempted to make poetry scientific, in hopes of resuscitating it. But from a historical standpoint, the attempt is unusual. Science and poetry have always shared certain values, such as honesty, intelligence, and open-mindedness. Great science and great poetry alike often result from a mixture of rigorous thought and imaginative intuition. For that matter, as was noted in the third chapter, poets have sometimes made use of scientific material; by the same token, scientists have sometimes written their works in meter to make them more memorable. Yet observers have traditionally believed that while the sciences address natural phenomena susceptible to quantitative analysis, the literary and humanistic arts address qualitative issues in human experience. In a well-known passage in the *Nicomachean Ethics* (1094b12ff.), Aristotle comments: "[I]t is the mark of an educated man to look for precision in each class of things just so far as the nature of the subject admits: it is evidently equally foolish to accept probable reasoning from a mathematician and to demand from a rhetorician demonstrative proofs."[4] Transferring this idea to a comparison of the scientific and literary disciplines, one might say that the two, despite their resemblances, have investigated different materials, operated by means of different techniques, and aimed at different degrees of conclusiveness.

This chapter will examine ways in which modern poetry has emulated science and the consequences of this emulation on prosodic practice. At the outset, one should bear in mind several points. One is that because many advances in modern science result from innovations in apparatus, experimental poets aim for technical novelties, hoping thereby to produce the kinds of "breakthroughs" and "discoveries" that modern science has made.

Another point concerns the specialized nature of modern science. Much modern science is not as readily accessible to the intelligent layman as is, say, Euclid's geometry or Newton's physics. As Alfred North Whitehead remarked in the twenties, "The new situation in the thought of today arises from the fact that scientific theory is outrunning common sense."[5] Poets who appeal to science to justify experimental procedures make this appeal partly because modern science supplies a model for a pursuit that is "difficult," that employs esoteric vocabulary and formulae, and that baffles conventional expectation. Here again, the "scientific" element in modern poetry reinforces the aesthetic element. The aesthetic belief that poetry should be elusive or obscure appears to find confirmation in modern science, many of the concepts of which resist the understanding of the non-specialist.

A final point is that, when explaining their methods by means of scientific concepts, experimental poets on occasion use those concepts in a rather loosely analogical or metaphorical fashion. Concepts which in science carry exact meanings and apply to specific contexts are relaxed and broadened in such a way that at times they actually lose their scientific character. On the one hand, this tendency gives experimental verse—and the various theories of it—a special liveliness and vitality. On the other hand, the tendency accounts for perhaps the most unsettling aspect of the modern movement: even while proclaiming its scientific character, it often derails into faddish superstitions and irrationalities. It is no mere accident of history that the triumph of experimental poetry and art in the first half of this century coincides with the triumph of reactionary pseudo-scientific political ideologies in the same period. Toward the end of the chapter, we will examine Thomas Mann's *Doctor Faustus,* which anatomizes this phenomenon.

1. Progressive Science,
Regressive Poetry?

It is in the seventeenth century, which Whitehead calls "the first century of modern science in the strict sense of the term,"[6] that one initially encounters the idea that science is progressing and poetry is stagnating. The idea is suggested by Pascal in the preface to his *Treatise on Vacuum,* both the treatise (which survives only in fragments) and the preface apparently having been composed between 1647 and 1651. Endeavoring to reconcile religion with the developing sciences, Pascal discriminates between those pursuits which must guide themselves by authority and precedent (e.g., history, grammar, jurisprudence, and, above all, theology) and those pursuits (e.g., physics, arithmetic, and medicine) which "must all receive continual augmentation in their progress to perfection. The ancients derived them only in their rudiments from their predecessors; and we shall merely transmit them to our posterity, in a state somewhat more matured than that in which they came down to us."[7] Though he does not make the point in so many words, Pascal in effect observes that science is capable of cumulative advances in which judicial, literary, philosophical, and moral enterprises cannot share.

Dryden seems to be the first major figure to examine this issue with specific reference to poetry. A member of the Royal Society, Dryden is keenly sensitive to the science of his day. His *Of Dramatic Poesy* explores the thesis that whereas the great minds of antiquity devoted themselves to poetry, the great minds of the Modern Age are devoting themselves to science. Crites is the character in the dialogue who most forcefully affirms this thesis; and though Dryden's judgments generally are felt to differ from Crites', Crites' particular argument about the impressiveness of modern science is consonant with views that Dryden expresses elsewhere.

Crites urges that every age is characterized by a certain intellectual talent, which gifted people share and exercise to perfect a specific endeavor. The specific endeavor examined in the dialogue is poetic drama, and Crites argues that in sixth and fifth century Greece the characteristic intellectual talent was poetic and dramatic, in consequence of which dramatic verse achieved at that time its high-water mark:

> Dramatic poesy had time enough, reckoning from Thespis (who first invented it) to Aristophanes, to be born, to grow up, and to flourish in maturity. It has been observed of arts and sciences, that in one and the same century they have arrived to a great perfection; and no wonder, since every age has a kind of universal genius which inclines those that live in it to some particular studies: the work then being pushed on by many hands, must of necessity go forward.
>
> (*ODP,* 1 : 25–26)

Crites then identifies the "universal genius" of the modern age as scientific and contends that the age's most significant accomplishments belong to science:

> Is it not evident in these last hundred years (when the study of philosophy [i.e., natural philosophy] has been the business of all the virtuosi in Christendom), that almost a new nature has been revealed

to us? that more errors of the school have been detected, more useful experiments in philosophy have been made, more noble secrets in optics, medicine, anatomy, astronomy discovered, than in all those credulous and doting ages from Aristotle to us? so true it is, that nothing spreads more fast than science, when rightly and generally cultivated.

(ODP, 1:26)

Running parallel to this argument is another one: just as the genius of antiquity devoted itself to drama and the genius of modern times is devoting itself to science, so ancient poetry is superior to modern poetry in the same way that modern science is superior to ancient science. Modern poets, Crites asserts, are inferior to their predecessors and simply imitate and refine on the achievements of the ancients: "[W]e do not only build upon their foundation, but by their models" (*ODP*, 1:25).

Mainly by citing the achievements of the Elizabethan and Jacobean stage, Neander refutes Crites' contention that ancient drama is superior to modern drama. Neander nevertheless speculates that Elizabethan and Jacobean playwrights have so exhausted the resources of the stage that contemporary playwrights have nothing to do. Of Shakespeare, Jonson, and Fletcher, Neander sadly remarks: "We acknowledge them our fathers in wit; but they have ruined their estates themselves before they came to their children's hands. There is scarce an humour, a character, or any kind of plot, which they have not blown upon [used]." Then, in words that have an almost twentieth-century ring to them, Neander suggests that poets must do something technically different or abandon verse: "This therefore will be a good argument to us either not to write at all, or to attempt some other way" (*ODP*, 1:85).

The novelty Neander proposes for drama is structural rhyme, which Dryden and his contemporaries were already using in their plays. Neander contends that contemporary playwrights should write in rhyme, because rhymed drama is not something upon which literary genius, at least in England, has previously exercised its powers. By writing in rhyme, Neander urges, contemporary dramatists are doing something that their great predecessors did not; and it is noteworthy that in stating this position, he uses a version of Crites' "universal genius" argument. "This way of writing in verse they have only left free to us," Neander says of the great Elizabethans and Jacobeans; "our age is arrived to a perfection in it which they never knew. . . . For the genius of every age is different" (*ODP,* 1:85). In other words, in rebutting Crites, Neander concedes and even adopts some of the terms of his argument. Nor is Neander's own argument much more favorable to contemporary poetic practice than is Crites'. Both say that the dramatic poetry of the past daunts by its excellence. The difference is that Crites refers to the ancient past, and Neander refers to the more recent past (and in this respect he clearly mirrors Dryden's feelings about Shakespeare).

Dryden ultimately seems, in his *Of Dramatic Poesy,* to come down on the side of modern verse. In addition, he pronounces contemporary poetic style to be better than that of earlier English verse. "All of them were thus far of Eugenius his opinion," Dryden comments at one point (*ODP,* 1:24), "that the sweetness of English verse was never understood or practiced by our fathers." And subsequently his confidence in the standards of his day was on occasion so strong as to have led him astray, as in the case of his refining translations of Chaucer. In a happier vein, his epigram on Milton indicates his enthusiasm for, and faith in the enduring value of, at least one contemporary poet.

On the other hand, in his later writings, Dryden sometimes voices negative sentiments about both modern and contemporary verse. Like Milton, who had called rhyme "the invention of a barbarous age," Dryden expresses mixed feelings about structural rhyme, especially about its use in longer works. As early as his prologue to *Aureng-Zebe* (1676), he confesses to growing "weary of his long-loved mistress, Rhyme" (*ODP,* 1:192); and in his 1684 preface to Roscommon's *Essay on Translated Verse,* Dryden implies that modern verse overall is inferior to ancient verse. Referring to the emergence of Poetry from medieval darkness, he writes:

> . . . Italy, reviving from the trance
> Of Vandal, Goth, and monkish ignorance,
> With pauses, cadence, and well vowell'd words,
> And all the graces a good ear affords,
> Made rhyme an art: and Dante's polish'd page
> Restor'd a silver, not a golden age.
> Then Petrarch follow'd, and in him we see
> What rhyme improv'd in all its height can be:
> At best a pleasing sound, and fair barbarity.
>
> (*ODP*, 2:15)

Admittedly, as in *Of Dramatic Poesy,* Dryden also argues here that modern and contemporary English poetry (and evidently English rhymed poetry in particular, to judge from the reference to the Restoration and to Roscommon himself) has special virtues. Further, he seems to suggest that contemporary English poetry not only excels continental vernacular poetries but approaches and restores the greatness of the poetries of the ancient world:

> The French pursu'd their steps; and Britain, last
> In manly sweetness all the rest surpass'd.
> The wit of Greece, the gravity of Rome
> Appear exalted in the British loom;
> The Muses' empire is restored again
> In Charles his reign, and by Roscommon's pen.
>
> (*ODP*, 2.15)

Nonetheless, there is a deep ambivalence in Dryden's attitudes. Though a partisan of modern poetry and its conventions, he is sensitive to the claims that it is not as good as earlier poetry. And he is especially sensitive to the claim that the poetry of his day is not advancing as science is advancing.

Dryden examines issues that were being debated during his lifetime in the Quarrel of the Ancients and Moderns. The Quarrel, which was mentioned in passing in an earlier chapter, may be briefly summarized. Though its origins lie in the Italian Renaissance, it did not assume full shape until it was taken up by French and English scholars of the second half of the seventeenth century, by which time the achievements of Galileo, Harvey, Descartes, and others had produced a widespread appreciation that science was establishing its independence of the authority of antiquity and the Middle Ages. The Quarrel consisted of comparisons of the accomplishments of the ancients and moderns in various sciences and arts. Verdicts issuing from these comparisons were not unanimous. The Quarrel's participants, however, tended to arrive at this conclusion: in fields susceptible to quantitative analysis (basically, the mathematical and physical sciences), the moderns were superior; in fields not susceptible to quantitative analysis (basically, the arts), the matter was left in doubt, or the ancients were judged superior. The best known English treatise dealing with the Quarrel, William Wotton's *Reflections upon Ancient and Modern Learning,* illustrates this conclusion. Wotton remarks:

> [O]f these Particulars [types of learning] there are Two Sorts: One, of those wherein the greatest part of those Learned Men who have compared Ancient and Modern Performances, either give up the Cause to the Ancients quite, or think, at least, that the Moderns have not gone beyond them. The other of those, where the Advocates for the Moderns think the Case so clear on their side, that they wonder how any Man can dispute it with them. *Poesie, Oratory, Architecture, Painting,* and *Statuary,* are of the First Sort; *Natural History, Physiology,* and *Mathematics,* with all their Dependencies, are of the Second.[8]

Though the Quarrel resembled in many respects an academic parlor game, its effect on poetry and the arts was considerable. It introduced a division between the arts and sciences, a division which is foreign to ancient, medieval, and Renaissance discussions of the subjects.[9] The Quarrel also fostered the tendency, which eventually contributed to Aestheticism, to study the fine arts collectively and apart from other intellectual disciplines. Moreover, the Quarrel led to the clarification and dissemination of the idea, suggested by Pascal, that science is capable of a progress unavailable to the arts. This idea in turn encouraged the idea that science builds on its achievements as a culture grows more sophisticated, whereas poetry achieves its fullest expression at a primitive societal stage and thereafter merely embroiders on its early accomplishments.

Eighteenth-century writers commonly voice this latter idea. For example, in his *New Science* of 1725, Giambattista Vico argues that there is a dichotomy between thought and imagination and that poetry embodies the latter to the exclusion of the former. Vico furthermore argues that cultural evolution is a process leading from imagination to intellect. Seen in this light, poetry represents a form of primitive racial consciousness that later gives way to rational thought. Vico says at the beginning of his study, "Throughout this book it will be shown that as much as the poets had first sensed in the way of vulgar wisdom, the philosophers later understood in the way of esoteric wisdom; so that the former may be said to have been the sense and the latter the intellect of the human race." Later taking issue with ancient and Renaissance critics who believed that poetic art had developed gradually and with the aid of reflection, Vico insists: "[I]t was deficiency of human reasoning power that gave rise to poetry so sublime that the philosophies which came afterward, the arts of poetry and of criticism, have produced none equal or better and have even prevented its production." Picturing Homer as an untutored bard, Vico adds, "Hence it is Homer's privilege to be, of all the sublime, that is, the heroic poets, the first in the order of merit as well as in that of age" (*CTSP,* 294, 298).

These themes are also sounded by Dr. Johnson, a writer whose views otherwise differ from Vico's. In the famous dissertation on poetry, in *The History of Rasselas Prince of Abyssinia* (1759), the character Imlac discusses the esteem in which early poets of a language are held by succeeding generations. Imlac suggests that one explanation of this situation may be that poetry develops virtually "at once" in a culture, while other pursuits involve knowledge "gradually attained":

> Wherever I went, I found that Poetry was considered as the highest learning, and regarded with a veneration somewhat approaching to that which man would pay to the Angelic Nature. And it yet fills me with wonder that, in almost all countries, the most ancient poets are considered as the best: whether it be that every other kind of knowledge is an acquisition gradually attained, and poetry is a gift conferred at once; or that the first poetry of every nation surprised them as a novelty, and retained the credit by consent which it received by accident at first; or whether, as the province of poetry is to describe Nature and Passion, which are always the same, the first writers took possession of the most striking objects for description and the most probable occurrences for fiction, and left nothing to those that followed them but transcription of the same events and new combinations of the same images. Whatever be the reason, it is commonly observed that the early writers are in possession of nature, and their followers of art: that the first excel in strength and invention and the latter in elegance and refinement.[10]

In the second half of the eighteenth century, a work appeared that significantly contributed to the belief that the earlier the poetry, the better it is. This work is Macpherson's translation, or pseudo-translation, of Ossian. The initial installment, *Fingal,* was published in 1762. Johnson's challenge to the genuineness of the poems, the revelation of Macpherson's fabrication of "original" manuscripts, and the findings of the MacKenzie committee in 1805 eventually undermined the authenticity of the Ossianic epics. For most readers today, the epics are simply curiosities. Nevertheless, for two generations, Ossian enjoyed a tremendous European vogue, even supplanting Homer, readers will recall, in the heart of young Werther. Many writers believed Ossian ring-ingly confirmed that poetry flourishes best in a primitive and non-rational culture, and they imitated Macpherson's prose-poetical effusions.

With regard to the imitations of Macpherson, it is interesting to note that the Ossian epics anticipate a development in later poetic practice. In their character as "translations," the epics be-came models of style. Despite the literary nationalisms that in-form much modern and contemporary European and American verse, poets frequently imitate writers in other literatures. This is hardly unprecedented. Horace, for instance, looks to Sappho and Archilochus for inspiration, Ben Jonson to Horace and Martial. The striking thing in our time is that many poets have looked to languages of which they lacked firsthand knowledge and, more important, have emulated the stylistic features of translations. In carrying a work from one language to another, translators often stagger under their burden. They often write in a strained man-ner and often are compelled merely to approximate the metrical qualities of their originals. If many contemporary poems are awkward and thorny in rhythm and diction and almost sound as if they were translations from some other language, it may be because their authors have been influenced, consciously or uncon-sciously, by the stilted diction and free rhythm to which trans-lators have frequently resorted.

Whereas Johnson simply noted the prestige of early poetry, writers in the Romantic period on occasion argued that poets should imitate primitive composition. As was suggested a mo-ment ago, Macpherson's work contributed to this development. By stressing the virtue of primitivism, however, Romantic writers placed themselves in a difficult position. It is hard to overlook the fact that our poetic tradition extends back nearly three thousand years. If one says that the primitive is necessarily the best and then sits down to write, one places oneself in the position of a runner in a hundred-yard dash who has several thousand entrants in the starting blocks ahead of him. Hence, a curious situation emerges in the Romantic period. Writers assert simultaneously a great faith in the poetic imagination and a profound anxiety that every vein in poetry itself has been completely mined. This condition, which is a notable feature of the modern movement as well, contributes to the elevation of organic poetic process over poetic product. That many poets place such emphasis on process results partly from the fact that they have little confidence in achieving significant products—that is, significantly fresh and excellent individual poems.

Coleridge exemplifies this situation. Though celebrating the imagination's power, Coleridge is doubtful of poetry's ability to do anything that has not been done before. Just as Wallace Stevens will later feel that "the Victorians had left nothing behind," Coleridge feels that the Augustans have exhausted many of the possibilities of poetry. This feeling is evident in a letter of 1814 in which Coleridge remarks:

> From the time of Pope's translation of Homer, inclusive, so countless have been the poetic metamorphoses of almost all possible thoughts and connections of thought, that it is scarcely practicable for a man to write in the ornamented style on any subject without finding his poem, against his will and without his previous consciousness, a cento of lines that had pre-existed in other works; and this it is which makes poetry so very difficult, because so very easy, in the present day. I myself have for many years past given it up in despair.[11]

In the Romantic period, a love-hate relationship also develops between poetry and science. An important document in the history of this relationship is Thomas Love Peacock's "Four Ages of Poetry" (1820), in which Peacock humorously argues that modern scientific progress has made poetry and poets obsolete:

> A poet in our times is a semibarbarian in a civilized community. He lives in the days that are past. His ideas, thoughts, feelings, associations, are all with barbarous manners, obsolete customs, and ex-

ploded superstitions. The march of his intellect is like that of a crab, backward. The brighter the light diffused around him by the progress of reason, the thicker is the darkness of antiquated barbarism, in which he buries himself like a mole.

(CTSP, 496)

Poetry, continues Peacock, "cannot claim the slightest share in any one of the comforts and utilities of life of which we have witnessed so many and so rapid advances" (*CTSP,* 496). It cannot claim a share, that is, in the triumphs of modern technology. And Peacock concludes:

> [I]ntellectual power and intellectual acquisition have turned themselves into other and better channels, and have abandoned the cultivation and the fate of poetry to the degenerate fry of modern rhymsters, and their Olympic judges, the magazine critics, who continue to debate and promulgate oracles about poetry, as if it were still what it was in the Homeric age, the all-in-all of intellectual progression, and as if there were no such things in existence as mathematicians, astronomers, chemists, moralists, metaphysicians, historians, politicians, and political economists, who have built into the upper air of intelligence a pyramid, from the summit of which they see the modern Parnassus far beneath them.

(CTSP, 497)

Peacock's essay highlights the way in which Aestheticism, in one respect, jeopardized the poetic art that it sought to liberate. Peacock's remarks are based on the Kantian triad of Scientific Understanding, Moral Reason, and Aesthetic Judgment. However, Peacock construes the triad not in a coordinate but a progressive manner. Early in a culture's history aesthetics prevail; later the ethical and natural sciences replace them. In other words, in freeing poetry from intellectual and moral concerns, Aestheticism placed it in a precarious position vis-à-vis the advancing physical and social sciences.

Romantic poets defended themselves against attacks like Peacock's, returning the hostile fire and pointing out that the influence of science on society was not always benign. Blake's engraving of Newton, Wordsworth's scientist botanizing on his mother's grave, and Keats' vision of "cold philosophy" clipping the angels wings and unweaving the rainbow all testify to the concern in the Romantic period with the possible detrimental effects of science. Further evidence of this concern is supplied by Shelley's *Defense of Poetry,* which was written in reply to Peacock's essay. The final third of Shelley's essay contains a prophetic warning that science, if its discoveries are not intelligently employed, may contribute to widespread social inequities and threaten the foundations of life itself.

At the same time, Romantic writers are haunted by the possibility of securing scientific validation for poetry. When, for example, Schiller argues that in the properly aesthetical work of art, form consumes content, he construes form in mathematical determinations of proportion. When Coleridge presents his doctrine of organic form, he does so in terms drawn from biology. Furthermore, the development of aesthetics reflects, among other things, the belief that an independent art might partake of the kind of progress achieved by independent science. One reason that writers seek to make poetry autonomous is that they hope that a poetry liberated from the claims of tradition will achieve insights comparable to those of a science that has been liberated from the weight of ecclesiastical imperatives and obsolete theory. Thus conceived, modern aesthetics complements modern science; the two together demolish antiquated views and usher in new ages of enlightenment.

In his preface to the Centennial Edition of *Leaves of Grass,* Whitman expresses this conception with particular force and relevance to poetic practice:

> Without being a scientist, I have thoroughly adopted the conclusions of the great savans and experimentalists of our time, and of the last hundred years, and they have interiorly tinged the chyle of all my verse, for purposes beyond. Following the modern spirit, the real poems of the present, ever solidifying and expanding into the future,

must vocalize the vastness and splendor and reality with which scientism has invested man and the universe. . . . Poetry, so largely hitherto and even at present wedded to children's tales, and to mere amorousness, upholstery and superficial rhyme, will have to accept, and, while not denying the past, nor the themes of the past, will be revivified by this tremendous innovation, the kosmic spirit, which must henceforth, in my opinion, be the background and underlying impetus, more or less visible, of all first-class songs.

(*CPSP,* 733–34)

This theme informs as well Whitman's preface to his earlier "As a Strong Bird on Pinions Free," in which he refers to "the entire revolution made by science in the poetic method" (*CPSP,* 723) and in which he advocates a literary crusade that will obliterate the antiquated heathenism of tradition-bound verse. Referring to his "Democratic Vistas," he writes of

creating in literature an *imaginative* New World, the correspondent and counterpart of the current Scientific and Political New Worlds,— and the perhaps distant, but still delightful prospect, (for our children, if not in our own day,) of delivering America, and, indeed, all Christian lands everywhere, from the thin moribund and watery, but appallingly extensive nuisance of conventional poetry.

(*CPSP,* 724)

Whitman thus states what has since become a common view: the literary past is largely irrelevant to the scientific present. Previous poetry consists primarily of "children's tales" and "mere amorousness, upholstery and superficial rhyme." Furthermore, Whitman not only asserts that the literary past is largely juvenile. He asserts as well that the literary present is scientifically enlightened, at least so far as it embraces "scientism." Similar assertions will appear time and again among subsequent poets. And they, like Whitman, will customarily identify metrical convention with some species of intellectual feudalism and non-metrical verse with some species of scientific progress.

240

The problem Dryden suggested is twofold: (1) Science is progressing and poetry is stagnating; (2) The poetry of the past daunts, by its excellence, the poetry of the present. Whitman in essence offers a twofold solution to the problem: (1) He asserts that modern poetry is scientific and that it is advancing as science is advancing; (2) He asserts that earlier poetry and poetic convention are irrelevant and even alien to modern poetry.

2. The New as the True: Novelty, Modern Verse, and Science

Modern poets have with unprecedented zeal sought novelty. Poets have always, of course, prized distinctive accomplishment, but, for earlier writers, the obligation to be morally instructive or to write in ways relatable to previous literary efforts tended to outweigh the claims of novelty. Moreover, so far as eloquence itself was considered a rare or divinely inspired gift, novelty was a tangential issue. A genuinely eloquent writer could not help but be novel. In addition, when earlier poets sought novelty, they did so with respect more to subject than to technique. When Milton announces, at the beginning of *Paradise Lost,* that he aims at "Things unattempted yet in prose or rhyme," he professes an ambitious novelty of topic. His epic will treat the Fall in order to "justify the ways of God to men." This novelty does not, however, extend to measure. As idiosyncratic as his long verse periods are, he writes in iambic pentameter; indeed, in defending his neglect of rhyme and the frequency with which he enjambs his line, he is at pains to point out that he is following the practice of ancient epic and "our best English tragedies."[12]

Modern poets, in contrast, often assert not only that novelty is a prerequisite of poetic art, but also that poets must specifically discover new techniques. Furthermore, it is argued that these techniques should be aggressively new; they should startle or shock the reader. In his "Reflections on *Vers Libre,*" the young Eliot contends: "In a sluggish society, as actual societies are, tradition is ever lapsing into superstition, and the violent stimulus of novelty is required" (*TCC,* 184). *Blast* is the appropriately entitled periodical in which Pound and Lewis promoted Vorticism. "Make It New" is one of Pound's better known rallying cries, and, for Pound, newness clearly involves new technique. Recalling in a late *Canto* the revolution that he helped to lead, he specifies that the key event concerned the mechanics of versification and the dismantling or destruction of the most familiar unit of conventional English poetry: "To break the pentameter, that was the first heave." [13]

Williams similarly emphasizes novelty. "Nothing is good save the new," he asserts. "If a thing have novelty it stands intrinsically beside every other work of artistic excellence" (*SE,* 21). As does Pound, Williams sees novelty primarily as novelty of technique; novelty means getting rid of old procedures and writing according to new ones. In his "Poem as a Field of Action" essay, he says: "I propose sweeping changes from top to bottom of the poetic structure. . . . I say we are *through* with the iambic pentameter as presently conceived, at least for dramatic verse; through with the measured quatrain, the staid concatenations of sound in the usual stanza, the sonnet" (*SE,* 281). And elsewhere he writes: "The unit of which the line has in the past been constructed no longer in our minds is permitted to exist. That is the thing which makes poems as they still continue to be written [i.e., poems in conventional meter] obsolete. A new measure has supplanted the old!" (*SL,* 332).

Sometimes the desire for novelty is accompanied by the desire to obliterate the past. In his lecture on modern poetry, Hulme laments the fact that poetry is not, like acting and dancing, an art whose performances can be witnessed only once. (Hulme is speaking before cinema and television made the recording of programs in the performing arts commonplace.) According to Hulme, if poems were performed once and then lost forever, the literary past would not be such a burden on the modern poet. He would be spared the worrisome strain of trying to write as well as his distinguished predecessors. Absent from Hulme's discussion is the traditional belief that if Homer and Shakespeare daunt us, they also inspire us and spur us on to write better than we might otherwise. Hulme evidently sees great poets of former times simply as impressive impediments:

> It would be different if poetry, like acting and dancing, were one of the arts of which no record can be kept, and which must be repeated for each generation. The actor has not to feel the competition of the dead as the poet has. Personally I am of course in favour of the complete destruction of all verse more than twenty years old.
>
> (*FS*, 69)

Hulme's comments recall Filippo Tommaso Marinetti's 1908–09 Futurist Manifesto. Marinetti energetically propounds the thesis that art should proceed by means of revolutions which, spaced at regular intervals of ten or so years, will periodically destroy previous art. Insisting that it is continually imperative to do away with the past—and, for that matter, to do away with the present as soon as it starts to slip into the past—Marinetti says:

> Therefore welcome the kindly incendiarists with the carbon fingers! . . . [The ellipses in this passage are Marinetti's own.] Here they are! . . . Here! . . . Away and set fire to the bookshelves! . . . Turn the canals and flood the vaults of museums! . . . Oh! let the glorious old pictures float adrift! Seize the pickax and hammer! Sap the foundations of the venerable towns!
>
> The oldest among us are thirty; we have thus at least ten years in which to accomplish our task. When we are forty, let others— younger and more daring men—throw us into the wastepaper basket like useless manuscripts! . . . They will come against us from far away, from everywhere, leaping on the cadence of their first poems,

clawing the air with crooked fingers and scenting at the academy gates the good smell of our decaying minds already promised to the catacombs of libraries.[14]

The particular association or linking of destruction and novelty—an association or linking that is especially evident in Hulme's and Marinetti's critical writings, develops partly out of Aestheticism. The distinguishing feature of novelty is that it is not like anything that preceded it. Novelty is thus aesthetically free of tradition and history. To the extent that novelty is violent and destructive, it also possesses the aesthetic virtue of immediacy; its force is that of an explosive present blowing away the past, an awareness of which supposedly "impedes" or "checks" the human spirit by connecting and committing it to something that is not itself. That a "liberation" from the past arguably places the human spirit in a bondage far more tyrannical than anything the past might impose is a matter that will be discussed toward the end of this chapter. For now it is necessary only to repeat a point made earlier: the denial or destruction of the past aided the practice of free verse, because such a denial or destruction obscured the fact that, for three millennia, fine poets of many different nations and temperaments had held that poetry fundamentally involved metrical composition.

Novelty and aesthetic organicism also complement each other. Many experimental poets argue that new poetry in general and free verse in particular express an irresistible evolutionary process. This argument—which also has a "scientific" element, so far as it reflects an interest in Darwin's theory of evolution—appears as early as Whitman's 1886 essay, "A Thought on Shakespere." Here Whitman urges: (1) that poetic forms organically decay over time, and (2) that new poetic forms are inevitably better than old ones. "Poetry, largely consider'd, is an evolution, sending out improved and ever-expanded types," says Whitman, adding that even Shakespeare's work has lost its relevance to the modern scientific and democratic world: "Superb and inimitable as all is, it is mostly an objective and physiological kind of power and beauty the soul finds in Shakespere—a style supremely grand of the sort, but in my opinion stopping short of the grandest sort, at any rate for fulfilling and satisfying modern and scientific and democratic American purposes" (*CPSP*, 823, 824). In a later note on Shakespeare, Whitman returns to this subject and again suggests evolution confirms—and even demands—new methods of writing: "Evolution is not the rule in Nature, in Politics, and Inventions only, but in Verse. . . . Then science, the final critic of all, has the casting vote for future poetry." [15]

In much the same manner, Hulme contends that poetic forms, like living organisms, are born, evolve, and die. He combines with this contention the argument that all artistic conventions exhaust themselves the way that musical styles do and the argument that earlier art is inevitably better than later art:

> A particular convention or attitude in art has a strict analogy to the phenomena of organic life. It grows old and decays. It has a definite period of life and must die. All the possible tunes get played on it and then it is exhausted; moreover its best period is its youngest.
>
> (*S*, 121)

Also revealing are comments that Tristan Tzara makes about modern art. Discussing its freedom and variety, Tzara asserts that these express not merely novelty, but a process of organic evolution. Furthermore, this evolution involves revelations, in Tzara's opinion, of noumenal essences indwelling in phenomenal appearances. Modern novelty thus represents, for Tzara, an advance on older art forms not simply because it has evolutionary superiority; novelty represents an advance because it leaves phenomena behind in order to explore noumena. At the risk of oversimplification, one might observe that this argument—which derives immediately from Kantian aesthetics and ultimately from Neoplatonism, has served as the basic defense for most types of abstractionism in the visual arts. Tzara writes:

The diversity of today's artists is a compressed jet of water scattered at crystal liberty. And their efforts create new limpid organisms, in a world of purity, with the aid of transparencies and of the materiality of construction of a simple image which is in the process of formation. They are carrying on the tradition; the past and its evolution are pushing them slowly, like a snake, towards their inner, direct consequences, beyond both surfaces and reality.[16]

If art is evolution, a poet must, to assure himself that he is evolving, keep changing. Pound expresses this view when he says: "No good poetry is ever written in a manner twenty years old" (*LE*, 11). Applied to metrics, such a statement means that it is necessary for poets continually to invent new prosodies. As Hulme puts it, in a comment referred to in this study's introduction, "Those arts like poetry, whose matter is immortal, must find a new technique each generation" (*FS*, 69).

This imperative contributes to the "isms" characteristic of the poetry and art of the early decades of this century; the champions of each "ism" pronouncing themselves the embodiment of the newest New and the rightful successor to the next-to-the-newest-New-but-nonetheless-now-old New. These isms reflect not only a concern with making art novel, but also with securing scientific validation for it. The futurists, for instance, appeal to Darwinian concepts of natural struggle. Pound refers imagism in part to modern psychology (and Hulme, arguably the first imagist poet, was a strong advocate of Bergsonian psychology); and Pound explains ideogrammic method in terms of modern biology. The surrealists avail themselves of Freud's psychoanalytic theories. Williams speaks of free verse as confirming, in the literary realm, Einstein's theories of relativity.

These observations lead to a more specific point. When modern poets seek novelty, they not only seek new techniques; they argue that such techniques will prove (or are) analogous to advances in scientific instrumentation and will enable poets to arrive at insights superior to previous insights. For instance, when

Pound discusses ideogrammic method, he suggests that it provides not merely a scientific directness of observation, but an instrumental improvement for verse-writing comparable to the improvement that inventions like the telescope supplied to scientific research. Pound urges that the ideogrammic method thus stands in relation to earlier poetics as modern science stands in relation to medieval natural philosophy:

> [A]ll your teachers will tell you that science developed more rapidly after Bacon had suggested the direct examination of phenomena, and after Galileo and others had stopped discussing things so much, and had begun really to look at them, and to invent means (like the telescope) of seeing them better. . . .
>
> By contrast to the method of abstraction, or of defining things in more and still more general terms, Fenollosa emphasizes the method of science, 'which is the method of poetry', as distinct from that of 'philosophical discussion', and is the way the Chinese go about it in their ideograph or abbreviated picture writing.
>
> (*ABC,* 20)

Williams, too, urges that the novelty of modern poetry should entail innovative instrumentation. By this means, according to Williams, modern poetry will make the kinds of advances that modern science is making. Williams says that "we have learned that to feel more we have to have, in our day, the means to feel *with*—the tokens, the apparatus. We are lacking in the means— the appropriate paraphernalia, just as modern use of the products of chemistry for *refinement* must have means which the past lacked." In addition, Williams consistently defines the chief task of modern poetry as being the experimental and scientific one of discovering new technical laws of versification to replace conventional meter. As he says in a letter to Kenneth Burke: "All one has to do is to discover new laws of the metric and use them. That's objective enough and little different from the practical deductions of an Edison" (*SE,* 284; *SL,* 257).

Williams also believes that discoveries of new metrical laws are inevitable and predictable in the way that certain scientific discoveries are inevitable once innovations or improvements in apparatus or measurement are made. This belief is evident in a letter Williams writes to Parker Tyler in 1946. Williams had delivered a public lecture and had apparently spoken of a "new way of measuring"; someone in the audience had asked Williams in the question-and-answer period following the lecture if he could explain this new procedure. Williams tells Tyler:

> Someone in the audience, I have seen him before, an older man, asked me if I thought I had given any evidence of the "new way of measuring" in anything I had read that night or in anything that I myself had written at any time. It was a fair question but one I shall have to postpone answering indefinitely. I always think of Mendelejeff's table of atomic weights in this connection. Years before an element was discovered, the element helium, for instance, its presence had been predicated by a blank in the table of atomic weights.
>
> (*SL*, 243)

What Williams and Pound are saying, in brief, is that poetry should have new instruments—a new telescope or a new microscope—or that the laws of versification should be studied with reference to something comparable to a new table of metrical weights and measures. For the experimentalists, free verse is thus, in part, just such an instrument, or it is at least the means by which a new instrument, a *novum organum* for poetry, will be forged.

One should make here a few remarks about relativity. This has been an influential concept in modern poetry. Though scientific relativity concerns the *relatedness* of different frames of reference, some modern poets have misinterpreted the concept to mean *subjectivity* of measurement. This misinterpretation has encouraged the writing of free verse: if measurement is subjective, all forms of versification or non-versification are equally valid, and every poet is free to measure lines according to his own inclinations or convenience.

In Williams especially, one sees relativity summoned as a justification for free verse. "Relativity applies to everything, like love, if it applies to anything in the world," he says in his "Poem as a Field of Action" lecture; with respect to poetry, he adds, "Thus from being fixed, our prosodic values should rightly be seen as only relatively true." In his "On Measure," he writes, "We have today to do with the poetic, as always, but a *relatively* stable foot, not a rigid one." In a letter to John C. Thirlwall, he looks back at his earlier life and offers a general assessment of himself as "a child of a new era in the world, the era which was to discover among other things the relativity of all knowledge." And in another letter to Thirlwall, Williams asserts (in a sentence whose syntax is slightly obscure but whose meaning is clear) that the revolution in poetry confirms and is confirmed by Einstein's theories: "It may seem presumptive to state that such an apparently minor activity as a movement in verse construction could be an indication of Einstein's discoveries in the relativity of our measurements of physical matter is drastic enough, but such is the fact" (*SE,* 283, 286, 340; *SL,* 328, 332).

Williams' appropriation of scientific relativity to assert the superiority of free verse has a recent counterpart. This involves a principle of quantum mechanics, Werner Karl Heisenberg's "uncertainty" or "indeterminacy" principle, which posits the impossibility of making simultaneous measurements of perfect accuracy of both the position and momentum of certain subatomic particles. The impossibility results from the fact that to detect a particle, one must bounce radiation off it, which itself affects the particle's position. Referring to this principle, some critics have urged that free verse is more scientifically valid than metrical composition because free verse is indeterminate. And some poets have scattered words over pages, on the theory that speech thus disposed is performing the verbal equivalent of quantum leaps.

Insofar as the appropriations of relativity and indeterminacy have stimulated discussions of the potentials of language and poetry, those appropriations have been useful and interesting. At the same time, however, one may find them troubling to the extent they have involved misunderstandings of the original scientific concepts. Relativity, at least as Williams uses the word, does not "appl[y] to everything." There could be no science if it did. In physics, for something to be "relative," it requires something to be relative to. Furthermore, one of the postulates of scientific relativity is the constancy of the speed of light, regardless of the motion of its source or the motion of someone observing it.

A similar misunderstanding seems to be reflected in Williams' remark about "the relativity of our measurements of physical matter" and his argument that free verse is an indication, in the poetic sphere, of this relativity of measurements. Scientific relativity concerns the interdependence of temporal, spatial, and kinematic phenomena; it does not posit that the measurement of them is "relative." When one speaks, for instance, of "relativistic mass" and "relativistic velocity," one does not mean that mass and velocity may be gauged according to the preferences of the observer. One means that, if the velocity of an object is sufficiently high, the mass of the object increases. This "relativistic" phenomenon, however, is itself measurable according to the equation $m_o = m\sqrt{(1-v^2/c^2)}$, where m_o is the rest mass, v is the velocity of the object, c is the velocity of light, and m is the relativistic mass.[17]

As for Heisenberg's principle, one might point out that it affirms simply that there is a limit to precise measurement and that this limit is reached at only an incredibly rarefied stage. One might also point out that quantum mechanics concern subatomic phenomena and that words are not subatomic particles.

There is a related matter. When Williams asserts that "[a] new measure has supplanted the old" but that he must "postpone answering indefinitely" what that new measure is, one may legitimately question his reasoning. Scientific discoveries may be quantifiably verified. If one contends that a cure for a disease has been found or a new discovery in physics has been made, experiments can be devised to confirm or refute the contention. Indeed, though there are cases of scientists who have advanced theories that later proved to be wrong,[18] most modern scientists would be chary of announcing particular discoveries until they had empirical or mathematical evidence to back up their discoveries. (Even Mendeleev's predictions were based on the already established knowledge of many elements and on the fact that the periodic recurrence of similar chemical and physical properties among these elements suggested the existence of additional, hitherto unobserved elements.) It is a different thing to advocate sweeping changes in poetic structure or to announce that one has discovered a new metric, and then to say that the evidence in support of the changes or the discovery does not exist or that its presentation must be indefinitely postponed. Demanding that such an argument be assented to and acted on is like ordering an astronaut into a never-before-tested rocket and blasting him off to an as yet unsighted planet.

One may feel similar reservations about appeals to evolution to justify violent innovation in the arts. One can reasonably argue that art should express natural dynamism. But it is well to remember that plant and animal species do not modify themselves because someone publishes a manifesto in a journal of natural history. They change for the most part in a comparatively gradual manner, usually retaining features of earlier stages of development.

It is also perhaps a less than sound procedure to think that any change in poetic technique is a change for the better and that poetry itself develops as surely as science can. Certainly in Western literature, weak and strong periods have alternated and fluctuated. If different readers were to graph poetic achievement from the Greeks to the present, they would no doubt come up with different results; yet it is likely that all readers would produce graphs that oscillated rather than ones that showed continuous (or always favorably punctuated) improvements.

The concept that verse and art can advance as science does is related to the faith, which itself results from the growth of science and technology in the Enlightenment and the nineteenth century, that the future will be in every way better than the past. If one holds this faith, one perhaps will naturally believe that it is unwise to try to shape the future's course or to criticize whatever it brings: one will see the future as being synonomous with progress, a force whose might makes right. And we may cite, in leaving this topic for the moment, Marinetti's vigorous summary of this faith:

> You ought to fear everything from the moss-grown past. All your hope should be in the Future.
>
> Put your trust in Progress, which is always right even when it is wrong, because it is movement, life, struggle, hope.
>
> And see that you do not go to law with Progress. Let it be an imposter, faithless, an assassin, a thief, an incendiary, Progress is always right.[19]

3. Impersonality and Skepticism: The Poet as Scientist

That "experimental" is an adjective commonly applied to modern poetry indicates not merely the degree to which modern poetry has emulated science. It indicates also the degree to which modern poets have emulated the scientist in the laboratory.

The application of the word "experiment" to poetry occurs as early as Wordsworth. In the Advertisement to the first edition of *Lyrical Ballads,* Wordsworth states: "The majority of the following poems are to be considered as experiments" (*SPP,* 443). And in his preface to the second edition, he says of the collection:

> It was published, as an experiment, which, I hoped, might be of some use to ascertain, how far, by fitting to metrical arrangement a selection of the real language of men in a state of vivid sensation, that sort

of pleasure and that quantity of pleasure may be imparted, which a Poet may rationally endeavour to impart.

(SPP, 445)

In speaking of "experiment," however, Wordsworth is not referring to scientific method. Rather, he signifies the word's more general meaning of "trial" or "testing." Though he is interested in science and even speculates about the possibility of treating contemporary scientific topics in verse, he does not suggest, as will later writers, that literary composition may be transformed into a species of science. Indeed, this development is not clearly evident until the second half of the nineteenth century.[20]

Émile Zola heralds this development, though he does so in connection with prose fiction rather than verse. In his 1880 *Experimental Novel,* he proposes a method for writing fiction derived from *Introduction to the Study of Experimental Medicine* by the physiologist Claude Bernard. Zola's work represents, in one respect, a version of Peacock's assertion that the modern age belongs to science and that conventional art is obsolete. "The return to nature," says Zola, "the naturalistic evolution which marks the century, drives little by little all the manifestation of human intelligence into the same scientific path" (*CTSP,* 647). But whereas Peacock suggests that imaginative literature should therefore silently retire into its own irrelevance, Zola contends that imaginative literature, if it will make itself scientific, can occupy a place in modern culture. He argues, in brief, that fiction must become a science, and the writer must become a scientist: "Now, science enters into the domain of us novelists. . . . In one word, we should operate on the characters, the passions, on the human and social data, in the same way that the chemist and the physicist operate on inanimate beings, and as the physiologist operates on living beings" (*CTSP,* 650).

Zola subsequently identifies the new experimental fiction he proposes with modern science in general. Moreover, he suggests experimental literature will represent an intellectual advance over classical and Romantic literature, just as modern scientific thinking represents an intellectual advance over scholasticism and theology:

> [T]he experimental novel is a consequence of the scientific evolution of the century; it continues and completes physiology, which itself leans for support on chemistry and medicine; it substitutes for the study of the abstract and the metaphysical man the study of the natural man, governed by physical and chemical laws, and modified by the influences of his surroundings; it is in one word the literature of our scientific age, as the classical and Romantic literature corresponded to a scholastic and theological age.

> (*CTSP*, 651)

When Zola, then, speaks of a kind of novel as being *experimentale,* the word is no longer neutrally descriptive. It is designed, as it is in many later discussions of the arts, to confer on its noun the prestige of science and the authority of the up-to-date.

During the modern movement, poets often see themselves as scientists and refer their procedures to the scientific laboratory. For instance, Pound announces at the outset of *ABC of Reading,* "The proper METHOD for studying poetry and good letters is the method of contemporary biologists, that is careful first-hand examination of the matter, and continual COMPARISON of one 'slide' or specimen with another" (*ABC,* 17). Paul Valéry observes: "With every question, before making any deep examination of the content, I take a look at the language; I generally proceed like a surgeon who sterilizes his hands and prepares the area to be operated on. This is what I call *cleaning up the verbal situation.* You must excuse this expression equating the words and forms of speech with the hands and instruments of a surgeon."[21] And speaking of Valéry, Eliot remarks that the great French poet "invented, and was to impose upon his age, not so much a new conception of poetry as a new conception of the poet. The tower of ivory has been fitted up as a laboratory. . . . The poet is comparable to the mathematical physicist, or else to the biologist or chemist. He is to carry out the role of scientist as studiously as Sherlock Holmes did."[22]

To be a "scientist" means, for the modern poet, to possess several related qualities. One of these is depersonalization. In *A Portrait of the Artist as a Young Man,* James Joyce's poet-hero Stephen Dedalus suggestively reflects on this quality. "The personality of the artist," Stephen says to Lynch towards the end of the novel, "at first a cry or a cadence or a mood and then a fluid and lambent narrative, finally refines itself out of existence, impersonalises itself, so to speak."[23] Yet the most famous discussion of the depersonalized poet is probably that provided by Eliot in his "Tradition and the Individual Talent." Specifically associating depersonalization with science, Eliot says, "The progress of an artist is a continual self-sacrifice, a continual extinction of personality. . . . It is in this depersonalization that art may be said to approach the condition of science" (*SE 1917–32,* 7). To illustrate his meaning, Eliot draws a metaphor from chemistry, suggesting that the mind of the poet resembles a catalytic agent. The poet's consciousness is, according to Eliot, comparable to a shred of platinum introduced into a chamber containing oxygen and sulphur dioxide; just as the platinum causes the formation of a new substance (sulphurous acid) while itself remaining unaltered, so the mind of the poet transmutes feelings into a work of art without being changed:

> [T]he mind of the mature poet differs from that of the immature one not precisely in any valuation of "personality," not being necessarily more interesting, or having "more to say," but rather by being a more finely perfected medium in which special, or very varied, feelings are at liberty to enter into new combinations.
>
> The analogy was that of the catalyst. When the two gases previously mentioned are mixed in the presence of a filament of platinum, they form sulphurous acid. This combination takes place only if the platinum is present; nevertheless the newly formed acid contains no trace of platinum, and the platinum itself is apparently unaffected;

has remained inert, neutral, and unchanged. The mind of the poet is the shred of platinum.

(SE 1917–32, 7)[24]

It is interesting to note that Eliot's impersonal poet functions unconsciously. Like "the shred of platinum," his mind is a "medium in which special, or very varied, feelings are at liberty to enter into new combinations." Throughout the poetic process, it remains "inert, neutral, and unchanged." Eliot once said of his best-known poem, "In *The Waste Land* I wasn't even bothering whether I understood what I was saying."[25] This statement, and his observations about the inert neutrality of the poet's mind during the process of composition suggest a way in which scientific and aesthetic tendencies in modern poetry reinforce one another. For if the poet is regarded as a scientifically depersonalized agent, with whose chemical-creative powers no conscious regulation interferes, he is free to compose spontaneously and automatically. He is free to write the "pure poetry' that, in Mallarmé's words, "implies the elocutionary disappearance of the poet, who cedes the initiative to the words, mobilised by the shock of their unevenness."[26]

Skepticism is another quality which modern writers seek for its scientific value. Recommending that authors adopt a detached attitude towards their material, Zola remarks: "All experimental reasoning is based on doubt, for the experimentalist should have no preconceived idea, in the face of nature, and should always retain his liberty of thought. He simply accepts the phenomena which are produced, when they are proved" (*CTSP*, 647). Explaining the principles of Dada, Tzara likewise advocates a total distrust of received procedures and opinion: "Dada places before action and above all: *Doubt. DADA* doubts everything."[27] Yeats relates that he and others associated with *The Savoy* magazine in the nineties were trying, in their iconoclasm, to claim the privilege of impartially analyzing all mental and spiritual phenomena, just as science had claimed the same privilege with respect to physical phenomena. "I think that had we been challenged," says Yeats, "we might have argued something after this fashion: 'Science through much ridicule and some persecution has won its right to explore whatever passes before its corporeal eye, and merely because it passes. . . . Literature now demands the same right of exploration of all that passes before the mind's eye, and merely because it passes.'"[28]

If the poet is scientifically skeptical as well as depersonalized, he is likely to hold himself aesthetically aloof not only from moral judgment, but from the literary past. He may well regard poetic conventions as a scientist might regard the doctrine of the four humors. Even if he adopts—as, for instance, Eliot and Pound do—a respectful view of the literary past, he may well consider it, from a practical standpoint, less as a body of materials worthy of emulation than as a repository of antiquated procedures. This attitude has had a special impact on versification, for the reason it has not only encouraged the practice of free verse, but has enabled many to treat those who have defended metrical convention as the poetic equivalents of flat-earth theorists.

This attitude is apparent in an essay which Eliot wrote in 1918 and in which he discusses Pound's *Little Review* anthology of modern French poetry. Pound's anthology includes work by vers-libristes such as Laforgue, Moréas, Stuart Merrill, and Remy de Gourmont; Eliot urges that English-language poets should adopt, under the imperative of scientific progress, the new methods developed in French. At this point in his career, one should note, Eliot appears to have held a less favorable opinion of Wordsworth than he later did, when he came to see Wordsworth's revolution as analogous to his own. Eliot says in his essay that the modern French poets have made "discoveries" in verse that have an objective validity comparable to discoveries in science and that any poet who fails to note and incorporate in his practice the implications of these discoveries dooms himself to poetic backwardness:

257

A poet, like a scientist, is contributing toward the organic development of culture: it is just as absurd for him not to know the work of his predecessors or of men writing in other languages as it would be for a biologist to be ignorant of Mendel or De Vries. It is exactly as wasteful for a poet to do what has been done already, as for a biologist to rediscover Mendel's discoveries. The French poets in question have made "discoveries" in verse of which we cannot afford to be ignorant, discoveries which are not merely a concern for French syntax. To remain with Wordsworth is equivalent to ignoring the whole of science subsequent to Erasmus Darwin.[29]

One should mention as well that scientific impersonality and skepticism are sometimes associated with poetic difficulty and with the idea, as Eliot puts it, "that it appears likely that poets in our civilization, as it exists at present, must be *difficult*" (*SE,* *1917–32,* 248). If the common reader finds the modern poet hard to understand, the poet, in the guise of a scientist, may point out that the common reader probably also finds the modern scientist hard to understand—the implication being that it is as wrong-headed to complain of difficulty in the modern poet as it is to complain of difficulty in the modern scientist. Pound says:

> The serious artist is usually, or is often as far from the aegrum vulgus as is the serious scientist. Nobody has heard of the abstract mathematicians who worked out the determinants that Marconi made use of in his computations for the wireless telegraph. The public, the public so dear to the journalistic heart, is far more concerned with the shareholders in the Marconi company.
>
> (*LE,* 47)

One might note that Pound's argument implicitly denies a traditional distinction between science and poetry. Customarily, the scientist speaks to a small community of fellow scientists, whereas the poet speaks to a more diverse audience. As Edward Bulwer-Lytton observes: "In science, address the few; in literature, the many. In science, the few must dictate opinion to the many; in literature, the many, sooner or later, force their judgment on the few."[30] Often fine poets do not immediately receive the public attention that they deserve; often when they do receive it, they must share it with inferior writers. As Horace says (*Epistles,* 2.1.63), "At times the public see straight; sometimes they make mistakes." This does not mean, however, that evaluation of poems should, like the evaluation of scientific theories, be entrusted to a small circle of "experts." Such an arrangement for poetry merely promotes coterie verse and the tyranny of the professional critic. What is more, it is arguably as foolish to value poetry simply on the basis of unpopularity and difficulty as to value it simply on the basis of popularity and facility.

The emphasis among modern poets on scientific impersonality and skepticism is understandable to the extent that they are reacting to the emotional excesses of much of the verse of the nineteenth century. However, as with other aspects of the modern movement, the experimentalists appear sometimes to generalize their impatience indiscriminately. They appear to overlook the fact that a great deal of poetry which incorporates ethical and moral judgment is neither "soft" nor "mushy." One should perhaps be suspicious about approaches to poetry aimed more at avoiding the shortcomings of a Shelley or a Swinburne than at achieving the depth and variousness of a Shakespeare or a Hardy.

In any case, the idea that poetry should scientifically shun ethical and moral evaluation may be contrasted with the assumption of the ancient rhetorical tradition that a poet or orator examines successively a *status coniecturalis,* a *status definitiva,* and a *status qualitatis.* The ancient idea that a poet or orator determines first the existence of something, then defines what it is, and, finally and most crucially, examines its moral implications is notably different from the modern outlook that holds in effect that the writer should arrest his work at the level of the *status definitiva.* Quintilian's argument (7.4.24) that "the real task of eloquence is to demonstrate *quality:* there lies its kingdom, there its power, and there its unique victory" is in the modern period turned on its head. For many moderns, such a demonstration is precisely what the author, the experimental author, seeks to avoid. As Zola puts it, "Experimental science [and by extension experimental fiction] has no necessity to worry itself about the 'why' of things; it simply explains the 'how'" (*CTSP,* 647).[31]

4. Data and Method: Poetry as Fact or Formula

When modern poets emulate scientific procedure, they emulate it in two principal ways. Either they pursue a methodology that has a rigidity considered to be scientific, or they collect and present particulars in a manner which they regard as analogous to scientific data gathering. We will examine the latter type of emulation first.

For some experimental poets, being scientific primarily entails the observation of particulars and, concomitantly, the suppression of abstract thought, on the ground that it might result in erroneous interpretations of the particulars. This circumstance accounts for an evident contradiction in the attitudes of the experimentalists toward science. Real modern science, especially modern physics, involves not only observation of natural phenomena, but hypothetical and theoretical reasoning as well.[32] Much experimental poetry, on the other hand, is anti-rational and anti-discursive. In other words, the science to which poetry appeals is, in this sense and context, not so much modern as it is Baconian.

Bacon's introduction to his *Novum Organum* (1620) contains statements that may clarify this point. Contending that the scholastic logic of his day offers no sure road to knowledge, and urging that scientists should instead follow an inductive experimentality, Bacon remarks:

Now my method, though hard to practice, is easy to explain; and it is this. I propose to establish progressive stages of certainty. The evidence of the sense, helped and guarded by a certain process of correction, I retain. But the mental operation which follows the act of sense I for the most part reject: and instead of it I open and lay out a new and certain path for the mind to proceed in, starting directly from the simple sensuous perception.[33]

This is, *mutatis mutandis,* the method of the Imagist poet and of subsequent poets who adopt, with variations, the Imagist program. The Imagists and their followers are concerned with "the simple sensuous perception," but reject "the mental operation which follows the act of sense."

To appreciate the resemblances between the aims of the Imagist poet and those of Bacon's investigator of nature, one need merely examine the principles expounded by leaders of the Imagist movement. For instance, Hulme says of poetic speech, "It is not a counter language, but a visual concrete one. It is a compromise for a language of intuition which would hand over sensations bodily. It always endeavors to arrest you, and to make you continuously see a physical thing, to prevent you gliding through an abstract process. . . . Images in verse are not mere decoration, but the very essence of an intuitive language." (*S,* 134, 135). These ideas appear as well in Pound, who advocates "[d]irect treatment of the 'thing' whether subjective or objective," and who warns the would-be poet, "Go in fear of abstractions" (*LE,* 3, 5). So, too, Williams observes: "The first thing you learn when you begin to learn anything about this earth is that you are eternally barred save for the report of your senses from knowing anything about it" (*SL,* 331); and in *Paterson* he urges, as a kind of poetic credo, "No ideas but in things."[34] In effect, then, Hulme, Pound, and Williams all are elevating, in Baconian fashion, sense perception over abstract thought.

The most Baconian of the modern sciences—those that are the most empirical and are based more on observation than on theoretical thought—are the life sciences of biology, biochemistry, zoology, and botany. It is not surprising, then, that poets advocating imagistic particularity have appealed especially to these sciences to explain and justify their work. (This is not to say that a poet like Williams may not appeal to theoretical physics a few sentences or pages after appealing to experimental chemistry.) The life sciences are more "aesthetic," in that they more involve sense perception, than physics and mathematics. Poets have additionally appealed to the life sciences for the reason that they entail the study of processes of growth and thus confirm, in the minds of some, the legitimacy of organic form. Pound especially appeals to biochemistry to explain his practices, asserting, for example, that art itself is a science that has special connections with chemistry and medicine: "The arts, literature, poesy, are a science, just as chemistry is a science. . . . The arts give us a great percentage of the lasting and unassailable data regarding the nature of man, of immaterial man, of man considered as a thinking and sentient creature. They begin where the science of medicine leaves off or rather they overlap that science" (*LE,* 42). Likewise, explaining ideogrammic method, he says:

> If so lately as the week before last one of the brighter scholars still professed ignorance of the meaning of "ideogram[m]ic" I must try once again to define that term, necessary to the said student if he still wishes to follow me or my meaning.
> Ernest Fenollosa attacked, quite rightly, a great weakness in western ratiocination. He pointed out that the material sciences, biology, chemistry, examined collections of fact, phenomena, specimens, and gathered general equations of real knowledge from them, even though the observed data had no syllogistic connection one with another.[35]

Pound's *Cantos* embody the method here described. The work is comprised of "collections of fact, phenomena, specimens" with "no syllogistic connection one with another." Much the same method governs other significant modern poems, such as Williams' *Paterson* and David Jones' *Anathemata;* Jones tellingly opens the preface to his work by quoting Nennius' remark, "I have made a heap of all that I could find."[36] In such poems, the poet provides a great deal of what Pound calls "observed data" with little or no rational organization or analysis of the data.

At this juncture, one should speak once more of correlations between scientific and aesthetic tendencies in modern verse. The bare "scientific" presentation of data well suits the "aesthetic" interest in suggestiveness. If one writes a poem which offers the reader imagistic details without indicating their significance, one has written a poem which may be said to suggest anything or perhaps nothing. One can thus claim both scientific precision, in the sense of avoiding possibly unreliable abstraction, and aesthetic freedom, in the sense of eluding definite (and therefore self-limiting) meaning.

It also should be observed that to the extent that the Imagists tend to exclude discursive reason from their enterprise altogether, they go beyond the position adopted by Bacon, who never suggested that science or philosophy should completely abandon theoretical or abstract thought. Nor is there anything Baconian in the Imagists' identification of immediate visual appearance with intuitive significance. This notion suggests less scientific examinations of nature than Neoplatonic discussions of pictographic (*symbolikē*) literary representation. Here it is illuminating to compare Pound's ideogrammic method with Plotinus' discussion (*Enneads,* 5.8.6) of hieroglyphics:

> [T]he wise of Egypt—whether in precise knowledge or by a prompting of nature—indicated the truth where, in their effort towards philosophical statement, they left aside the writing-forms that take in the detail of words and sentences—those characters that represent sounds and convey the propositions of reasoning—and drew pictures instead, engraving in the temple-inscriptions a separate image for every separate item: thus they exhibited the absence of discursiveness

in the Intellectual Realm. For each manifestation of knowledge and wisdom is a distinct image, an object in itself, an immediate unity, not an aggregate of discursive reasoning and detailed willing.[37]

Like Pound, who considers Chinese characters as "ideograph or abbreviated picture writing' (*ABC,* 20), Plotinus praises writing which communicates nondiscursively. Like Pound, who says "that there are two kinds of written language, one based on sound and the other on sight" (*ABC,* 20), and who urges that the latter is superior (for poetry at least) to the former, Plotinus asserts the superiority of hieroglyphics over discourse involving "words and sentences." Both Plotinus and Pound advocate, that is, visual discourse in preference to composition based on the representation of sound. That neither hieroglyphics nor Chinese characters in fact comprise a visual language is not relevant here. What is crucial is that a mystical type of communication is presented as possessing a higher value than discursive communication possesses. What is peculiarly "modern" about Pound's presentation is that he urges that such mystical communication is "THE METHOD OF SCIENCE" (*ABC,* 26).

This mixture of science and mysticism appears as well in Pound's early discussion, in his "Retrospect" essay, of the "Image." Connecting imagism with science (the science here, however, is psychology), he explains:

> An 'Image' is that which presents an intellectual and emotional complex in an instant of time. I use the term 'complex' rather in the technical sense employed by the newer psychologists, such as Hart, though we might not agree absolutely in our application.
>   It is the presentation of such a "complex" instantaneously which gives that sense of sudden liberation; that sense of freedom from time limits and space limits; that sense of sudden growth, which we experience in the presence of the greatest works of art.
>
>   (*LE,* 4)

What Pound seems to be suggesting is a poetic method whose "scientific" character is designed to produce a mystical experi-

ence. The mere presentation of an "Image" is seen as being sufficient to release a flood of insight.[38]

It may appear curious that Pound, while advocating that poetry should be "musical," also urges that it should be written so as
to convey visual images rather than sounds. No communication
would seem less musical than that based on pictographic representations of objects. Yet if one reads Pound with care, one gradually realizes that in his terms, a musical poem is, in a crucial way,
like a poem which is imagistic. Pure sound and pure image both
elude statement, and hence they achieve the same aesthetic immediacy. Both musical poetry and imagistic poetry "liberate" speech
from its verbal condition.

The appropriation of *haiku* by the Imagists deserves comment
here. The verse form in the original Japanese generally followed
definite conventions.[39] These included the reference to the season
in which the poem was written and the so-called breaking word
that marked the crux or turn of the poem, not to mention the
metrical convention of the five-seven-five syllabic measure. Furthermore, *haiku* assumed and alluded to a considerable body of
literary and religious tradition. These factors enabled the reader
to recognize the meanings of the physical details presented by the
poet. In practicing *haiku* during the modern movement, poets
such as Pound, Flint, and Amy Lowell retained something of the
superficial character of the form. However, they did not retain the
conventions that gave meaning to the traditional Japanese *haiku,*
nor did they invent conventions of their own to replace the absent
originals. Thus the form that in Japanese was a means for intel-
ligible, if often indirect, statement became in English a vehicle for
ineffability and symbolism.

Poets concerned with data frequently express a related concern
with the fragmentation of data, with the breaking down of observed detail into component parts. The theory behind this practice is that, just as breaking down chemical or biological material
into its component elements produces clearer knowledge of
matter, so breaking down literary materials will produce similar

knowledge. This theory appears with special frequency in Pound. In his original first *Canto,* he announces, "I have many fragments," and he evidently felt the value of the poem as a whole was that it served as "a rag-bag" for the fragments.[40] A related idea informs his praise of Stravinsky and George Antheil. For Pound, the value of their music appears to derive from its fragmentary nature. This fragmentation, he contends, represents a kind of scientific atom-smashing of conventional notes, and thus it illuminates the essential qualities of the constituents of music: "[V]ia Stravinsky and Antheil and possibly one other composer, we are brought to a closer conception of time, to a faster beat, to a closer realisation or, shall we say, 'decomposition' of the musical atom."[41]

One may recall at this point that Eliot characterizes *The Waste Land,* the most celebrated poem of the modern movement, as "These fragments I have shored against my ruins."[42] This description could cover many other works produced in this century. It is as if, for many modern writers, the fragmentary alone is "true" and "pure" in the sense of containing its own irreducible essence. Nor is fragmentation in modern poetry simply scientifically motivated. It is aesthetically motivated as well because the fragment, like the unmediated image, is suggestive rather than definite.

Turning specifically to versification, one may note that if the fragment is prized more than the whole, the poet may well be drawn to experiment with free verse. Free verse is itself fragmentary, since it is customarily compounded of fragments of rhythm. Here again, Pound's comment, "To break the pentameter, that was the first heave," is significant. It indicates the value he and other modernists placed on breaking apart, in virtually a physical manner, metrical conventions.

If experimental poets sometimes construe their works as scientific presentations of data, so they sometimes construe their works as scientific exercises in what Pound calls "METHOD." This tendency is reflected not only in the "ism" movements already mentioned. It is reflected also in the compositional formulae that certain modern poets have devised with a view to endowing their works with a kind of mathematical validation.

These formulae must be distinguished from traditional principles of proportion. These principles, such as perspective in painting, rhythm in music, and meter in poetry, assist the artist in organizing his work. But they offer only general directives. Though they supply frameworks for composition, the artist who adopts them is free to explore and arrange a variety of different materials in a variety of different ways. Once certain basic requirements of structure are met, the details of the work may, as the artist composes, be treated as need or preference or even accident dictates.

The modern formulae, on the other hand, are usually private principles devised by an artist to insure, before composition begins, both the general nature and the individual features of his finished work. Furthermore, the work itself is regarded as a sort of geometrical demonstration; its success depends on its adherence to its own self-created and self-contained procedures. Its relationship to a world of experience external to itself, and its relationship to other works and conventions, are essentially irrelevant.

Poe provides an early instance of this type of formula. In his "Philosophy of Composition," he discusses the manner in which he prearranged his writing of "The Raven." He announces that "the work proceeded, step by step, to its completion with the precision and rigid consequence of a mathematical problem"; and he prescribes, in discussing the steps in this process, a precise recipe for making a poem. Poe argues that a work in verse should ideally: (1) be approximately one hundred lines long; (2) convey an impression of Beauty; (3) be Melancholic in tone; (4) employ, as a central device, a one-word refrain (Poe comments that he chose for "The Raven" the word "Nevermore" because he believes the refrain "must be sonorous and susceptible of protracted empha-sis" and because a long *o* is "the most sonorous vowel" and *r* "the most producible consonant"); (5) have as its subject the death of a beautiful lady [literally, (2) plus (3) equals (5): Beauty plus Melan-choly equals Beautiful Dead Lady]; (6) have as its speaker the bereaved lover of the deceased. Only after having constructed this formula, Poe remarks, did he begin writing; even here, he did not start with the first stanza but with the climactic one: "Here then the poem may be said to have its beginning—at the end, where all works of art should begin" (*ER,* 15, 18, 20).

Whether Poe actually composed "The Raven" in the fashion that he outlines is not important. What is important is that Poe holds up the formula as, to refer to the title of his essay, a philoso-phy of composition.

Such a procedure encourages literary automatism. Once a for-mula has been concocted, the poem manufactures itself. Hence, as odd as it may seem at first, formulae of this type suit the aesthetic ideals of organic spontaneity. Vegetable expression is uncon-scious. Equally unconscious is a mathematical equation. Instinc-tive immediacy and formulaic predetermination thus become, so to speak, two sides of the same coin.

This compatibility of the unconsciously spontaneous and the formulaically predetermined is evident in Breton's program for surrealist writing. Advising the surrealist writer how to compose, Breton says:

> Write quickly without any previously chosen subject, quickly enough not to dwell on, and not to be tempted to read over, what you have written. . . . Punctuation of course necessarily hinders the stream of absolute continuity which preoccupies us. But you should particularly distrust the prompting whisper. If through a fault ever so trifling there is a fore-warning of silence to come, a fault, let us say, of inattention, break off unhesitatingly the line that has become too, lucid. After the word whose origin seems suspect you should place a letter, any letter, *l* for example, always the letter *l,* and restore the arbitrary flux by making that letter the initial of the word to follow.[43]

Breton's concept of "arbitrary flux" recalls Rimbaud's remark in his letter to Paul Demeny: "Le Poète se fait *voyant* par un long, immense et raisonné *dérèglement* de *tous les sens*" (The poet makes himself a visionary by a long, immense and reasoned *derangement* of *all the senses*.)[44] Though Rimbaud underscores the derangement, equal emphasis should perhaps be laid on the epithets: the derangement is "reasoned." Extreme freedom is systematized.

In their prescriptions, Poe and Breton are painstakingly specific; their formulae possess unusual clarity. Nevertheless, a similar tendency to construe poetry in arbitrary formulae characterizes many other writers. Pound, for example, urges in his *Spirit of Romance:* "Poetry is a sort of inspired mathematics, which gives us equations, not for abstract figures, triangles, spheres, and the like, but for the human emotions."[45] This notion is repeated, with different terminology, by Eliot in his *Hamlet* essay, in which he asserts that emotion in poetry cannot be expressed straightforwardly, but rather requires an "objective correlative," that is, "a set of objects, a situation, a chain of events which shall be the formula of that *particular* emotion; such that when the external facts, which must terminate in sensory experience, are given, the emotion is immediately evoked" (*SE 1917–32,* 124–25).

Both the search for formulae, and the use of formulae to explain or validate experimentality, appear also in discussions of modern visual art. A revealing instance is supplied by Wassily Kandinsky. In his 1911 *Concerning the Spiritual in Art* and in his 1938 essay "Concrete Art," he elaborates a system for abstract painting, according to which colors are assigned specific emotional and tonal properties. And it is interesting to note that when, in *Concerning the Spiritual in Art,* he discusses abstraction in painting, he not only appeals to a quasi-mathematical formula, but also defends abstractionism in general on the grounds that it is musically expressive and embodies noumenal essence as opposed to phenomenal appearance:

> [T]he various arts are drawing together. They are finding in Music the best teacher. With few exceptions music has been for some cen-

turies the art which has devoted itself not to the reproduction of natural phenomena, but rather to the expression of the artist's soul, in musical sound.

A painter, who finds no satisfaction in mere representation, however artistic, in his longing to express his inner life, cannot but envy the ease with which music, the most non-material of the arts today, achieves this end. He naturally seeks to apply the methods of music to his own art. And from this results that modern desire for rhythm in painting, for mathematical, abstract construction, for repeated notes of colour, for setting colour in motion.[46]

Among other things, Kandinsky's remarks indicate a connection between nonrepresentational painting and non-metrical verse: both reflect a desire for a musicality of expression which is, simultaneously, spiritually ineffable and scientifically precise.

Setting forth his system for abstract painting, Kandinsky argues that colors have intricate correspondences with sounds produced by musical instruments and with emotions that those sounds suggest. He reproduces and compresses this system in "Concrete Art," saying:

> YELLOW, for example, possesses the special capacity to "ascend" higher and higher and to attain heights unbearable to the eye and the spirit; the sound of a trumpet played higher and higher becoming more and more "pointed," giving pain to the ear and to the spirit. BLUE, with the completely opposite power to "descend" into infinite depths, develops the sounds of the flute (when it is light blue), of the cello (when it has descended farther), of the double bass with its magnificent deep sounds; and in the depths of the organ you "see" the depths of blue. GREEN is well balanced and corresponds to the medium and the attenuated sounds of the violin. When skillfully applied, RED (vermillion) can give the impression of strong drum beats.[47]

In other words, according to Kandinsky, it is possible for a painter, using the system outlined, to render exactly in paint states of mind and spirit without having to resort to conventional representations of people and objects.

270

If Kandinsky's assigning of musical values to colors seems fanciful, nonetheless it has great resonance for our discussion, because the most famous of all modern precompositional formulae is musical. This formula is the twelve-tone system, according to which the composer organizes the twelve notes of the chromatic scale in a set tone row and then, in composing his piece, repeats the order of the tone row throughout his entire composition. Since the tone row is symmetrically expanded by its inversion, its retrograde form, and its retrograde inversion—and since a note, while restricted from appearing out of sequence, may be sounded in any octave when its turn comes round (e.g., a higher C may be substituted for the middle C in the original sequence)—there is extensive room for variations. These variations, nevertheless, are wholly determined by the tone row, and they derive their legitimacy from its authority.

Schönberg is the best known exponent of this theory of "serial" composition. We will now turn to Thomas Mann's *Doctor Faustus,* which examines the theory and analyzes the significance, for modern art in general, of such formulae.

5. *Superstition and Experiment*

The hero of Mann's novel is a composer named Adrian Leverkühn. A gifted artistic revolutionary, Leverkühn is dissatisfied with music's traditional resources. Like many artistic revolutionaries of our century, however, he has the power only to destroy the conventional. He lacks the generative ability to invent something new to stand in place of the old. To escape this predicament, he enters into a pact with the devil. In exchange for Leverkühn's soul, Lucifer liberates the composer from artistic sterility.

A crucial scene in the novel occurs in its twenty-second chapter when Leverkühn is walking in the country one afternoon with Serenus Zeitblom, his closest friend and the narrator of the novel.

Leverkühn speaks of having earlier in his career written a song that "is entirely derived from a fundamental figure, a series of interchangeable intervals, the five notes B, E, A, E, E-flat, and the horizontal melody and the vertical harmony are determined and controlled by it. . . . It is like a word, a key word, stamped on everything in the song."[48] Yet, suggests Leverkühn, the song was not satisfactory: the tonal space afforded by the five notes was too confined; the word was too short. The composer goes on to speculate about expanding his original figure, and in the course of his speculations, he discusses compositional possibilities that were explored in real life by Schönberg, Berg, and Webern:

> One would have to go on from here [the five-tone row] and make larger words out of the twelve letters, as it were, of the tempered semitone alphabet. Words of twelve letters, certain combinations and interrelations of the twelve semitones, series of notes from which a piece and all the movements of a work must strictly derive. Every note of the whole composition, both melody and harmony, would have to show its relation to this fixed fundamental series. Not one might recur until the other notes have sounded. Not one might appear which did not fulfil its function in the whole structure. There would no longer be a free note. That is what I would call 'strict composition.'
>
> (*DF*, 191)

Zeitblom is impressed by the composer's reflections, but he registers a reservation about the system outlined to him:

> A striking thought. . . . Rational organization through and through, one might indeed call it. You would gain an extraordinary unity and congruity, a sort of astronomical regularity and legality would be obtained thereby. But when I picture it to myself, it seems to me that the unchanged recurrence of such a succession of intervals, even when used in different parts of the texture, and in rhythmic variations, would result in a probably unavoidable serious musical impoverishment and stagnation.
>
> (*DF*, 191–92)

Zeitblom raises the further objection that in determining the work entirely by precompositional formula, the real composition would be done, in effect, prior to composition. The selection of the sequence of notes of the tone row would be a sort of substitute for the creative act of actual composition. Once the composer has established the tone row, all the details of his unwritten composition would be settled. "When he went to work," Zeitblom comments, "he would no longer be free" (*DF,* 193).

Leverkühn replies, "Bound by a self-imposed compulsion to order, hence free," to which Zeitblom, who is a classical scholar, returns: "Well, of course the dialectic of freedom is unfathomable. But he could scarcely be called a free inventor of his harmony. Would not the making of chords be left to chance and accident?" Leverkühn answers, "Say, rather, to the context [of the composition in which the chords figured]. The polyphonic dignity of every chord-forming note would be guaranteed by the constellation [of the notes]." And he suggests that, like traditional composers, he aims "to resolve the magic essence of music into human reason" (*DF,* 193).

Zeitblom, however, will not be evaded and responds:

> You want to put me on my honour as a humanist. . . . Human reason! And besides, excuse me; 'constellation' is your every other word. But surely it belongs more to astrology. The rationalism you call for has a good deal of superstition about it—of belief in the incomprehensibly and vaguely daemonic, the kind of thing we have in games of chance, fortune-telling with cards, and shaking dice. Contrary to what you say, your system seems to me more calculated to dissolve human reason in magic.
>
> (*DF,* 193–94)

Leverkühn, who suffers from chronic headaches, puts his hand to his brow, and says: "Reason and magic . . . may meet and become one in that which one calls wisdom, initiation; in belief in the stars, in numbers" (*DF,* 194). His voice trails off. Zeitblom, seeing that his friend is in pain, does not pursue the argument. The curtain closes on the scene.

It has seemed advisable to quote so extensively from Mann's novel because it acutely anatomizes a disturbing consequence of modern attempts to endow art with scientific novelty and validity: the attempts have often derailed into superstition and irrationality. Feeling the possibilities of his art limited (partly as a result of historical circumstances, partly as a result of his own temperament), Leverkühn sells his soul to the devil for the gift of composing a "new" music. This music, as Mann describes it, possesses great theoretical complexity. The complexity, however, is invidious. It has, as Zeitblom points out, the appearance of reason, yet it is not reasonable in the least. It is merely arbitrary and programmatic.

Though Mann sympathizes with his hero's plight, he stresses that what Leverkühn does is morally and artistically horrifying. In his *Genesis of a Novel,* Mann discusses the writing of *Doctor Faustus* and speaks of the novel's

> central idea: the flight from the difficulties of the cultural crisis into the pact with the devil, the craving of a proud mind, threatened by sterility, for an unblocking of inhibitions at any cost, and the parallel between pernicious euphoria ending in [Leverkühn's] collapse with the nationalistic frenzy of Fascism.[49]

In composing *Doctor Faustus,* Mann says that he set out "to write nothing less than the novel of my era, disguised as the story of an artist's life, a terribly imperilled and sinful artist."[50]

Mann's novel underscores a fact sometimes overlooked in considerations of modern verse. Though the experimentalists frequently claimed that they represented progress, their movement carried a strain of reactionary violence. This is not, I stress, to suggest that all the experimentalists were reactionary. Williams, for example, believed profoundly in democratic principles; one of the most appealing qualities of his verse is its sympathy for the common working men and women whom he, as a practicing physician, knew and cared for. Yet a number of leading modernists—Gabriele D'Annunzio, Marinetti, Lewis, Pound, and

Louis-Ferdinand Céline—were apologists for Nazism or Fascism and its leaders. Mann's novel is presented as a memoir that Zeitblom is writing during the darkest days of World War II; as he looks back upon his long friendship with Leverkühn, Zeitblom realizes that just as the composer has yielded to pseudo-scientific magic in art, so has Germany sold its soul for the pseudo-scientific ideology of Nazism.

Only with these considerations in mind can one rightly examine the claims of modern poetry to scientific superiority. C. P. Snow's famous "Two Cultures" lecture is misguided to the extent that it fails to take account of how deeply the vocabulary of modern science has affected modern art. At the same time, Snow is correct in noting that the understanding of modern science which most modern artists possess is limited. Often their "science" is at best metaphoric and at worst propagandistic. Snow is also correct in warning that we do not have, in poetry and prose fiction, quantifiable means of determining when new procedures are or are not producing good results. It is one thing to explore revolutionary methods. It is another to assert that they have scientific validity and therefore supersede time-tested conventions. To adopt this latter course is perhaps to deceive oneself into believing in nonexistent discoveries and to encourage one's followers to pursue a course that leads them further and further away from any possibility of substantial achievement. As Snow comments, with a view to the years 1914–50, "Literature changes more slowly than science. It hasn't the same automatic corrective, and so its misguided periods are longer."[51]

One other observation should be set forth here. Scientific works become dated, and, in our age especially, they become dated quite quickly. Few scientists today read Newton's *Principia* or Einstein's "On the Electrodynamics of Moving Bodies." The ideas in these works are available in more convenient texts which also incorporate more recent developments in the fields that they address. Paradoxically perhaps, it is students of intellectual history, not physicists, who are most likely to read the writings of

Newton and Einstein now. Great literature, in contrast, does not become dated. If one were to distill, condense, and present in more "economical" guise Shakespeare's *Measure for Measure* or Robinson's "The Clerks," one would destroy them. A poem's power to instruct, uplift, and console resides in its unique expression of intelligence and its unique comeliness of form.

Therefore, to urge that the poet, like the scientist, should concentrate his attention on the latest works in his field is to misunderstand poetry. The great works of the past—the works which hold esteem year in and year out, century in and century out—offer the best guides for composition. Imposing on poetry the "scientific" doctrine that the newest is the truest thus deprives contemporary art of its richest supports and resources. This is especially true of those who impose the doctrine on the pretense of being great friends and champions of contemporary work.

A related matter concerns the nature of scientific discovery. Even Einstein felt that, had he not been born, his special theory of relativity would have been discovered, more or less around the time that he had discovered it, by other investigators and would have been presented in much the same form that he presented it.[52] One may feel that Einstein was being overly modest in this observation. Yet much scientific discovery has an aspect of inevitability. Developing knowledge and apparatus almost insure concomitant advances of insight. In contrast, had Sappho not been born, no one would have written her beautiful lyric to Aphrodite. Had Virgil not been born, no one would have written the *Georgics*. Had Keats and Emily Dickinson not been born, no one would have written "To Autumn" or "Farther in Summer than the Birds." One may invent all the isms one wishes. The fact remains, however, that great poetry is not inevitable; nor can it be wrenched into being by tyrannical acts of will. It seems to result from a providential gift of talent to an individual and to the patient cultivation of that talent by the individual. We are right to esteem science and to wish to understand it. But if we value poetry, we will recognize that its masterworks come about under somewhat different conditions and according to somewhat different processes than scientific masterworks do.

The arts and sciences have traditionally had healthy points of contact. Some artists, such as Leonardo, Dürer, and Goethe, have been immeasurably enriched as artists by their scientific knowledge. And there are works—Vesalius' *De humani corporis fabrica* being an often-cited example—in which art and science are magnificently joined. Yet it would be wise to remember what a great mathematician once said about literary studies; "[I]n proportion as anyone endeavours to make of Dialectic or Rhetoric, not what they are, faculties, but sciences, to that extent he will, without knowing it, destroy their real nature, in thus altering their character, by crossing over into the domain of sciences, whose subjects are certain definite things."

The writer here is Aristotle (*Rhet.* 1.4.5–7). The point he is making is that literature deals with qualitative issues of life for which, as he says elsewhere (1.2.12), "we have no systematic rules." Poetry must maintain connections with and an appreciation of philosophy and science to remain vigorous. But poets should probably not strain after a specious appearance of scientific method for the sake of novel effect. To the degree that such attempts have divorced poetry from meter, they have divorced poetry from perhaps its most "scientific" quality—meter being scientific in the sense that its procedures can be rationally imparted to and shared among a community of interested students. To the degree that the attempts have dislocated poetry from comprehensible subject matter and have forced it into obscurantisms of one sort or another, they have divided poetry from its most vital and distinctive function—the simultaneously vivid and comprehensive examination of human experience.

Before moving on to the concluding section of this study, I should like to point out several of the interrelationships between the various elements that contributed to the modern revolt against meter. For instance, the identification of meter with scansion, and the consequent notion that metrical composition was intrinsically overly emphatic and "metronomic" tied in, in the experimentalists' thinking, with the aesthetic doctrine that all art, including poetry, should aim for a musical indefiniteness of form and matter. The experimentalists' view tied in as well with the feeling that "verse" was itself vaguely contemptible and that "poetry" needed a new structural basis. The desire for a more prosaic speech in verse reflected not simply the experimentalists' admiration for the modern novel, but also their desire to emulate science, since prose itself had been, from the time of the founding of the Royal Society, the language of scientific exactitude. So, too, the aesthetic insistence on the liberty of the poet was strengthened, in the minds of the modern revolutionaries, by their image of the scientist who, working in defiance of conventional thought and understanding, achieved breakthroughs and discoveries. Similarly, the suspicion that metrical composition necessarily produced poems that were stuffy and Victorian, and that free verse would produce fresh and streamlined poems, found evident confirmation in the model of science and in its ever-improving, ever-innovative apparatus. The interest in organic form also tied in with science insofar as modern ideas about organic form were influenced by Darwin and the theory of evolution. Finally, the aesthetic concept that artistic composition is best performed unconsciously was reinforced by the scientific idea that progress is inevitable and that the artist who unquestioningly entrusts himself to progress and novelty will secure achievements unavailable to an artist working in a conscious manner and in a traditional mode.

Other interrelationships have been drawn in these pages. Still others could be drawn. The crucial thing is to note how these ideas and conditions, like tributary streams, came together and formed a torrent that swept many poets away from the conventions that had governed their art for millennia.

It remains to discuss briefly the present status of meter and to suggest that it is of no less value today to poets and readers than it ever was.

Conclusion

At the beginning of this book, I cited Mallarmé's observation, made in 1891, that for the first time since the beginning of poetry poets had ceased to write in meter. Later in the interview in which that observation appears, Mallarmé makes additional comments worth noting. He suggests—again, this is in 1891— that the *vers libre* movement has run its course and that poets will soon return to meter. Though sympathetic to the vers-libristes, Mallarmé urges that conventional metric in general and the Alexandrine line in particular remain as vital as ever. As for *vers libre* itself, it has simply provided, in Mallarmé's view, an interlude in which versification could be examined and refreshed:

I still believe, personally, that, with the miraculous knowledge of verse and with the superb instinct for rhythmic pause which such masters as Banville possess, the alexandrine can be infinitely varied and can reproduce all possible shades of human passion. . . . But, after all, it was a good thing to give our perfect and traditional poetic instrument a little rest. It had been overworked.[1]

Mallarmé's remarks raise a significant issue. Many of those most closely involved with the poetic experiments of the modern movement did not expect free verse to last. The medium was regarded as a temporary expedient or as the expression of a passing phase. Even those who were dogmatically opposed to conventional meter hoped that a new metric would emerge when the old had been cleared away. The free verse movement seemed, in Williams' words, "a formless interim" (*SL,* 129); it was not considered an end in itself, but was to lead to a "new way of measuring" (*SL,* 243).

What happened was different from what the leaders of the modern movement anticipated. Their revolution triumphed. But a new metric did not emerge. And the inheritors of the legacy of the modern movement, their numbers growing from decade to decade, simply went on writing without meter. The interim period was repeatedly and indefinitely extended. Originally a means of examining the old measures or of testing whether new measures were possible, free verse itself became a "form." Whereas the early experimentalists had pursued heterodox versification in the interests of poetic purity, their followers employed such procedures in an increasingly casual fashion, the revolution having undermined the metrical tradition and metrical awareness that gave the procedures significance in the first place.

During the modern movement, traditional versification continued to be practiced, and practiced brilliantly, by Frost and Yeats, as it was later to be brilliantly practiced by Auden, Cunningham, Richard Wilbur, Philip Larkin, and Thom Gunn. In addition, following the Second World War, there was a metrical revival. This, however, was short-lived. In the late fifties, after the publication of Allen Ginsberg's *Howl* and with Lowell's abandonment of traditional form for free verse, poetry again swung away from meter. The antipathy to meter in this period grew to be especially vehement, and it became almost universal when it was reinforced by iconoclasms of the sixties. It received additional reinforcement from the burgeoning creative writing programs in universities and from the increasing curricular emphasis on contemporary literature. These developments created powerful groups with vested interests in the view that the human mind and poetry had, in our time, undergone vast and irrevocable changes and that those who questioned this view were subversive and should be ostracized from the literary community.

Today, one almost hesitates to say that most poets write unmetrically: such a statement suggests that they know what meter is, which does not appear to be the case. Rather, it seems that versification, as it has been understood for millennia, is for the majority of contemporary poets an irrelevant matter. And looking back across our century, one may feel that metrical tradition resembles a signal which has been growing fainter and fainter.

As alarmed as they were at this trend, the modern movement's leaders were powerless to affect its course. Their predicament was that of successful revolutionaries in any field: having claimed special liberties for themselves, they found it difficult to persuade their followers to adopt a more restrained approach. Their predicament also reflected their misunderstanding of their revolution. They saw the kind of poetry they desired to avoid more clearly than the kind they wanted to write and, consequently, placed more emphasis on the destruction of the old than on the creation of the new. They construed their revolution as a reformation of style, not realizing that more—the very status of versification—was involved. I have analyzed here some of the historical and intellectual factors that contributed to this situation. In addition, there was an important human factor, the influence of which is difficult to assess. The modern movement's leaders were uneasy about writing free verse and they sometimes refused to recognize what they were doing. Eliot's assertion, "*Vers libre* does not exist" (*TCC,* 183), indicates, among other things, the degree to which he wished to deny that he was engaged in procedures that differed fundamentally from those of earlier poets. So, too, the many remarks, in Pound's and Eliot's critical writings, about "tradition" indicate how deeply they wished to see their revolution as an affirmation of literary culture rather than as a disruption of it. (These remarks also perhaps indicate their shrewd perception that the best way to forestall traditionalist objections to their revolution was to claim that they themselves were the true traditionalists: they thus might hope to deprive the opposition of grounds from which to argue.)

Misunderstanding their revolution, the modern movement's leaders also misunderstood their debt to Aestheticism. Without meaning to, they intensified the severance of poetry from understanding and reason. This severance continues to characterize verse today. If a street-paver, brain-surgeon, plumber, or airline pilot rejected regulatory procedures as being inhibiting, he would in short order prove a menace to those he served and a disgrace to his profession. Yet many poets assume this attitude toward poetry. This situation testifies to a quality mentioned earlier, namely, the hypnotic power of the doctrine of autonomous art and of its circular theory that rules for art are unnecessary because art is like nothing else and that art is like nothing else because it needs no rules.

An observation about the philosophical background of Aestheticism is in order. Kant's narrowing of metaphysics into a study of consciousness has had serious consequences for all humanistic and civic arts. The transformation has led to Hegel's concept of "God as he is alive and present in the subjective consciousness" (*CTSP,* 526). If a person thinks that subjective consciousness expresses divinity, he may well argue that he is free to violate any and all conventions on the grounds that the god within compels him to do so. The unhappy history of this century has taught us to be suspicious of individuals who, claiming that their private visions embody political destiny or spiritual truth, initiate policies opposed to time-tested standards of decency. Many still unblinkingly accept, however, radical subjectivism in poetry. This situation in part results, again, from the aesthetic severance of art from other pursuits: ideas that would cause us the gravest doubts and move us to immediate rebuttals, if we were to encounter them in different contexts, are taken less seriously—are even treated as piquant eccentricities—when encountered in poetry.

Several observations should be made about contemporary attitudes towards versification. The first is that though some commentators have contended that free verse is intrinsically "democratic," one should be skeptical of this contention, if only for the reason that certain of the leading experimentalists were apologists for Nazism or Fascism. As was stressed in the last chapter, it would be wrong to throw any blanket judgment over the political views of experimental poets. (It would also be wrong to throw blanket judgments over poets wishing to retain traditional versification.) Yet it is useful to bear in mind the politics of a Pound or a Lewis when, as so often happens, one hears it said that free verse is libertarian and enlightened and that traditional verse is reactionary and regressive.

There is a related issue. If it is true that almost anyone can write free verse, the same thing may be said of many activities, such as doing the dishes, that one would not necessarily characterize as democratic or free. And in one key sense, free versification is more "dictatorial" than traditional versification. I will do what I will do, the free verse poet says to his audience, and it is not yours to wonder why. He versifies by fiat. In contrast, meter is, as Wordsworth eloquently observes, like common law. Its basic statutes are few and clear; it asks obedience of and offers rewards to all poets equally. Here again, a word about Aestheticism is in order. The aesthetic emphasis on the subjective experience of the artist has contributed to the belief that free verse is libertarian. If one is considering poetry solely in terms of the poet, free verse is certainly liberating in some ways. If, however, one thinks of poetry as involving readers, too, the character of free verse grows ambiguous: it may deprive the reader of elements of the art that bring him pleasure and intellectual stimulation.

Furthermore, meter is liberal in the sense that the standards of craft supplied by meter encourage an open-minded examination and evaluation of poems. An intelligent or sensitive reader, that is, can readily judge whether the metrical poet is genuinely in command of his medium, or whether he is ineptly engaging in awkward inversions of syntax and forced rhymes and clichés to fit his scheme. In free verse, on the other hand, the very absence of formal standards demands that the poet's self-expression be accepted on its own terms, however arbitrary and obscure they may be.

In addition, and in a more general sense, there is a troubling aspect of the the characterization of nonmetrical verse as "free." This adjective may appeal to feelings more related to political and personal experience than to poetic technique. Believing that all people should have a voice in how they are governed and should be allowed to develop their talents, we are drawn to the idea of "freedom" in poetry. In the introduction to this study, I mentioned Aldington's remark, "We fight for it [free verse] as for a principle of liberty." Insofar as Aldington is striking a blow for free expression, one can agree readily with his statement. At the same time, one may wonder what, precisely, "liberty" has to do with the craft of versification. We must defend our liberty to say *what* we believe. But *how* we say it is not fundamentally a matter of liberty or lack of liberty; it is a matter of rhetorical strategy, of effective presentation. In this respect, the terms of Aldington's argument seem somewhat misplaced.

One may feel similarly troubled about characterizations of

meter as a restriction on freedom of expression. The concluding sentence of the entry for "Metre" in the latest edition of *The Oxford Companion to English Literature* informs us, "Verse in the 20th cent. has largely escaped the straitjacket of traditional metrics."[2] Reading such a statement, one scarcely knows how to respond. To write in meter is undeniably to place obligations on speech; one can no longer say anything one chooses when one chooses. Yet one may pause and wonder why, if traditional metrics were indeed a straitjacket, so many poets of such great intellectual curiosity and independence and of such lively and diverse gifts wrote in meter for so long. It seems terribly simple-minded to say of a medium that allowed for the poems of Homer and Virgil and Dante and Shakespeare that it is a straitjacket.

The phrase "free verse" might also be profitably scrutinized. If there is a disturbing element in Eliot's discrimination between "poetry" and "verse," it is that it in effect claims both terms for free verse and undermines the claims of metrical composition to either. The discrimination suggests a scheme according to which free verse is "poetry" and is also, as free verse, "verse." By the same token, the discrimination deprives metrical composition not only of its claim to "poetry," but makes it share its claim to "verse" with free verse. Metrical composition, that is, is reduced to being merely a species of verse—a "non-free" and "non-poetic" one. As was suggested in the introduction, it is fruitless to frame restrictive definitions of poetry. But it might have been useful if, at some point in the modern movement, people had set aside the question of whether free verse was poetry and examined the more modest issue of whether it was verse, which by definition is, or at least used to be, speech reconciled to measure.

One might also comment on the view that American poets are obliged to write free verse. A typical expression of this view is provided by the contemporary poet Robert Bly: "As Whitman saw, the rhymed metred poem is, in our consciousness, so tied to the feudal stratified society of England that such a metered poem refuses to merge well with the content of American experience. We therefore have no choice but to write free verse."[3] This statement should be questioned. Meter has nothing in particular to do with medieval England. Meter is common to the poetries of many different societies and goes back to prehistoric times.

Furthermore, it is misinformed to describe conventional accentual-syllabic measure as "feudal." At one level, the history of versification in the West involves the establishment, the temporary loss, and the recovery, in altered linguistic contexts, of isosyllabic measure. "Isosyllabic measure" refers simply to versification in which lines or stanzas exhibit syllabic equivalence or correspondence, and in which each syllable is accountable to a particular stichic or strophic arrangement. This system of versification established itself in pre-Homeric times and was practiced by ancient poets for over a millennium. Naturally, the system permitted certain liberties, just as certain liberties have been permitted in isosyllabic measures in modern languages. For instance, the ancient poet might at points resolve a long syllable into two shorts or contract two shorts into a long. In a related fashion, the poet writing in English may, say, occasionally substitute an anapest for an iamb in an iambic line, or he may mix standard iambic tetrameters with "headless" tetrameters lacking their initial unaccented syllable. Though, strictly speaking, such variations disrupt the syllable count, they have traditionally been allowed as long as the ear can reconcile them to the metrical pattern.

The system of isosyllabic measure was to a great extent lost in late antiquity and the Middle Ages, when the classical quantitative measures were supplanted by accentual ones. In the later Middle Ages and the Renaissance, the system was gradually recovered. In English, this recovery did not occur completely until the second third of the sixteenth century, and the recovery involved a prosody based not, as the ancient one was, on syllable length and syllable count, but on syllable accent and syllable count. (And as was noted in the introduction, though the accentual-syllabic system prevailed, it did not preclude the practice of a looser rhymed accentual verse in certain types of poetry, such as ballads.)

Seen in an historical context, free verse is thus more medieval than traditional English meter. Williams' variable foot, for example, is a kind of indeterminate accentual verse. Because there is no regular grouping of accented syllables and no structural alliteration to point the placement of accents, Williams' versification differs from that of the old Germanic tradition. Yet it suggests that tradition because it is anisosyllabic.

Perhaps it also bears repeating that it is wrong to suggest that free verse is distinctly American. If much English proto-*vers libre,* like Christopher Smart's *Jubilate Agno* and Blake's prophetic poems, was either unknown or uninfluential until this century, there nevertheless remain the King James Psalms, Macpherson's Ossianic epics, and Tupper's *Proverbial Philosophy,* all of which influenced early developments in free verse. No less significant is the fact that, in addition to the French experimentalists of the final two decades of the nineteenth century who influenced Eliot and Pound, there were English writers in the same period— among them Henley, Fiona Macleod/William Sharp, and Edward Garnett—who composed experimental poetry. Though this poetry is now largely forgotten, it received attention and exerted some influence in its day, at least according to Ford (*TTR,* 210). In a more general vein, one might note again that the ostensibly native theories advocated by many American free versers are influenced by European Aestheticism and, behind that, Neoplatonism.

Another point could be raised. Without criticizing Poe and Whitman themselves, one might say a few cautionary words about the standard Poe-Whitman approach to our literature. This approach—which treats extreme peculiarity, whether of the tortured or the bold and buoyant variety, as our distinctive contribution to Western literature—is an invention of European critics. While acknowledging the contributions of French and German students of American poetry, one might regret that they have often looked to our shores for an intellectual holiday. Poe's literary theory and Whitman's literary practice are important parts of our heritage. But they are not the only parts. European (and American) critics may talk of an "American" tradition in poetry, as if this were a single massive flood upon which every poet in our country is obliged to launch his bark. Yet poets should be allowed to chart their own courses, whether these lead them to free or metrical verse. They should not be made to feel compelled to write in exaggerated and mannered fashions simply to pay homage to Poe and Whitman.

This country, it should be added, has a long and rich tradition of metrical verse. It seems wrongheaded to deny this tradition or to suggest that the experience it depicts is not American. Emily Dickinson's verse is distinctly of our nation; she did not write about the Royal Family or the Charge of the Light Brigade, any more than Robinson or Frost wrote about cricket matches. It is true that the meters of this rich native tradition are the same as those used by English poets. This circumstance, however, is a result of the fact, denied though it sometimes is, that we speak English. Our vocabulary, our grammar, and our syntax are English. We have idioms that are our own; we have subjects that are our own. We should use these. But we cannot construct a prosody from them.

This last statement brings up an issue touched upon in the introduction and the first chapter. If one wants to invent a new prosody, one must invent a new language. Metrical systems, like languages themselves, come into being gradually. Metrical conventions get established, generally speaking, because they suit, to varying degrees, patterns of speech. It is right to insist that a poet must be inventive in using his medium. It would seem folly, however, to insist that he invent his medium. Williams is highly ambitious when he says: "I must make the new meter out of whole cloth" (*SL*, 313). But his ambition is misguided. The medium is determined by and is a property of the language. It is this general character of the medium that makes possible its use by a variety of different poets communicating with a variety of different readers.

Furthermore, the fluid character of language insures that conventional meters are continually renewed. Though metrical forms are, in the abstract, constant over time, as speech habits alter, the sounds of specific poems written in metrical forms likewise alter. As a language changes, it is inevitable that effects produced in its metrical system will also change. Ben Jonson's "Inviting a Friend to Supper," Pope's "Epistle to Dr. Arbuthnot," Robert Bridges' "Elegy: The Summer-House on the Mound," and Edgar Bowers' "Wandering" are all in heroic couplets. But each falls differently on the ear. Each registers an individual voice speaking in a particular time. The same can be said of the blank verse of Coleridge's "Frost at Midnight," Wallace Stevens' "Sunday Morning," and Richard Wilbur's "Mind-Reader." And not the least pleasing feature of a fine contemporary poem in meter is this: it enables one to hear a voice which—in its phrasing and the rhythm of its thought—is distinctively of one's day and yet which at the same time recalls the cadences and shapes of speech that characterized earlier masters working at earlier stages in the language.

Today, in the absence of agreed upon standards of versification, poetry often is judged exclusively with respect to its intentions or subject matter. Frequently, poets characterize themselves or are characterized by critics according to political views or ethnic backgrounds or sexual preferences. Poets are thus classified as "ecologists," "feminists," "gay activists," "native Americans," "black poets," and so forth. Under this rubric, writers who adopt meter are given their own little label—"formalists." It is good that poets should write of issues and causes that they believe are important. Classifying poetry by the causes it addresses, however, trivializes meter: the practice confuses what is extrinsic to poetic structure with what is intrinsic to it. In addition, it pretends that meter represents merely one more item in the smorgasbord of contemporary styles.

This notion also distorts past poetic achievement. It would be absurd to call Sophocles, Petrarch, or Keats a "formalist." And it is misleading to suggest that writing *in form* and writing *about something* are mutually exclusive enterprises. To reiterate a point made earlier, meter is neutral. It is a means by which poets can make what they say more forceful and memorable. Indeed, if poets care about an issue, they should want to give it the best possible treatment. The poet who says his subject is too urgent to submit to meter may be deceiving himself. If we care about what we say, if we want to communicate it to others, if we want them to consider it as having more than ephemeral interest, we should aim to make what we say as memorable as possible.

These comments raise an additional point. One often hears it said that our lives and our age are not suited to the conventions which in the past have made great poetry possible and without which, in all probability, great poetry cannot be written. One should stress that our world would be much smaller and poorer if earlier poets had adopted this attitude. If one takes as a cardinal principle of composition that it is impractical to seek the level of excellence that made people delight in earlier poetry, one should probably put away pen and paper.

There is a related matter. We live in an age that is in many ways profoundly disturbing. But every age is difficult. When we look at the past, we do not (and in some cases do not have the opportunity to) look too closely. In consequence, we do not see that the sources for individual and collective unhappiness and unease exist in all times. One must admit and face the terrors of the day. But to say that we confront such unprecedentedly trying conditions that we are at liberty to abandon conventional restraint may be to commit an act of spiritual vanity. Those who tell us that we should write in a crazy fashion because our times are crazy may be inviting us to collaborate with the very forces that we should resist.

This argument may be carried a step further. When Wyndham Lewis says that great art is no longer possible, one may well ask, Who could have predicted in 1560 that Shakespeare would be born? Who could have anticipated, at that rather undistinguished point in English literary history, the extraordinary work that he and contemporaries like Jonson and Donne would be producing before the century was out? Who could have predicted at Pope's death that Wordsworth would be born twenty-six years later? As long as the human spirit responds to measure, someone will come to use measure beautifully, and, in the process, delight and instruct mankind.

Young writers should be apprised of these views. It is not correct to tell them, as seems to have been the case in many "creative writing" workshops in our universities in recent years, that meter is no longer viable. Nor is it correct to evade fundamental questions of versification by referring to "structure" and "form" without relating these terms to the concept of metrical arrangement. It has long been apparent that the new metric that was supposed to emerge from the experimental movement did not emerge; the variety of competing schools and outlooks has long since reached a point of saturation. If a young poet wishes to write something that has a chance of distinguishing itself from the great mass of short poems currently being published, if the young poet wishes to write something that may not only be glanced at but read and remembered with affection and enthusiasm, he or she would be well-advised to consider the possibility of writing in meter. It may be significant that though Larkin, Louise Bogan, and Cunningham wrote comparatively little, they have devoted audiences. Part of the reason for this devotion is that they wrote well in meter.

It is also time to entertain the idea that free verse is no longer novel. As was mentioned in the introduction to this book, Dujardin commented of the French *vers libre* movement that by 1889, "The battle had been, in effect, won"[4]; as early as 1917, Eliot referred slightingly to "the popular American magazines, whose verse columns are now largely given over to *vers libre*" (*TCC*, 184). It may also be time to realize that free verse has long been official art and that some of its partisans have suffered from the reactionary intolerance to which partisans of any official art are liable. Indeed, because the medium has no positive principles for its proponents to defend, some of them have tended to maintain a defensive revolutionary vehemence while, so to speak, living in the palace. This attitude has discouraged attempts to place the free verse movement in some kind of historical perspective and to assess it.

And an assessment of free verse may now be called for. The medium has been around for a little over a century. Its original practitioners hoped to broaden poetry's range of subject matter, to make the diction of verse more natural, and to discover a new metric. The last of these hopes has been conclusively disappointed. What is more, if one reads the poems in current literary journals and in the collections of verse being published, one may well feel that the hopes for a fresher diction and subject matter have been disappointed, too. In fact, in the absence of meter, many poets seem to have adopted a highly mannered diction to distinguish their work from prose. In this sense, the effect of free verse has been contrary to its intentions.

It might be added that if one seeks novelty in mere device, even if genuine novelty be found, this novelty must exhaust itself very quickly. Lamenting in 1982 that video games were destroying the market for pinball machines, the pinball pioneer Harry Williams observed: "It's a funny thing to be at the birth of a business and then maybe at its demise. . . . But we're in the novelty business. And novelty means one thing—sooner or later you get tired of the novelty of it."[5]

The only novelty sure to last in poetry is the novelty of talent. Moreover, the alert poet cannot help but be novel: his subjects are the manners and morals and aspects of his world and fellow creatures, and these are always changing. The idea that to be novel, one has to invent a "METHOD" in the Poundian sense is not only wrongheaded; it is unnecessary.

It is important to emphasize, finally, that poetry can and should fulfill an important role in our culture. Even in an age remarkable for its science, our individual and collective well-being and happiness depend on how thoughtfully and sensitively we respond to qualitative issues in human experience. Science can define for us the nature of the rings around Saturn or identify a microorganism that causes a certain disease. Such discoveries are rightly prized. But science cannot teach us how to live in the world and in society. Science cannot even teach us how to use its discoveries humanely and intelligently. Wanting to live well, we need guidance in both private matters relating to personal relationships and in public questions of social and political relationships. Poetry preeminently supplies this guidance. Neither abstracted to philosophical precept nor confined to the literalness of history, poetry can speak with special vividness and comprehensiveness.

The poetry of the past can elevate and console us. But it cannot do this as fully and richly as poetry of the present. Only the poetry of the present speaks of our life and time. And though the poetry of Shakespeare or Emily Dickinson can connect us with the past, only the poetry of our time can connect us with the future and give us the indispensable hope that something that we say will matter to our descendants and will enable them to live more intelligently and happily than otherwise they might. Only the poetry of our time can offer the prospect that, after we and those we love have returned to dust, some reader somewhere will be moved by lines that bear witness to us and will commit our words to heart and mind that we may live again.

What is most essential to human life and to its continuance remains a love of nature, an enthusiasm for justice, a readiness of good humor, a spontaneous susceptibility to beauty and joy, an interest in our past, a hope for our future, and, above all, a desire that others should have the opportunity and encouragement to share these qualities. An art of measured speech nourishes these qualities in a way no other pursuit can. Taking heart in this reflection, we may appropriately close with Frost's lyric, "The Aim Was Song":

> Before man came to blow it right
>   The wind once blew itself untaught,
> And did its loudest day and night
>   In any rough place where it caught.
>
> Man came to tell it what was wrong:
>   It hadn't found the place to blow;
> It blew too hard—the aim was song.
>   And listen—how it ought to go!
>
> He took a little in his mouth,
>   And held it long enough for north
> To be converted into south,
>   And then by measure blew it forth.
>
> By measure. It was word and note,
>   The wind the wind had meant to be—
> A little through the lips and throat.
>   The aim was song—the wind could see.

LIST OF ABBREVIATIONS

ABC	Ezra Pound. *ABC of Reading*. New York: New Directions, 1960.
BL	Samuel Taylor Coleridge. *Biographia Literaria*. Eds. James Engell and W. Jackson Bate. Princeton: Princeton University Press, 1983.
CJ	Immanuel Kant. *The Critique of Judgement*. Trans. James Creed Meredith. Oxford: Oxford University Press, 1969.
CP	Ford Madox Ford. *Collected Poems*. Introduced by William Rose Benet. New York: Oxford University Press, 1936.
CPSP	Walt Whitman. *Complete Poetry & Selected Prose and Letters*. Ed. Emory Holloway. London: Nonesuch, 1971.
CTSP	Hazard Adams, ed. *Critical Theory Since Plato*. New York: Harcourt Brace, 1971.
CW	Frank MacShane, ed. *Critical Writings of Ford Madox Ford*. Lincoln, NB: University of Nebraska Press, 1964.
DF	Thomas Mann. *Doctor Faustus*. Trans. H. T. Lowe-Porter. New York: Knopf, 1948.
EL	Ralph Waldo Emerson. *Essays and Lectures*. Texts selected and notes supplied by Joel Porte. New York: Library of America, 1983.
ER	Edgar Allan Poe. *Essays and Reviews*. Selected by G. R. Thompson. New York: Library of America, 1984.

FS	T. E. Hulme. *Further Speculations*. Ed. Sam Hynes. Minneapolis: University of Minnesota Press, 1955.
LE	T. S. Eliot, ed. *The Literary Essays of Ezra Pound*. New York: New Directions, 1968.
ODP	George Watson, ed. *John Dryden: Of Dramatic Poesy and Other Critical Essays*. In Two Volumes. London: Dent, 1967.
OPP	T. S. Eliot. *On Poetry and Poets*. London: Faber, 1957.
S	T. E. Hulme. *Speculations*. Herbert Read, ed., with a frontispiece and foreword by Jacob Epstein. London: Routledge, 1965.
SE	William Carlos Williams. *Selected Essays of William Carlos Williams*. New York: New Directions, 1969.
SE 1917–32	T. S. Eliot. *Selected Essays 1917–1932*. New York: Harcourt Brace, 1932.
SL	John C. Thirlwall, ed. *The Selected Letters of William Carlos Williams*. New York: New Directions, 1984.
SPP	Jack Stillinger, ed. *William Wordsworth: Selected Poems and Prefaces*. Boston: Houghton Mifflin, 1965.
TCC	T. S. Eliot. *To Criticize the Critic*. New York: Farrar Straus, 1965.
TN	Byron Vazakas, *Transfigured Night*. New York: Macmillan, 1946.
TTR	Ford Madox Hueffer. *Thus to Revisit*. New York: Dutton, 1921.

NOTES

Introduction

1. Mallarmé, *Selected Prose Poems, Essays, and Letters*, trans. Bradford Cook (Baltimore: Johns Hopkins University Press, 1956), 18. The French text may be found in Stéphane Mallarmé, *Igitur, Divagations, Un Coup de Dés* (Paris: Gallimard, 1976), 388.

2. George Saintsbury, *A History of English Prose Rhythm* (London: Macmillan, 1912), 469–72.

3. Édouard Dujardin, *Les Premiers Poètes du Vers Libre* (Paris: Mercure de France, 1922), 37. Where, in the present book, no other translator is indicated, the translation may be assumed to be mine, as it is in this case. For a recent discussion of Vielé-Griffin and the preface to *Joies,* see Raffaele Scalamandrè, *F. Vielé-Griffin e il Platonismo* (Rome: Edizioni di Storia e Letteratura, 1981), 65ff.

4. *Selected Prose Poems, Essays, and Letters*, 44.

5. Cicero, *Orator,* trans. H. M. Hubbell, Loeb Classical Library [LCL], Cambridge, MA: Harvard University Press, 1971. Future references to this work will be to this edition.

6. Ford Madox Hueffer, *Thus to Revisit*, 201. This work will hereafter be referred to as *TTR*.

7. T. S. Eliot, *On Poetry and Poets*, 37. This work will hereafter be referred to as *OPP*.

8. T. S. Eliot, ed., *The Literary Essays of Ezra Pound*, 3. This work will hereafter be referred to as *LE*.

9. John C. Thirlwall, ed., *The Selected Letters of William Carlos Williams,* 325. This work will hereafter be referred to as *SL*.

10. T. E. Hulme, *Further Speculations*, ed. Sam Hynes, 69. This work will hereafter be referred to as *FS*.

11. Ralph Waldo Emerson, *Essays and Lectures,* 70. This work will hereafter be referred to as *EL.*

12. Cf. Milton Hindus, ed. *Walt Whitman: The Critical Heritage* (London: Routledge, 1971), 90ff., 95, 110, 204, Saintsbury comments of *Proverbial Philosophy* "that the form, chiefly through Whitman's transformation, has been largely used since; that the principle of it—the revolt of rhythm against metre—is very much alive at the present day; and that Martin Farquhar Tupper . . . is, in literary history, not a mere cypher." (*The Cambridge History of English Literature,* Vol. 13, ed. A. W. Waller [Cambridge: Cambridge University Press, 1916], 151). See as well Derek Hudson, *Martin Tupper: His Rise and Fall* (London: Constable, 1949), 43: "[T]here is little doubt that Walt Whitman (whom Tupper incidentally abominated) was influenced by Tupper's innovation—and that the free versifiers in general, down to T. S. Eliot, who have so thoroughly familiarised us with this form, or lack of form, have all been moving (horrified though they may be to hear the news) under the original impulse of Martin Tupper." Though Hudson overstates the case, his remarks, like those of Saintsbury's and those of Whitman's early readers, may help to remind us of Tupper's significance.

On at least one occasion, in 1847, Whitman himself wrote enthusiastically about Tupper, though this was in connection with *Probabilities, An Aid to Faith,* not *Proverbial Philosophy* (*The Uncollected Poetry and Prose of Walt Whitman,* ed. Emory Holloway [New York: Peter Smith, 1932], 1 : 136).

13. *Some Imagist Poets* (Boston: Houghton Mifflin, 1915), vi. The preface to this volume, and the matter of its authorship, are discussed in Jean Gould, *Amy: The World of Amy Lowell and the Imagist Movement* (New York: Dodd, Mead, 1975), 176.

14. *Les Premiers Poètes du Vers Libre,* 9. Victor Hugo speaks of *vers libre* in his 1827 preface to *Cromwell.* He uses the term, however, in a general sense: "[W]e would like a free verse (*un vers libre*), frank, straightforward, daring to say all without prudery, to express all without affectation." And though advocating a freer handling of the caesura in the Alexandrine line and a freer use of enjambment, Hugo nevertheless insists that French poetry remain "faithful to rhyme," which he describes as "that supreme grace of our poetry, that generator of our meter" (P. Moreau and J. Boudout, eds. *Victor Hugo, Oeuvres Choisies*

[Paris: Librairie Hatier, 1950], 1 : 186). When, in contrast, poets use the term in the late 1880s and the 1890s, they do so, as Dujardin indicates, with reference to verse not only free of classical conventions governing matters such as hiatus, elision, caesura, and enjambment, but free of isosyllabic measure and rhyme as well.

15. *The Compact Edition of the Oxford English Dictionary* (Oxford: Oxford University Press, 1971), 1 : 1784, the entry for "Metre." See as well 2 : 2550, the entry for "Rime."

16. Aristotle, *The Poetics,* trans. W. Hamilton Fyfe (LCL, Cambridge, MA: Harvard University Press, 1982).

17. James Gibson, ed., *The Complete Poems of Thomas Hardy* (New York: Macmillan, 1978), 12.

18. T. V. F. Brogan, *English Versification, 1570–1980* (Baltimore: Johns Hopkins University Press, 1981), 402–16. Recent works offering prosodic analyses of free verse include: Charles O. Hartman, *Free Verse: An Essay on Prosody* (Princeton: Princeton University Press, 1980); Derek Attridge, *The Rhythms of English Poetry* (London: Longman, 1982), 316–24; Stephen Cushman, *William Carlos Williams and the Meanings of Measure* (New Haven: Yale University Press, 1985).

19. For a discussion of Ennius and the development of the Latin hexameter, see A. Cordier, *Les Débuts de L'Hexamètre Latin* (Paris: Librairie Philosophique, 1947) esp. 79–81. A standard work on experiments with quantitative verse in the Elizabethan period is Attridge, *Well-weighed Syllables* (London: Cambridge University Press, 1974).

Chapter 1

1. Harvey Gross, ed., *The Structure of Verse* (New York: Ecco Press, 1979), 262.

2. Aristotle, *The "Art" of Rhetoric,* trans. John Henry Freese (LCL, Cambridge, MA: Harvard University Press, 1975). All future references to this work will be to this edition.

3. Cf. Richard Bentley's *A Dissertation upon the Epistles of Phalaris:*

Every living language, like the perspiring bodies of living creatures, is in perpetual motion and alteration; some words go off, and become obsolete; others are taken in, and by degrees grow into common use; or the same word is inverted to a new sense and notion, which in tract of time makes as observable a change in the air and features of a language, as age makes in the lines and mien of a face.

Alexander Dyce, ed., *the Works of Richard Bentley* (London: Francis Macpherson, 1836), 2:1. I am indebted to Paul G. Naiditch for this reference.

4. For a comparison of Greek and Latin meter, see M. L. West, *Greek Metre* (Oxford: Oxford University Press, 1982), 186–90; Nabokov's comparison of English and Russian tetrameters appears in his *Notes on Prosody* (New York: Pantheon, 1964), esp. 51–69.

5. Jack Stillinger, ed., *William Wordsworth: Selected Poems and Prefaces*, 457–58. This work will hereafter be referred to as *SPP*.

6. T. S. Eliot, *To Criticize the Critics*. This work will hereafter be referred to as *TCC*.

7. Ford's evaluation of himself as a poet is, both for its modesty and accuracy, worth noting: "I attach little importance to myself as a poet. But I do attach importance to myself as a 'specimen'" (*TTR*, 198). One study which stresses the influence of Ford's thought on the modern movement in verse is Herbert N. Schneidau, *Ezra Pound: The Image and the Real* (Baton Rouge: LSU Press, 1969). See especially chapter one, "Imagism as Discipline: Hueffer and the Prose Tradition," 3–37.

8. Ford Madox Ford, *Collected Poems*. This work will hereafter be referred to as *CP*.

9. Frank MacShane, ed., *Critical Writings of Ford Madox Ford*. This work will hereafter be referred to as *CW*.

10. Byron Vazakas, *Transfigured Night*, xiv, ix. This work will hereafter be referred to as *TN*.

11. T. E. Hulme, *Speculations*, 133. This work will hereafter be referred to as *S*. Hulme's remarks about the "sloppiness" of the Romantics occur in *S*, 126: "I object even to the best of the romantics. . . . I object to the sloppiness which doesn't consider that a poem is a poem unless it is moaning or whining about something or other."

12. William Carlos Williams, *Selected Essays of William Carlos Williams*, 281, 284. This work will hereafter be referred to as *SE*.

13. In D. A. Russell and M. Winterbottom, eds., *Ancient Literary Criticism* (Oxford: Oxford University Press, 1972).

14. Diogenes Laertius, *The Lives and Opinions of Eminent Philoso-*

phers, trans. C. D. Yonge (London: George Bell, 1905). Future references to *Lives and Opinions* will be to this edition unless otherwise noted.

15. *The Poetics,* trans. W. Hamilton Fyfe (Cambridge, MA: Harvard University Press, 1982). Though Sophocles' observation about himself has been subject to differing interpretations—for example, Gerald F. Else (*Poetics* [Ann Arbor: University of Michigan Press, 1970]) translates, "portrayed people the way they ought to be portrayed"—the meaning of his judgment of Euripides is clear.

16. "Longinus," *On the Sublime,* trans. W. Hamilton Fyfe (LCL, Cambridge, MA: Harvard University Press, 1982). Future references to "Longinus" will be to this edition.

17. References to the Greek text of *The Frogs* will be to W. B. Stanford's edition (London: Macmillan, 1958). The translation used is that of David Barrett, *The Wasps, The Poet and the Women, The Frogs* (New York: Penguin, 1980).

18. Horace, *Satires, Epistles and Ars Poetica,* trans. H. Rushton Fairclough (LCL, Cambridge, MA: Harvard University Press, 1978). Future references to Horace's satires and epistles will be to this edition. I have also consulted C. O. Brink's edition of the *Ars Poetica* (Cambridge: Cambridge University Press, 1971).

19. Cf. Vasari's Life of Michelangelo:

> Another time, a painter had executed a scene in which many of the details were copied from other pictures and drawings, and indeed there was nothing original in it. The painting was shown to Michelangelo, and after he had looked at it a close friend of his asked for his opinion.
>
> "He has done well," Michelangelo commented, "but at the Day of Judgement when every body takes back its own members, I don't know what that picture will do, because it will have nothing left."

Giorgo Vasari, *Lives of the Artists,* a selection translated by George Bull (Harmondsworth: Middlesex, Penguin, 1972), 427–28.

20. T. S. Eliot, "The Poet who Gave the English Speech," *The Listener,* April 15, 1931, 621, 622.

21. George Watson, ed., *John Dryden: Of Dramatic Poesy and Other Critical Essays.* This work will hereafter be referred to as *ODP.*

22. A good general account of the Quarrel is provided in R. F. Jones, *Ancients and Moderns* (St. Louis: Washington University Press, 1961). Though some scholars have dated the beginning of the Quarrel with

reference to Fontenelle's *Digression sur les Anciens and les Modernes* of 1688 and Perrault's *Parallèle des Anciens et des Modernes* of 1688–96, it is generally agreed that these works, important as they are, focused on concerns that had already had considerable development.

23. Cf. West, *Greek Metric,* 135–37.

24. William Frost, ed., *Selected Works of John Dryden* (New York: Holt, 1967), 243.

25. Timothy Steele, "An Interview with J. V. Cunningham," *The Iowa Review* 15 (Fall 1985): 15.

26. Ezra Pound, *ABC of Reading,* 203–04. This work will hereafter be referred to as *ABC.*

27. Cf. Quintilian's observation (9.4.115) that "the poet in writing a verse considers the metre as a whole, and does not concentrate his attention on the six or five individual feet that constitute the verse." *Institutio Oratoria,* trans. H. E. Butler (LCL, Cambridge, MA: Harvard University Press, 1969). All future references to Quintilian will be to this edition unless otherwise designated.

28. William B. Hunter, Jr., ed., *The Complete Poetry of Ben Jonson* (New York: Norton, 1968), 20; David M. Vieth, ed., *The Complete Poems of John Wilmot, Earl of Rochester* (New Haven: Yale University Press, 1968), 120; J. E. Austen Leigh, *A Memoir of Jane Austen* (London: Bentley and Son, 1871), 55; E. A. Robinson, *Collected Poems* (New York: Macmillan, 1945), 95; *Selected Poems of Robert Frost,* introduction by Robert Graves (New York: Holt, 1963), 194; Thom Gunn, *Moly and My Sad Captains* (New York: Farrar Straus, 1973), 52.

29. Julius Caesar Scaliger, *Poetices Libri Septem,* introduction by August Buck (Stuttgart: Friedrich Frommann, 1964), 56. Cf. Frost's comment, in his "Figure a Poem Makes": "The possibilities for tune from the dramatic tones of meaning struck across the rigidity of a limited meter are endless." (*Selected Poems,* 1–2.) Cf. as well Yvor Winters' essay, "The Audible Reading of Poetry," in his *The Function of Criticism* (Denver: Swallow, 1957), 81–100. An excellent account of traditional English versification and of rhythmical variation within metrical norm is provided by James McAuley, *Versification: A Short Introduction* (East Lansing: Michigan State University Press, 1966).

30. Paull Franklin Baum, ed., *Sidney Lanier: The Science of English Verse and Essays on Music* (Baltimore: John Hopkins University Press, 1945). (This is Volume II in *The Centennial Edition of the Works of Sidney*

Lanier, gen. ed. Charles R. Anderson.) For Lanier's use of musical time and metronomic measure to analyze English versification, see especially 51ff. and 106ff. Richard Webb and Edwin R. Coulson, *Sidney Lanier: Poet and Prosodist* (Athens, GE: University of Georgia Press, 1941), 73–103, discuss the response to and influence of *The Science of English Prosody.* Lanier's influence seems to have waned after he was attacked in perhaps unfairly severe but acute terms by Saintsbury in *A History of English Prosody,* first published in 1906–10. Saintsbury's remarks may be found in his *History* (New York: Macmillan, 1923), 3:493–97. Earlier attempts to describe prosody in terms of musical notation, such as Joshua Steele's *Essay Towards Establishing the Melody and Measure of Speech* (1775) do not appear to have had the impact on the practice and criticism of verse that Lanier's work had.

31. Janet Adam Smith, "Tom Possum and the Roberts Family," *The Southern Review* 21 (Autumn 1985): 1067.

32. Wallace Stevens, *The Necessary Angel* (New York: Vintage, 1951), 26.

Chapter 2

1. *Diodorus of Sicily,* Vol. V, trans. C. H. Oldfather (LCL, Cambridge, MA: Harvard University Press, 1950).

2. Demetrius, *On Style,* trans. W. Rhys Roberts (LCL, Cambridge, MA: Harvard University Press, 1982). Future references to Demetrius will be to this edition unless otherwise designated.

3. The standard work on ancient prose rhythm is Eduard Norden, *Die Antike Kunstprosa,* 5th Ed. (Stuttgart: Teubner, 1958). With respect to Latin prose rhythm, a standard work is Tadeusz Zielínski, *Das Clauselgesetz in Ciceros Reden* (Leipzig: Dieterich, 1904).

4. Dionysius of Helicarnassus, *On Literary Composition,* trans. W. Rhys Roberts (London: MacMillan, 1910). Future references to the work will be to this edition. Recently, another edition of the work has appeared in Dionysius' *Critical Essays,* vol. 2, trans. Stephen Usher (LCL, Cambridge MA: Harvard University Press, 1985).

5. Cicero, *De Oratore,* trans. H. Rackham (LCL, Cambridge, MA: Harvard University Press, 1977). Future references to this work will be to this edition unless otherwise designated.

6. This and the following passage are taken from Michael Winter-bottom's translation in *Ancient Literary Criticism,* 262–63.

7. It is worth citing Crassus' observations about the natural readiness with which people appreciate rhythm in speech:

> But do not let anybody wonder how these things can possibly make any impression on the unlearned crowd when it forms the audience, because in this particular department as in every other nature has a vast and indeed incredible power. For everybody is able to discriminate between what is right and what wrong in matters of art and proportion by a sort of subconscious instinct, without having any theory of art or proportion of their own; and while they can do this in the case of pictures and statues and other works to understand which nature has given them less equipment, at the same time they display this much more in judging the rhythms and pronunciations of words, because these are rooted deep in the general sensibility, and nature has decreed that nobody shall be entirely devoid of these faculties. And conse-quently everybody is influenced not only by skilful arrangement of words but also by rhythms and pronunciations. For what proportion of people under-stands the science of rhythm and metre? yet all the same if only a slight slip is made in these, making the line too short by a contraction or too long by dwelling on a vowel, the audience protests to a man.
>
> (3.195–96)

The aural sensitivity of ancient audiences appears to have been extraor-dinary. At the same time, in an discussion of versification cited at the conclusion of this chapter, Dr. Johnson makes points (*Rambler,* no. 86), quite similar to Cicero's, with respect to English ears.

8. Among works on prose rhythm in the Middle Ages, the following may be cited: Gudrun Lindholm, *Studien zum Mittellateinischen Pro-sarhythmus* (Almqvist & Wiksell: Stockholm, 1963); Dag Ludwig Nor-berg, *Manuel Pratique de Latin Médiéval* (Paris: Picard, 1968). For the development of structural rhyme in Latin prose and poetry, see Louis Palanca, *Prose Artistry and the Birth of Rhyme in St. Zeno of Verona* (Jericho, NY: Exposition Press, 1972). For a general consideration of medieval theories of poetry and prose, see Ernst Robert Curtius, *Euro-pean Literature and the Latin Middle Ages,* trans. Willard R. Trask (Princeton: Princeton University Press, 1973), esp. 147–54.

9. Cf. Curtius, 148–51.

10. Dante Alighieri, *Le Opere Minori,* ed. Enrico Bianchi (Florence:

Salani, 1936), 464. The translation of the passage is by A. G. Ferrers Howell and Philip H. Wicksteed, and appears in O. B. Hardison, Jr., Alex Preminger, Kevin Kerrane, Leon Golden, eds., *Medieval Literary Criticism* (New York, Unger, 1974), 170.

11. R. Warwick Bond, ed., *The Complete Works of John Lyly* (Oxford: Oxford University Press, 1902, 1 : 241.

12. Dante Alighieri, *The Divine Comedy,* trans. with a Commentary by Charles S. Singleton (Princeton: Princeton University Press, 1970–75). Singleton has an interesting discussion of this line in his Commentary 2 : 643.

13. Giovanni Boccaccio, *Decameron,* ed. Mirko Bevilacqua (Rome: Riuniti, 1980), 327, 333. The translation is by G. H. McWilliam, and appears in *The Decameron* (Harmondsworth, Middlesex: Penguin, 1981), 325, 330.

14. Evelyn S. Shuckburgh, ed., *Sir Philip Sidney, An Apologie for Poetrie* (Cambridge: Cambridge University Press, 1912), 12.

15. Ioan Williams, ed., *The Criticism of Henry Fielding* (London: Routledge & Kegan Paul, 1970), 251.

16. Edgar Allan Poe, *Essays and Reviews,* 15. This work will hereafter be referred to as *ER*.

17. For a good consideration of the fate of the long poem in the Romantic period, see Edgar Wind, *Art and Anarchy* (New York: Vintage, 1969), 140–42. Even one of the Romantic period's finest extended works in verse, Wordsworth's remarkable *The Prelude,* shows signs of what Wind calls "the collapse of the long poem." After finishing in 1805 a draft of his poem, which was originally intended to be simply the introductory part of *The Recluse,* Wordsworth revised the work for decades; nor was the work published until after his death, the very choice of a title being left to his widow. It may be significant that Pushkin's *Eugene Onegin,* which some observers believe the greatest long poem of the nineteenth century, was written by a poet who, though alert to developments in European Romanticism, was geographically and intellectually removed from some of its more vexing influences and who also was a gifted writer of prose fiction.

18. Richard Aldington, ed., *The Portable Oscar Wilde* (New York: Viking, 1946), 57–58.

19. Pound's debt to Swinburne, and the shift of his allegiance from Swinburne to Browning, are well documented and discussed in Michael

John King, ed., *Collected Early Poems of Ezra Pound,* with an introduction by Louis L. Martz (New York: New Directions, 1976).

20. Daryl Hine and Joseph Parisi, eds., *The Poetry Anthology 1912–1977* (Boston: Houghton Mifflin, 1978), 45.

21. Ibid., 48.

22. T. S. Eliot, *Selected Essays 1917–1932,* 285. This work will hereafter be referred to as *SE 1917–32.*

23. Ezra Pound, *Selected Poems* (New York: New Directions, 1957), 61.

24. W. B. Yeats, *Essays and Introductions* (New York: Macmillan, 1961), 499.

25. J. E. Spingarn, ed., *Critical Essays of the Seventeenth Century* (Bloomington: Indiana University Press, 1957), 2:118, 132.

26. Hudson, *Martin Tupper: His Rise and Fall,* 43, notes that Tupper was reluctant to call *Proverbial Philosophy,* which was his first literary success, poetry. Nor does his audience seem to have initially considered it poetry. Because, however, Tupper subsequently not only kept expanding the work, but also published many poems in traditional measures, people came to designate, in a retrospective fashion, *Proverbial Philosophy* as poetry, and Tupper himself felt compelled to accept this designation. Hudson remarks:

> As time went on, and as the public saw Tupper continually expressing himself in the conventional metres in short poems . . . the tendency increased to class "Proverbial Philosophy" also under the heading "Poetry"—a practice in which Tupper eventually acquiesced, though he always preferred his own expression "rhythmics."

27. William Ernest Henley, *Poems* (New York: Scribner's, 1904). The page, unnumbered, is the recto of the third leaf of the book.

28. Cited in Roberts' edition of *On Literary Composition,* 192–93.

29. Alex Preminger, ed., Frank J. Warnke and O. B. Hardison, Jr., assoc. eds., *Princeton Encyclopedia of Poetry and Poetics* (Princeton: Princeton University Press, 1974), 289. Cf. Yvor Winters, *In Defense of Reason* (Chicago: Swallow, 1947), 116. Winters speaks—as do other writers of *vers libre*—of approximating while avoiding meter and of treating rhythmical units larger than the line as the fundamental forms of versification: "My own free verse was very often balanced on this particular tight-rope [near but not in iambic measure]. During the

period in which I was composing it, I was much interested in the possibility of making the stanza and wherever possible the poem a single rhythmic unit, of which the line was a part not sharply separate."

30. W. H. Gardner and N. H. MacKenzie, eds., *The Poems of Gerard Manley Hopkins* (New York: Oxford University Press, 1967), 47, 48–49.

31. For Williams' discussion of the variable foot, see *Princeton Encyclopedia of Poetry and Poetics,* 289.

Poe evidently felt that a "caesura" in the middle or at the termination of a line of English verse functioned, or might function, in a manner analogous to the ambiguous or "anceps" last syllable in the spondaic sixth foot of the classical hexameter—that syllable which should, strictly speaking, be long but which may, according to the poet's discretion, be short, on the theory that the pause at the line-end makes up for the deficiency of length.

Williams' essay on Poe in *In the American Grain* does not exhibit any special concern with Poe's metrical theories. Nor does Williams mention Poe in discussing his discovery of the variable foot (Williams Carlos Williams, *I Wanted to Write a Poem,* reported and edited by Edith Heal [New York: New Directions, 1978], 82).

Possibly, Williams' theory of the variable foot was influenced by Yvor Winters' essay, "The Scansion of Free Verse," which was published in Winters' *Primitivism and Decadence* more than a decade before Williams' discovery and which in fact discusses Williams' work. Speaking of his own free verse and of his attempts to make a system of scansion for it, Winters writes: "The foot which I have used consists of one heavily accented syllable, an unlimited number of unaccented syllables, and an unlimited number of syllables of secondary accent. This resembles the accentual meter of Hopkins, except that Hopkins employed rhyme. He appears to have had the secondary accent, or subordinate and extrametrical 'foot,' in mind, when he spoke of 'hangers' and 'outrides'" (*In Defense of Reason,* 112).

32. Isocrates, *The Works of Isocrates,* Vol. 3, trans. Larue van Hook (LCL, Cambridge, MA: Harvard University Press, 1945). Subsequent references to Isocrates will be to this edition unless otherwise indicated.

33. *Princeton Encyclopedia of Poetry and Poetics,* 289.

34. *History of English Prose Rhythm,* 1–9.

35. Interview reprinted in James Scully, ed., *Modern Poetics* (New York: McGraw-Hill, 1965), 233, 232.

36. Ibid., 232.

37. Cf. Conrad Aiken's 1918 review of Ford's *On Heaven*. Aiken quotes Ford's statement, in his preface to the collection, "*Vers libre* is a very jolly medium in which to write and to read, if it be read conversationally and quietly. And anyhow, symmetrical or rhymed verse is for me a cramped and difficult medium—or an easy and uninteresting one." Aiken then comments (Frank MacShane, ed., *Ford Madox Ford: The Critical Heritage* [London: Routledge, 1972], 70, 71–72):

> This is a plausible and intriguing theory. At first glimpse it seems only natural that in a freer and more discursive medium the poet should find himself better able to fix upon the more impalpable nuances of feeling. But a steadier inspection leaves one not quite so sure. If one can convey subtler moods in free verse than in symmetrical verse, might one not logically argue that prose could be subtler still than either? And we should have reached the conclusion that poetry should employ, to reach its maximum efficiency, not only the language but also the rhythms of prose—in other words, that it should *be* prose.

Cf. as well Robert Graves' short essay, "Vers Libre," which appears in his *On English Poetry* (London: Heinemann, 1922), 45–49, and in which Graves remarks that *vers libre* is "only our old friend, Prose Poetry, broken up in convenient lengths."

38. Samuel Johnson, *Selected Writings,* ed., with an introduction and notes by R. T. Davies (London: Faber, 1965), 102.

An examination of modern prose rhythm is beyond the scope of this study. One might mention, however, that in this century prose writers as well as poets have grown increasingly indifferent or hostile to rhythm. And it may be significant that, in some modern prose, rhythmical organization is shunned on the same grounds that metrical arrangement is shunned in modern verse—the desire to appear "sincere" or "natural" rather than "artificial."

Chapter 3

1. Donald Davie, *Purity of Diction in English Verse* (London: Routledge & Kegan Paul, 1967), 5, 6.

2. Calvin Bedient, *Eight Contemporary Poets* (Oxford: Oxford University Press, 1974), 29, 30.

3. Plato, *Phaedrus,* trans. Harold North Fowler (LCL, London: Heinemann, 1923). Future references to the *Phaedrus* will be to this edition. Many have felt that it is with a certain irony that Socrates treats, especially in the *Ion,* the association of poetry with *mania.* Many have felt a similar quality characterizes the passage in Horace's *Satire* 1.4 cited below. Whether Socrates and Horace are being ironic is not relevant, however, to the matter at hand. The fact that they discuss the ideas is sufficient to show that, even if they did not take them entirely seriously, others did.

4. See the entries for these words in *A Greek-English Lexicon,* (Oxford: Oxford University Press, 1977), comp. H. G. Liddell and Robert Scott, rev. and augmented by Henry Stuart Jones, with the assistance of Robert MacKenzie. The authors indicate that *poiēsis* was often used with a noun that more precisely defined the kind of "making" being mentioned. See also the entry for "Poetry" in the *OED,* in which it is noted that Ingram Bywater observes, "The relation of the word to L. *poetria,* Gr. ποιήτρια, poetess, is not clear."

5. *The Works of Isocrates,* Vol. II, trans. George Norlin.

6. Guiliana Lanata, *Poetica Pre-Platonica* (Florence: La Nuova Italia, 1963).

7. Plato, *The Republic,* trans. Paul Shorey (LCL, Cambridge MA: Harvard University Press, 1946). Future references to this work will be to this edition.

8. My translation.

9. Lanata, 5.1. Cf. *Timaeus* (47D–E), trans. R. G. Bury (LCL, London: Heinemann, 1929). All future references to the *Timaeus* will be to this edition.

10. Gerald F. Else, "Imitation in the Fifth Century," *Classical Philology* 53 (1958): 73–90.

11. Plato had suggested this discrimination earlier, in *Phaedo* 61 A–B, where Socrates tells of how, wishing to write poetry before he dies, he has been spending his time in prison versifying some of Aesop's fables. Socrates relates that he initially wrote a hymn to Apollo, but reflecting that "a poet, if he is really to be a poet, must compose myths (*mythous*) and not speeches (*logous*), since I was not a maker of myths (*mythologikos*), I took the myths [in the sense of "fables" or "stories"] of Aesop,

which I had at hand and knew, and turned into verse (*epoiēsa*) the first that I came upon" (trans. H. N. Fowler, LCL). Socrates seems to feel, that is, that to write a genuine poem, it is not enough merely to produce verses. One should also tell a story. By the same token, Socrates' account implies that if verse without story is not fully poetry, neither is a story without verse. Both verse and story are required. (Though Socrates does not speak of *mimēsis* on this occasion, he does use the word *mythos,* the word that Aristotle will apply to "plot," the vehicle by means of which dramatic or epic imitation is presented.)

12. References to the Greek text of the *Poetics* will be to Else, *Aristotle's Poetics: The Argument* (Cambridge, MA: Harvard University Press, 1957). The English translation used is Else's *Aristotle: Poetics* (Ann Arbor: University of Michigan Press, 1970), which is a revision of his earlier translation in *Aristotle's Poetics: The Argument.*

13. Else suggests (*Aristotle: Poetics,* 108–09) that Aristotle himself distinguishes epic from history on the grounds of metricality when he says, in the twenty-third chapter of his treatise (1459a17), that epic "is narrative and imitates in verse" (*diēgēmatikēs kai en metrō mimētikēs*). Else remarks, that is, that this phrase is perhaps to be understood as the first part of an incomplete comparison, the implied second half of which is "as opposed to history, which does the same thing in prose." Aristotle's context is unclear, however. Though the twenty-third chapter contrasts the methods of epic composition and historical composition, it may be that Aristotle is merely noting that epic imitates in a single meter (hexameter), as opposed to tragedy which, though employing mainly iambic trimeter for dialogue, also uses lyric forms in choral passages and also on occasion uses other metrical forms. Though this latter inter-pretation does not wholly suit the grammar of Aristotle's sentence, it arguably parallels an earlier statement that Aristotle makes (1449b11) about epic and tragedy. If Else's interpretation is correct, it would indicate, as does *Rhetoric* 3.8. and Aristotle's praise of Empedocles in *On Poets,* that he at times follows the popular view of identifying poetry with metricality, however much his general argument in the *Poetics* strains to counter this view.

14. Strabo, *Geography,* trans. Horace L. Jones (LCL, Cambridge MA: Harvard University Press).

15. *Ancient Literary Criticism,* 538. For other comparisons of poetry

and history, see Petronius, *Satyricon* 118, Polybius 2.5.9–16, Plutarch, *Moralia* 348A–B.

16. One might also think of Aristotle's remarks about imitation and plot as involving an elevation of content over form or of things over words. In this regard, one might consider a celebrated anecdote about Menander, who was a pupil of Theophrastus, Aristotle's successor as Head of the Academy, and who may have been the one great ancient poet that had firsthand knowledge of the *Poetics*. The anecdote is recorded by Plutarch *(Moralia,* 347E–F). When a friend observed to Menander that he had not finished a comedy for an approaching festival, Menander is reported to have replied, "By heaven, I have really composed the comedy: the plot's all in order *(ōkonomētai gar hē diathesis).* But I still have to fit the lines *(stichidia,* ["verses"]) to it." Commenting on this episode, Plutarch says that it illustrates that "poets consider the subject matter *(pragmata)* more necessary and vital than the words *(logōn)."* *(Plutarch's Moralia,* Vol. IV, ed., Frank Cole Babbitt [LCL, Cambridge, MA: Harvard University Press, 1936]. Future references to the *Moralia* will be to this edition, and to the translations of Babbitt, who edited the first five volumes in the edition.)

The distinction here is between content and words. To use terms that Aristotle employs (1450a10–14) in discussing the elements of tragedy, the distinction is between the things that drama imitates—including plot and character—and the means by which it imitates—including verbal expression and song, metrical and melic composition. What Menander suggests in a practical setting, and what Aristotle perhaps urges in a theoretical one, is that the matter of a play has precedence over the means by which the matter is embodied. Nevertheless, the means— the words, the verses—are still important. They are concurrent with the matter, which could not exist without them.

17. Jonathan Barnes, ed., *The Complete Works of Aristotle* (Princeton: Princeton University Press, 1984), 2:2419. The translators of the fragment are Barnes and Gavin Lawrence.

18. For a recent discussion of the *Tractatus Coislinianus,* which may or may not derive from the lost book on Comedy, see Richard Janko, *Aristotle on Comedy, Towards a Reconstruction of Poetics II* (London: Duckworth, 1984). It is interesting that, at the beginning of the *Tractatus,* the author divides poetry into mimetic and non-mimetic species,

adding that in discussing Comedy he is concerned only with the mimetic.

19. For this passage, I have used Michael Winterbottom's translation, which appears in *Ancient Literary Criticism*, 393, and I have checked Winterbottom's Oxford text of the *Institutes* against Butler's Loeb edition.

20. See the entries for "Versificator" in P. G. W. Clarke, *Oxford Latin Dictionary* (Oxford: Oxford University Press, 1982), and in Charlton T. Lewis and Charles Short, *Harper's Latin Dictionary* (New York: American Book Company, 1907).

21. Terentianus Maurus, *De Litteris Syllabis Pedibus et Metris,* ed. with notes, Lawrence Santeni, finished by David Jacob Van Lannep (London: H. Bohn, 1825); Justin, *Epitoma Historiarum Philippicarum Pompei Trogi,* ed. Otto Seel (Leipzig: Teubner, 1935).

22. The transmission of the *Institutes* is discussed by Jean Cousin, *Recherches sur Quintilien: Manuscripts et Editions* (Paris: Société d'édition "Les Belles Lettres," 1975). Cousin has an extended consideration (pp. 50–69) of Poggio and the manuscript at St. Gaul.

23. Aeneas Silvius, *De Liberorum Educatione,* trans. Joel Stanislaus Nelson (Washington D.C.: Catholic University of America Press, 1940), 183–85. This work is Volume 12 in Catholic University of America's *Studies in Medieval and Renaissance Latin Language and Literature.*

24. Henry Herbert Stephan Croft, ed., *The Boke Named the Gouernour Deuised by Sir Thomas Elyot, Knight* (London: Kegan Paul, 1883), 120.

25. George Thilo and Hermann Hagen, eds., *Servii Grammatici Qui Feruntur In Vergilii Carmina Commentarii* (Leipzig: Teubner, 1891), 1 : 129.

26. For a good account of the controversy surrounding Lucan, see Eva Matthews Sanford, "Lucan and his Roman Critics," *Classical Philology* 26 (July, 1931); 233–57.

27. John of Salisbury, *Policraticus,* ed. with a commentary by Clements C. I. Webb (Oxford: Oxford University Press, 1909). The subsequent reference to John of Salisbury is also to this edition.

28. Charles G. Osgood, *Boccaccio on Poetry* (New York: Liberal Arts Press, 1956), 67. For the Latin text, see Giovanni Boccaccio, *Genealogie Deorum Gentilium Libri,* ed., Vicenzo Romano, Bari, Laterza, 1951.

29. *Numerandus* appears in Quintilianus, *Institutiones Oratoriae,* with a commentary by Raphael Regius, Venice, Bonetus Locatellus,

1493 (Regius specifically notes that other texts read *imitandus*), and Quintilianus, *Institutiones Oratoriae,* Venice, Aldus, 1514. *Annumerandus* appears in *Oratoriarū Institutionū,* Paris, Claude Chavallon, 1527. This is not a comprehensive survey; the texts mentioned are among the holdings of Quintilian in UCLA's Department of Special Collections. In modern texts of the *Institutes,* from Carl Halm's landmark edition forward, *imitandus* is given without exception.

30. For discussions of Renaissance literary criticism, see Bernard Weinberg, *A History of Literary Criticism in the Italian Renaissance* (Chicago: The University of Chicago Press, 1961), and Baxter Hathaway, *The Age of Criticism: The Late Renaissance in Italy* (Ithaca, NY: Cornell University Press, 1962 [reprint ed. Westport, CN: Greenwood, 1972]).

31. Barnardino, Partenio, *Della Imitatione Poetica* (Munich: Wilhelm Fink, 1969), 93.

32. Lodovico Castelvetro, *Poetica D'Aristotele Vulgarizzata E Sposta,* ed. Werther Romani (Rome: Laterza, 1978), 1:45.

33. Ibid., 1:48.

34. Ibid., 1:175.

35. *Les Oeuvres de Pierre Ronsard, Texte de 1587,* new ed., introduction and notes by Isidore Silver (Chicago: Librairie Marcel Didier, 1966–70), 4:15, 16.

36. Ibid., 4:17–18.

37. Ibid., 4:18.

38. *Oeuvres Choisies de Pierre de Ronsard,* notes and commentary by C.-A. Sainte Beuve, reviewed and augmented by M. Louis Moland (Paris: Librarie Garnier, 1890), 350.

39. Torquato Tasso, *Discorsi Dell'Arte Poetica E Del Poema Eroico,* ed. Luigi Poma (Rome: Laterza, 1964), 121.

40. Alonso López Pinciano, *Philosophía Antigua Poética,* ed. Alfredo Carballo Picazo (Madrid: Biblioteca de Antiguos Libros Hispánicos, 1953), 1:203, 204–05.

41. Hazard Adams, ed., *Critical Theory Since Plato,* 141. Hereafter this work will be referred to as *CTSP.* The translation from J. C. Scaliger is F. M. Padelford's; the original text is in Buck's edition of *Poetices,* 5.

42. Giovanni Pietro Capriano, *Della Vera Poetica* (Munich: Wilhelm Fink, 1968), ch. 3, p. 8 (no page numbers in text).

43. Allan H. Gilbert, *Literary Criticism Plato to Dryden* (Detroit: Wayne State University Press, 1962), 287. Gilbert's translation.

44. *Apologie,* 10, 11.

45. Ibid., 12.

46. Ibid., 35–36.

47. *Poetica,* 1:254.

48. *Philosophía Antigua Poética,* 1:203–4, 206–7.

49. *Poetica,* 1:255.

50. *Apologie,* 12.

51. *Philosophía Antigua Poética,* 1:207, 208.

52. Cited in Weinberg, 1:302.

53. *Medieval Literary Criticism,* 54.

54. Giovanni Antonio Viperano, *De Poetica Libri Tres* (Munich: Wilhelm Fink, 1967), 65.

55. Cited in Weinberg, 1:620.

56. Francesco Patrizi da Cherso, *Della Poetica,* ed. Danilo Aguzzi Barbagli (Florence: Instituto Nazionale di Studi Sul Rinascimento, 1969), 2:113, 195.

57. Gilbert, 247.

58. *Philosophía Antigua Poética,* 1:206.

59. Cited in Weinberg, 1:246.

60. Agostino Michele, *Discorso in cui contra l'opinione di tutti i più illustri scittori del arte poetica chiaramente si dimostra come si possono scivere con molto lode le comedie e le tragedie in proso,* Venice, 1592, 40. I am grateful to the Library of the University of Illinois at Urbana-Champaign for providing me with a microfilm copy of this work. Michele is discussed in detail by Hathaway, 105–11.

61. *Discorso,* 41.

62. Montaigne, *Oeuvres Complètes,* eds. Albert Thibaudet and Maurice Rat, introduction and notes by Maurice Rat (Paris: Gallimard, 1962), 169–70.

63. Gilbert, 306n.

64. John Buxton, ed., *Poems of Michael Drayton* (London: Routledge and Kegan Paul, 1953), 1:154.

65. J. E. Spingarn, ed., *Seventeenth Century Critical Essays* (Bloomington: Indiana University Press, 1968), 2:3, 11.

66. Ibid., 2:73.

67. George W. Robinson, "Joseph Scaliger's Estimates of Greek and

Latin Authors," *Harvard Studies in Classical Philology* 29 (1918): 158, 171.

68. Cited in entry for "Versifier" in the *OED*.

69. Gilbert, 672.

70. George Sherburn, ed., *The Correspondence of Alexander Pope* (Oxford: Oxford University Press, 1956), 1 : 109−10.

71. Ibid., 1 : 110.

72. *Selected Writings*, 325.

73. Samuel Taylor Coleridge, *Selected Poetry and Prose*, ed. with an introduction and notes by Elisabeth Schneider (San Francisco: Rinehart Press, 1971), 371. Cf. Coleridge's well-known definition of poetry: "prose = words in their best order;—poetry = the *best* words in the best order."

74. Ibid., 289−90.

75. George Saintsbury, *A History of Elizabethan Literature* (London: Macmillan, 1920) (1st ed., 1887), 41.

76. Matthew Arnold, *Selected Poetry and Prose*, with an introduction by Frederick L. Mulhauser, (New York: Holt, 1953), 318.

77. Ibid., 117.

78. A. E. Housman, *Selected Prose*, ed. John Carter, (Cambridge: Cambridge University Press, 1961), 170−71.

79. Marjorie Perloff, "One of the Two Poetries," *PN Review* 19 (1980): 48. Wells' poem appears in his *The Winter's Task* (Manchester: Carcanet, 1977), 39.

80. "One of the Two Poetries," 48.

81. david antin, *talking at the boundaries* (New York: New Directions, 1976). The page on which the prefatory poem appears faces the copyright page and is not numbered.

82. "One of the Two Poetries," 48.

83. *The Collected Essays of J. V. Cunningham* (Athens, OH: Swallow/ Ohio University Press, 1976), 406.

84. *The Collected Poems and Epigrams of J. V. Cunningham* (Athens, OH: Swallow/Ohio University Press, 1971), 43.

Chapter 4

1. William Carlos Williams, *Paterson* (New York: New Directions, 1963), 224.

2. *Princeton Encyclopedia*, 289. Cf. Williams' statement that "each speech having its own character, the poetry it engenders will be peculiar to that speech also in its own intrinsic form" (*SE*, 256).

3. Paul Oskar Kristeller, *Renaissance Thought and the Arts* (Princeton: Princeton University Press, 1980), 163–227.

4. Petri Caramello, ed., *Summa Theologiae* (Rome: Marietti, 1952–56).

5. Discussions of this matter appear in Raymond Klibansky, Erwin Panofsky, and Fritz Saxl, *Saturn and Melancholy* (London: Nelson, 1964), and Rudolf and Margot Wittkower, *Born Under Saturn* (New York: Norton, 1963).

6. Karl Aschenbrenner and William B. Holther, eds., *Reflections on Poetry: Alexander Gottlieb Baumgarten's Meditationes philosophicae de nonnullis ad poema pertinentibus* (Berkeley: University of California Press, 1954), 78; original text in appendix, 39.

7. Immanuel Kant, *The Critique of Judgement,* 13. This work will hereafter be referred to as *CJ*. For citations of the original German text, I have used the edition of the *Critique* (Otto Buek, ed.) in Vol. V of Kant's *Werke,* Berlin, Bruno Cassirer, 1914.

8. For a detailed discussion of the background of this matter, see Hiram Caton's study of Descartes, *The Origin of Subjectivity* (New Haven: Yale University Press, 1973).

9. Margaret Peterson, *Wallace Stevens and the Idealist Tradition* (Ann Arbor: UMI Research Press, 1983), 17–36, provides an excellent discussion of the process by which Kantian aesthetics were transformed from a largely philosophical context into a largely artistic one. For Coleridge's relationship to Kant and to the German Idealist tradition, see G. N. G. Orsini, *Coleridge and German Idealism* (Carbondale: Southern Illinois University Press, 1969), Thomas McFarland, *Coleridge and the Pantheist Tradition* (Oxford: Oxford University Press, 1969), and Norman Fruman, *Coleridge: The Damaged Archangel* (New York: Braziller, 1971).

10. David Simpson, ed., *German Aesthetic and Literary Criticism* (Cambridge: Cambridge University Press, 1984), 120. The translation is by Albert Hofstadter.

11. James Engell and W. Jackson Bate, eds., *Biographia Literaria,* 1:252. All references in this chapter to the *Biographia* will be to this edition, hereafter designated as *BL*.

12. Samuel Taylor Coleridge, *Miscellanies, Aesthetic and Literary,*

collected and arranged by T. Ashe (London: Bell, 1911), 48. This passage is perceptively discussed by Peterson, 30.

13. W. J. Bate, *Criticism: The Major Texts* (San Diego: Harcourt Brace, 1970), 386.

14. *Miscellanies, Aesthetic and Literary,* 46, 48.

15. Herman Melville, *Moby-Dick,* ed. with an introduction and commentary by Harold Beaver (Harmondsworth, Middlesex: Penguin, 1980), 261, 262.

16. Poe's notorious hostility to didactic verse logically issues from his Kantian principles. If Poe's criticism often appears to be exaggerated, the exaggerations are mostly of tone, not substance. He is in many respects squarely in the mainstream of the literary theory of the last two hundred years.

17. Walter Pater, *The Renaissance,* ed. with notes by Donald L. Hill, Berkeley, University of California Press, 1980, xx. The first edition was published in 1873; the second edition, augmented by the "School of Giorgine" chapter, was published in 1877.

18. Cf. Wesley Trimpi's great study *Muses of One Mind* (Princeton: Princeton University Press, 1983), xi–xii:

> At its best, literary theory articulates the ways to achieve and maintain the delicate balance between the cognitive, the judicative, and the formal intentions of literature. . . . When a literary theory fails to recognize and resist any tendencies toward imbalance, it will gradually reduce literature to its cognitive 'philosophical' intention, or to its exhortatory 'rhetorical' intention, or to its purely formal 'mathematical' intention. . . . Too exclusive a preoccupation with the definition and transmission of knowledge leads to an abstract didacticism. Too exclusive a preoccupation with the means of persuasion leads to the exploitation of language for the sake of display or of psychagogic manipulation. Too exclusive a preoccupation with the structural principles leads to one type or another of 'formalism'.

19. *Apologie,* 50.

20. Friedrich Schlegel, *Dialogue on Poetry and Literary Aphorisms,* trans. Ernst Behler and Roman Struc, (University Park, PA: Penn State University Press, 1968), 140–41.

21. Walt Whitman, *Complete Poetry & Selected Prose and Letters,* 574. Hereafter this work will be referred to as *CPSP.*

22. Wallace Stevens, *Opus Posthumous*, ed. with an introduction by Samuel French Morse (New York: Knopf, 1969), xxxvii.

23. Arthur Symons, *The Symbolist Movement in Literature*, with an introduction by Richard Ellmann (New York: Dutton, 1958), 5.

24. T. S. Eliot, *The Sacred Wood* (London: Methuen, 1969), viii. It is interesting that it is partly on Kantian grounds that Eliot contends that most of Kipling's poems are not poetry. When Eliot says, "For Kipling the poem is something which is intended to *act*" and depreciates his work as "instrumental" (*OPP,* 238, 250), his argument is much like one that Kant makes. "*Beauty* is the form of *finality* in an object, so far as perceived in it *apart from the representation of an end,*" states Kant in the *Critique of Judgment,* and he adds that we cannot rightly call ancient artifacts beautiful, even if time has hidden from us the "functional" or "instrumental" purpose that they served. The bare indication that they once served utilitarian ends means that we cannot judge them in a truly aesthetic manner: "A flower, on the other hand, such as a tulip, is regarded as beautiful, because we meet with a certain finality in its perception, which, in our estimate of it, is not referred to any end whatever" (*CJ,* 1.80).

25. *Opus Posthumous,* 180.

26. See especially M. H. Abrams, *The Mirror and the Lamp* (New York: Oxford University Press, 1971), 184ff., and Orsini, *Organic Unity in Ancient and Later Poetics* (Carbondale: Southern Illinois University Press, 1975).

27. *The Complete Work of Raphael,* introduction by Maro Salmi (New York: Harrison House, 1969), 623. Goethe's original text may be found in *Italienische Reise,* new ed. by Heinz Nicolai (Baden: Horst Hermann, 1959), 459.

28. *German Aesthetic and Literary Criticism,* 152.

29. Martin F. Tupper, *Proverbial Philosophy* (London: E. Moxon, 1876), 351.

30. Vivian de Sola Pinto and Warren Roberts, eds., *The Complete Poems of D. H. Lawrence* (London: Heinemann, 1964), 1 : 182.

31. Ibid., 1 : 182.

32. Ibid., 1 : 185.

33. Thomas Middleton Raysor, ed., *Coleridge's Miscellaneous Criticism* (Cambridge, MA: Harvard University Press, 1936), 89.

34. Geoffrey Keynes, ed., *The Letters of William Blake* (London: Rupert Hart-Davis, 1956), 85.

35. Herschel B. Chipp, ed., with contributions by Peter Selz and Joshua C. Taylor, *Theories of Modern Art* (Berkeley: University of California Press, 1970), 412.

36. Robert Creeley, ed., *Selected Writings of Charles Olson* (New York: New Directions, 1966), 22, 23.

37. Ibid., 20, 21.

38. *The Science of English Verse and Essays on Music,* 275, 276.

39. Paul Valéry, *Cahiers,* ed. by Judith Robinson (Paris: Gallimard, 1974), 2:931, 933.

40. DeWitt H. Parker, ed., *Schopenhauer: Selections* (New York: Scribners, 1956), 176–77.

41. Ibid., 182.

42. Stéphane Mallarmé, *Divagations,* ed. Edmond Jaloux (Geneva: Albert Skira, 1943), 220.

43. Cited by Charles Baudelaire, *Oeuvres Complètes,* preface, introduction, and notes by Marcel A. Ruff (Paris: Éditions du Seuil, 1968), 516.

44. *The Renaissance,* 106, 109. Hill calls attention in a note (391) to the similarity between Pater's elevation of music and the ideas advanced by Wagner in his *Letter on Music.* Hill also cites the passage from Wagner quoted above.

45. Cf. George Thomson, *Greek Lyric Metre* (Cambridge: Cambridge University Press, 1929), 1–2, who comments on the great age of Greek choral composition that:

> If poetry and music commonly went hand in hand, there was no question but that poetry was the mistress and music the handmaid. We know little of Greek music, but what we know confirms this view. There was no harmony; the choir sang in unison to the accompaniment often of a single instrument—sometimes to the lyre and flute combined. The words of the singer were the dominant element, and often reached, both in sense and in rhythm, a degree of elaboration rarely equalled in the poetry of other ages. The music which accompanied such poetry was necessarily simple.

46. *The Renaissance,* 108.

47. Paul Verlaine, *Oeuvres Poétiques Complètes,* ed., Y.-G. Le Dantec, rev. Jacques Borel (Paris: Gallimard, 1962), 326.

48. *The Symbolist Movement in Literature,* 69.

49. Richard Ellmann and Robert O'Clair, eds., *The Norton Anthology of Modern Poetry* (New York: Norton, 1973), 1160.

50. Hugo Ball, "Sound Poems," trans., Eugene Jolas *Transition* 25 (Fall 1936): 159.

51. Ibid., 159.

52. Cited in O. B. Hardison, Jr., "Dada, the Poetry of Nothing, and the Modern World," *Sewanee Review* 92 (Summer 1984): 390. Hardison also quotes Ball's statement about sound poems, though he misattributes it to Jolas. (Hardison frankly confesses confusion about the matter, noting that Rudolf Klein attributes the statement to Ball.) Because Jolas translated Ball's discussion for *Transition,* of which he, Jolas, was editor, some people evidently were led to ascribe what Ball wrote to Jolas. One might also mention that Isidore Isou's *lettrisme* movement exhibits tendencies, similar to those in the Dada movement, to escape meaning altogether. Not unlike the Dadaists, Isou contended that words were unnecessary for poetic expression, mere letters on a page being sufficient, in Isou's view, to create poetry. Raoul Hausmann's brief history of phonetic and abstract poetry may be found cited in Hans Richter, *Dada: Art and Anti-Art* (New York: Oxford University Press, 1978), 118–21.

53. *Theories of Modern Art,* 383. The translation is by Ralph Manheim.

54. T. S. Eliot, *The Use of Poetry and the Use of Criticism* (London: Faber, 1980), 151.

55. Mallarmé, *The Poems,* trans., with an introduction by Keith Bosley (Harmondsworth, Middlesex: Penguin, 1977), 255, 257.

56. Because purposely elusive or difficult modern poems invite and support different critical interpretations, they have sometimes enjoyed special attention from critics. At the same time, poets might be cautioned, by an occurrence late in Eliot's career, against placing too much emphasis on the desirability or legitimacy of a wide variety of critical responses. Eliot often maintained the view that "what a poem means is as much what it means to others as what it means to the author" (*The Use of Poetry and the Use of Criticism,* 130). When in 1952, however, *Essays in Criticism* published an interpretation of *The Waste Land* sug-

gesting that the poem concerned a homoerotic infatuation between the speaker and a young man who had died by drowning, Eliot was extremely upset and threatened to sue the journal for libel if it did not destroy the issues in which the article appeared. This episode is related in Peter Ackroyd, *T. S. Eliot: A Life* (New York: Simon and Schuster, 1984), 309.

57. Cf. McAuley, *Versification: A Short Introduction,* 28–29: "Speech uses a wide gamut of stress; but [English] metre deals in only two values: accented and unaccented. The two-value system is an abstraction from the live flexible movement of spoken language." Cf. as well Quintilian (9.4.84), who observes in discussing prose rhythm that "there are degrees of length in long syllables and of shortness in short. Consequently, although syllables may be thought never to involve more than two time-beats or less than one, and although for that reason in metre all shorts and all longs are regarded as equal to other shorts and longs, they none the less possess some undefinable and secret quality, which makes some seem longer and others shorter than the normal." Finally, Cf. Otto Jespersen who in his "Notes on Metre" says: "The ancients recognized only longs and shorts though there are really many gradations of length of syllables. In the same way most of the moderns, while recognizing that stress is the most important thing in modern metres, speak of two grades only. . . . But in reality there are infinite gradations of stress" (Harvey Gross, ed., *The Structure of Verse* [New York: Ecco Press, 1979], 109, 110).

58. *Personae,* 103.

59. *Poems,* 255.

60. *Selected Writings of Guillaume Apollinaire,* trans. with a critical introduction by Roger Shattuck (New York: New Directions, 1971), 227, 228.

61. *Selected Writings,* 22.

62. For a penetrating analysis of the difficulties of trying to base English metric on quantity, see Housman's review of William Johnson Stone's *On the Use of Classical Measures in English,* which appears in J. Diggle and F. R. D. Goodyear, eds., *The Classical Papers of A. E. Housman* (Cambridge: Cambridge University Press, 1972), 2:484–88. On the subject of musical scanning, see Nabokov, *Notes on Prosody,* 4, where Nabokov says about his investigations of other works on prosody:

"I have of course slammed shut without further ado any such works on English prosody in which I glimpsed a crop of musical notes or those ridiculous examples of strophic arrangements which have nothing to do with the structure of verse."

63. *Goethe on Art,* selected, edited and translated by John Gage (Berkeley: University of California Press, 1980), 11. Cf. chapter 5 of part seven of Tolstoy's *Anna Karenina,* in which Levin attends the Wagnerian *King Lear of the Heath* fantasia. "In the *entr'acte* Levin and Pestsov fell into an argument on the merits and demerits of the Wagnerian tendency in music. Levin maintained that the mistake of Wagner and his followers lay in trying to make music enter the domain of another art, just as poetry goes wrong when it tries to depict the features of a face, which is the function of painting." Trans. Rosemary Edmonds (Harmondsworth, Middlesex: Penguin, 1983), 717.

64. *Selected Writings,* 15.

65. Wyndham Lewis, *Blasting & Bombardiering* (London: Eyre & Spottiswoode, 1937), 264–65.

Chapter 5

1. *Blasting and Bombardiering,* 261.

2. Ian F. A. Bell, *Critic as Scientist: The Modernist Poetics of Ezra Pound* (London: Methuen, 1981), offers a detailed discussion of the scientific background of Pound's poetics.

3. W. H. Auden, *The Dyer's Hand and Other Essays* (New York: Vintage, 1968), 81.

4. *Complete Works,* 2:1730. The translation is by W. D. Ross, rev. by J. O. Urmson.

5. Alfred North Whitehead, *Science and the Modern World* (New York: The Free Press, 1967), 113–14.

6. Ibid., 1.

7. *The Miscellaneous Writings of Pascal* trans. George Pearce, (London: Longman, 1849), 112.

8. William Wotton, *Reflections upon Ancient and Modern Learning,* 2d. ed., (London: Peter Buck, 1697), 19. My thanks to Kathy Donahue of UCLA's Biomedical Library for helping me to locate a copy of this volume.

9. Cf. Kristeller, *Renaissance Thought and the Arts,* 193–96. Cf. as well J. B. Bury, *The Idea of Progress* (New York: Macmillan, 1932), 78–126.

10. Samuel Johnson, *The History of Rasselas Prince of Abyssinia,* ed., Gwin J. Kolb (New York, Appleton-Century-Crofts, 1962), 22–23.

11. Earl Leslie Griggs, ed., *Collected Letters of Samuel Taylor Coleridge* (Oxford: Oxford University Press, 1956–71), 3:469–70.

12. *The Complete Poems of John Milton,* notes by Thomas Newton (New York: Bonanza Books, 1936), 2, x.

13. Ezra Pound, *The Pisan Cantos* (New York: New Directions, 1948), 96.

14. *Theories of Modern Art,* 288. The translation is by Joshua C. Taylor.

15. Walt Whitman, *Complete Poetry and Collected Prose,* texts selected and notes supplied by Justin Kaplan (New York: The Library of America, 1982), 1270. This volume contains (1060–61) Whitman's short article on "Darwinism." Here Whitman speaks of Darwin's theory of evolution as "a counterpoise to yet widely prevailing and unspeakably tenacious, enfeebling superstitions." At the same time, Whitman the spiritualist is troubled by the anti-spiritualist element of the theory, saying, "In due time the Evolution theory will have to abate its vehemence." Generally speaking, so far as evolution supports the notion of literary change, Whitman favors it; so far as it discourages spiritualistic conceptions about human origins and destiny, Whitman seems not to favor it.

16. Tristan Tzara, *Seven Dada Manifestos and Lampisteries,* trans. Barbara Wright (London: John Calder, 1977), 56.

17. John Dainith, ed., *Dictionary of Physics* (New York: Barnes and Noble, 1982), 162; Subjectivistic misinterpretations of relativity appear to have begun quite early. In 1925 Whitehead complains (*Science and the Modern World,* 118) that philosophical discussion has suffered from metaphorical and inaccurate uses of the concept: "[T]he relativity of space and time has been construed as though it were dependent on the choice of the observer." Helen Pinkerton Trimpi once suggested in conversation that Einstein's own attempts to supply visual aids to enable the layman to understand relativity may have contributed to this problem. Einstein's train-and-embankment model may be cited. The body in the speeding train and that on the embankment are simply serving

instrumental purposes, not representing individual mental processes. Failure to understand this, however, leads to a view of relativity that, though perhaps happily humanized, is stripped of its mathematics. It leads to the view that, because events simultaneous for the observer in the train are not simultaneous to the observer on the embankment, perception is subjective; and it leaves out the fact the discrepancy can be mathematically determined. Whitehead remarks (118) that, in explaining relativity, "It is perfectly legitimate to bring in the observer, if he facilitates explanations. But it is the observer's body that we want, and not his mind. Even this body is only useful as an example of a very familiar form of apparatus."

Teachers of physics have debated whether one should try to explain relativity without at least some reference to the mathematics that are central to it. (See Geoffrey Dorling, "Approaches to the Teaching of Special Relativity" in A. P. French, ed., *Einstein: A Centenary Volume* [Cambridge, MA: Harvard University Press, 1979], 245–60.) That the concept has so frequently been misinterpreted to mean subjectivity would indicate that accounts of relativity should not neglect its mathematics.

18. Cf. Martin Gardner, *Fads and Fallacies in the Name of Science* (New York: Dover, 1957).

19. F. T. Marinetti, *Selected Writings,* ed. with an introduction by R. W. Flint, trans. by Flint and Arthur A. Coppotelli (New York: Farrar Straus, 1972), 82.

20. Coleridge in his *Biographia* speaks in the same vein. Recalling the genesis of *Lyrical Ballads* and Wordsworth's Advertisement to the first edition, Coleridge refers to the collection "as an *experiment,* whether subjects, which from their nature rejected the usual ornaments and extra-colloquial style of poems in general, might not be so managed in the language of ordinary life as to produce the pleasureable interest, which it is the peculiar business of poetry to impart" (*Selected Poetry and Prose,* 285).

21. Paul Valéry, *The Art of Poetry,* trans. Denise Folliot, with an introduction by T. S. Eliot (Princeton: Princeton University Press, 1985), 53–54.

22. Ibid., xix–xx.

23. James Joyce, *A Portrait of the Artist as a Young Man* (New York: Viking, 1964), 215.

24. Schopenhauer anticipates Eliot's argument that poetry results from a process analogous to chemical precipitation. In his *World as Will and Idea,* Schopenhauer observes: "As the chemist obtains solid precipitates by combining perfectly clear and transparent fluids; the poet understands how to precipitate, as it were, the concrete, the individual, the perceptible idea, out of the abstract and transparent universality of the concepts by the manner in which he combines them. . . . The skill of a master, in poetry as in chemistry, enables us always to obtain the precise precipitate we intended" (*CTSP,* 483). Pater employs a similar metaphor in discussing criticism, saying that "the function of the aesthetic critic is to distinguish, to analyse, and separate from its adjuncts, the virtue by which a picture, a landscape, a fair personality in life or in a book, produces this special impression of beauty or pleasure, to indicate what the source of that impression is, and under what conditions it is experienced. His end is reached when he has disengaged that virtue, and noted it, as a chemist notes some natural element, for himself and others" (*The Renaissance,* xx–xxi).

25. *The Norton Anthology of Modern Poetry,* 458.

26. *Divagations,* 221.

27. *Seven Dada Manifestos and Lampisteries,* 38.

28. *W. B. Yeats, Autobiographies* (London: MacMillan, 1956), 325–26.

29. T. S. Eliot, "Contemporanea," *The Egoist,* 5 (June–July 1918): 84. This passage is cited and discussed from a different point of view by Bell, 82.

30. Edward Bulwer-Lytton, *Caxtoniana* (New York: Harper & Brothers, 1864), 428.

31. For a detailed discussion of the concept of quality in ancient literary theory, see Trimpi, *Muses of One Mind,* 243–84. See, too, my article in a different vein, "Matter and Mystery: Neglected Works and Background Materials of Detective Fiction," *Modern Fiction Studies* 29 (Autumn 1983): 435–50. A recurring theme, among mystery writers from Dickens to Raymond Chandler, is that the detective story, which is centrally concerned with testing conjecture and defining fact, should also examine qualitative issues in human experience.

32. Cf. Richard Morris, *Dismantling the Universe: The Nature of Scientific Discovery* (New York: Simon and Schuster, 1983), esp. chapter five, "The Primacy of Theory," 103–27.

33. Francis Bacon, *Essays, Advancement of Learning, New Atlantis and Other Pieces,* sel. and ed. by Richard Foster Jones (New York: Odyssey Press, 1937), 267–68.

34. *Paterson,* 9. The statement also appears, with a lower case "n" at its head, on 6.

35. Ezra Pound, *Guide to Kulchur* (New York: New Directions, 1968), 27–28.

36. David Jones, *The Anathemata: Fragments of an Attempted Writing* (New York: Chilmark, 1963), 9.

37. Plotinus, *The Enneads,* trans. Stephen Mackenna, rev. by B. S. Page with a foreward by E. R. Dodds and an introduction by P. Henry (London: Faber, 1956). Plotinus' discussion of hieroglyphic writing is quoted by Trimpi, *Muses of One Mind,* who comments (185): "This passage lays down in the barest possible terms the presuppositions of all subsequent symbolist theories of the literary and the visual arts."

38. Bell notes (137) "Pound's efforts to assimilate the formulae of science to the mysticism of the pagan and medieval worlds."

39. For a discussion of *haiku,* see Bashō, *The Narrow Road to the Deep North and Other Travel Sketches,* trans. with an introduction by Nobuyuki Yuasa (Harmondsworth, Middlesex: Penguin, 1983), 9–19.

40. *The Poetry Anthology,* 46. The characterization of the form of Browning's *Sordello* and of the *Cantos* as "a rag-bag" appears on 45, in a passage which was cited in chapter two.

41. Ezra Pound, *Antheil and the Treatise on Harmony with Supplementary Notes* (Chicago: Pascal Covici, 1927), 148.

42. T. S. Eliot, *The Complete Poems and Plays 1909–1950* (New York: Harcourt Brace, 1962), 50.

43. *Theories of Modern Art,* 413.

44. Arthur Rimbaud, *Oeuvres Complètes,* ed., Antoine Adam (Paris: Gallimard, 1972), 251.

45. Ezra Pound, *The Spirit of Romance* (Norfolk, CN: New Directions, 1952), 5.

46. Wassily Kandinsky, *Concerning the Spiritual in Art,* trans. with an introduction by M. T. H. Sadler (New York: Dover, 1977), 19.

47. *Theories of Modern Art,* 347–48. Kandinsky's synesthetic color-tonal system recalls Joris-Karl Huysmans' *Against the Grain,* a novel whose hero, the Duc Jean des Esseintes, has in his apartments (see ch. 4) a cabinet with small kegs of alcoholic beverages, each of which repre-

sents a musical instrument. Gin and whiskey are like 90-proof cornets and trombones, asinette is like a flute, kummel an oboe, kirsch a trumpet, marc-brandy a tuba. Des Esseintes can thus drink sonatas and symphonies, just as, presumably, Kandinsky could paint a violin concerto or a wind quintet.

48. Thomas Mann, *Doctor Faustus,* 191. Hereafter this work will be referred to as *DF.*

49. Thomas Mann, *The Genesis of a Novel,* trans. Richard and Clara Winston (London: Secker & Warburg, 1961), 28.

50. Ibid., 34.

51. C. P. Snow, *The Two Cultures and the Scientific Revolution* (Cambridge: Cambridge University Press, 1959), 8.

52. *Einstein: A Centenary Volume,* 5.

Conclusion

1. *Selected Prose Poems, Essays, and Letters,* 21.

2. Margaret Drabble, ed., *The Oxford Companion to English Literature,* 5th edition, (Oxford: Oxford University Press, 1985), 644.

3. Stuart Friebert and David Young, eds., *A FIELD Guide to Contemporary Poetry and Poetics* (New York: Longman, 1980), 37–38.

4. *Premiers Poètes du Vers Libre,* 37.

5. Alan Citron, "Pinball—the Industry Goes 'Tilt'," *The Los Angeles Times,* 10 December 1982.

INDEX

Abrams, M. H., 318 n.26
Ackroyd, Peter, 321 n.56
Aeschylus, 46–47
Aestheticism: background of, 174–88; connections of, with scientific elements of modern verse, 225, 262, 277–78; contributions of, to free verse, 11–13, 171–223; definition of, 174; influence of, on attitudes towards versification, 11–13, 172–73, 282, 283–84; and novelty, 244–45; pioneers of, 172; and rise of music to primary art, 203–08
Aiken, Conrad, on Ford's verse, 308 n.37
Aldington, Richard, 17, 41, 284
American literary nationalism, ascription of free verse to, 16
Antheil, George, Pound on, 266
Antin, David, 166–68
Apollinaire, Guillaume, on free verse, 220–21
Areopagus circle, 27
Ariosto, Ludovico, 71
Aristophanes, 46, 112
Aristotle, 45, 114–69 *passim,* 226–27; on custom of defining poets with respect to their meters, 114–15; difference between history and po-etry, 115–18; on imitation, 20, 111, 114–19, 140; on importance of plot, 118; on literature as dealing with qualitative issues, 277; on meter, 22, 72–73, 118–19; on rhythm as property of prose, meter as property of verse, 31, 72–73; on prose rhythm, 72 ff; Renaissance conflation of, with Quintilian, Plutarch, and Servius, 10, 131–49; and organic form, 192
Arnold, Matthew, 17, 160–61
Ashbery, John, 212
Attridge, Derek, 299 n.18, n.19
Auden, W. H., 226, 280
Austen, Jane, 61, 62
Autonomy, as characteristic of modern poetry, 11–13, 203–04
Averroës, 131–32

Bacon, Francis, 247, 260–61
Ball, Hugo, poetry of, 212
Baudelaire, Charles, 208
Baumgarten, Alexander Gottlieb, 172, 174, 176
Beaumont, Francis, 146
Bedient, Calvin, 110
Bell, Ian F. A., 322 n.2, 326 n.38
Bellow, Saul, 107